'Nostalgic and funny. Anyone who grew up loving football in the 90s has a special place in their heart for Kevin Keegan and The Entertainers, and Andrew Nagy captures the joy, passion and pain of that period beautifully. Newcastle fans in particular will love this book.'

Sam Parker, GQ

'Fever Pitch for Geordies. A love letter to the greatest nearly team in history. Highly recommended.'

George Caulkin, The Athletic

'As enjoyable as putting five past Manchester United.'

Andy Jaye, Adopted Geordies podcast

'Loved it to the Toon and back.'

Ben Jacobs, sports broadcaster

THE BATTLE FOR NEWCASTLE UNITED

Kevin Keegan, Mike Ashley and One Man's Search for Football Salvation

ANDREW NAGY

pitch

First published by Pitch Publishing, 2025
1

Pitch Publishing
9 Donnington Park,
85 Birdham Road,
Chichester, West Sussex,
PO20 7AJ

www.pitchpublishing.co.uk
info@pitchpublishing.co.uk

A CIP catalogue record is available for this book from the British Library.

ISBN 978 1 83680 160 3

Typesetting and origination by Pitch Publishing

MIX
Paper | Supporting responsible forestry
FSC™ C016779
www.fsc.org

Printed and bound on FSC® certified paper in line with our continuing commitment to ethical business practices, sustainability and the environment.

Printed and bound in India by Replika Press Pvt. Ltd.

Contents

To my wife, Alexandria, who inspires me every day, and my dad, József, who took me to St James' Park and started this whole thing off in the first place.

Introduction
Welcome to Hell

HAVE YOU ever wondered what it would be like if you fell out of love with your favourite football team? If, one day, the fixture list that had given you so much joy now filled your boots with a genuine, bone-shaking dread? I have, and it's horrible.

Allow me to explain.

Towards the end of Mike Ashley's ownership at Newcastle United, I found myself in the midst of an existential crisis. There had been many bloodcurdling low points during the course of his 14 years in charge of the club, some of which you'll read about in the pages of this book. But a meek surrender in the 2020 League Cup quarter-final at Brentford stung more than most. It was three days before Christmas, and the first time we had inched past the second round of this particular tournament in four seasons. I had every right to have been painfully aggrieved at our 1-0 loss, and for blowing what was considered such a 'reasonable' draw and chance at Wembley. But rather than moving through my tried and tested sequence of Magpies matchday emotions (rage, acceptance, sadness, rage again, bitter confusion and, finally, blind optimism), I offered little more than tame resignation. My response had been coming.

Supporting Newcastle has never been what you might call an exercise in glory. In the 40 years since my first match, the honours have been pretty slim. I have seen us win the Championship (the second tier) three times, achieve two second-placed finishes in the Premier League, and reach a grand total of three cup finals – losing them all without scoring a single goal. A staggering 30 different clubs have won a major honour in England since we last held a trophy aloft, and 19 of them aren't even in the top division any more. It's embarrassing to call our recent triumphs 'honours', really. At best they should be described as 'all right bits', followed by an audible sigh.

In many ways that lack of success never bothered me. Not in the grand scheme of things. I was devastated by every defeat, and eternally frustrated by our ability to choke at the merest hint of top-tier silverware, but it didn't make me love the club any less. For a time I believed that we would only win a trophy after I was dead, as if my own mortality was inherently linked to the team's success. Full disclosure: I still think that occasionally. But the truth was that, win or lose, it didn't make much difference to my support. Following Newcastle United wasn't something that I did, it was fundamentally who I was. At least until Ashley turned up, and the whole thing unravelled into one long pride-sucking, dream-crushing, utterly hopeless trudge to nowhere.

So, one day something inside of me just snapped. I was done, finished, and secretly wondered if it could be all over for good. Whether it was possible to simply grow out of football. That unknown existence absolutely terrified me.

It wasn't always this way. In 1992, Kevin Keegan became the manager and the club embarked on a joyful five-year adventure packed with fantasy football, kamikaze tactics, gun-toting Colombians and, in 1996, one of the most dramatic climaxes to a Premier League campaign ever seen. Keegan transformed more than just the fortunes of a football club, too, and after decades of neglect the city itself was suddenly revitalised, with life on Tyneside embodying the good times at St James' Park.

The idea for this book came when I tried to reconcile those two disparate threads in my life, at a point when my obsession was starting to crumble. The wide-eyed, anything-is-possible optimism of Kevin Keegan versus the deep down and dirty despair of Mike Ashley. For that reason you'll find that the chapters in *The Battle For Newcastle United* follow a dual narrative. One chapter Keegan, the next Ashley. One chapter: *gettin!*, the next: *bloody hell, man*. Two storylines with one overall aim: to see whether it really was possible to fall out of love with the football team that had defined my very existence.

It should be said that this isn't a forensic account of Ashley's financial practices while owner, or indeed the inner workings – and outer turmoil – of the eventual takeover that, in 2021, made us the richest club on the planet. People far smarter than me will tackle those subjects. This book is about being a fan, plain and simple. It's about trying to explain the depths of an obsession that a huge number of people will never know anything about, and why, as I approach 50 years of age, the results of my football team still matter so very much to me. But while this book is about Newcastle United, I dearly hope that just some of it appeals to other supporters, too. Fandom is built upon tribalism, but I always think that the football community has more to unite than divide it, and that's something truly worth celebrating.

In many ways *The Battle For Newcastle United* is also about my own salvation. I hoped that, by going back over 40 years of memories, I could rediscover the spark that ignited my passion in the first place. Maybe it was still possible to find the light I carried as a kid, when following the fortunes of my football team still felt like fun. Perhaps that will resonate with you, too, if you have become just a little bit disillusioned with the modern game. I hope that this book reminds you of why you fell in love with football to begin with. That, away from the astronomical finances, the breakaway super leagues, and the unfathomable offside laws, you can think that maybe, just maybe, the greatest days at your club might still be yet to come.

1

Return of the King

8 February 1992
Newcastle United 3 Bristol City 0
Kelly (2), O'Brien

It was only midday, but Steve Tillberry had already had eight wanks. At least, that was his claim as we played football on the pitch across the road from my house. As the statement hung in the air like a teasing John Barnes cross, I was baffled at how it was only met with shrugs and laughs from the other kids.

The sheer logistics alone were mind-bending. 'He must have been at it from about 6am to be hitting those sorts of numbers,' I thought, as the ball cannoned off a rusting goalpost and into the wild undergrowth beyond. Not impossible for a 16-year-old boy, sure, but certainly no walk in the park. On the flip side, childhood is a time for dreaming. If this was accurate then he had truly set a benchmark for us all.

I realise that this topic might not be what you were expecting from a football book – and certainly not so early on (not that any book's wank-related chapters are ever truly set in stone), but all stories have to start somewhere. If this book is ever made into a movie, then Dame Judi Dench or

Sir Ian McKellen will be required to narrate that opening, offering the gravitas it deserves.

At the time, I put my friend's Herculean efforts down to the events of the previous week's local news. Admittedly, masturbating to the events of the day wasn't what you'd call standard, but we were living in exceptional times. It was Saturday, 8 February 1992, and three days earlier Kevin Keegan had been announced as the new manager of Newcastle United.

A TV programme called *Northern Life* was often the dull backdrop to my childhood in the mining village of Sacriston, County Durham. A weekday show featuring grey-suited presenters, a grey studio, and a grey theme tune, it signalled the end of *Grange Hill* or *Byker Grove*, a swift change of channel, and the beginning of having to be quiet because 'the news is on'. Even thinking about it now makes me want to storm off to my bedroom, and I'm 48. But on 5 February 1992 it might as well have been *Top of the Pops* as far as I was concerned. I couldn't take my eyes off it.

The format of a news programme hasn't really changed much over the years. A sliding scale of events, read pretty much in order of importance: it starts with a war, and ends with a ferret driving a tiny Hummer. But on that day – the holiest of days – their schedule was out of the window. Keegan's return *was* the news. The *lead* news – not just some sports story pegged on at the very end of the programme. That was the gravity of the situation.

The two-minute segment showed a rather nervous-looking Keegan fidgeting through a press conference – name tags on the desk written wonkily in big marker pen – as he issued a rallying cry in typically ebullient fashion.

'There's no job in football I've ever wanted,' said Keegan, his voice a little shaky. 'This is the only job I've ever wanted. I'm not gonna make any statements that you lot [the press] can throw back in my face, but I will say that we're gonna turn this club around.' It was all at once contradictory and compelling, and easily the most electrifying moment of my young life. Still not what you would describe as 'wanking material', of course, but electrifying, nonetheless.

At the risk of derailing this chapter so early on, I think it's highly unlikely that anyone has ever had a wank over football. Not to football news, at least. If you were going to, you would probably save it up for an overhead kick or a sublime no-look pass. People often try to imply some sort of correlation between the beautiful game and sex. Like asking your partner to wear a football shirt in the bedroom. What if I accidentally think about the bruising, former Newcastle centre-forward Billy Whitehurst? And what if that actually makes it better? And why did his name pop so quickly into my head? What if I start to get aroused at the match, generally? There must be rules about that. My mate Spugsy once got a blowjob while watching a Newcastle game (at home, not in the ground) believing it to be some sort of Holy Grail life moment. He climaxed just as Carl Cort scored the winner and he has never been the same since. But such randomness aside, I can find no real evidence to support the supposed football-arousal equation.

Ten years previously, Kevin Keegan had taken a huge leap of faith by joining Newcastle United as a player. The two-time European Footballer of the Year (now Ballon d'Or) had just enjoyed two successful seasons in the top flight with Southampton, following three seasons in Germany with Hamburg after he had left Liverpool. He was still an England international. So, dropping down a division to help a painfully average Newcastle United was a seismic shock. He would eventually help galvanise the club, dragging them back up to the First Division at the second attempt. They finished fifth in Keegan's first season of 1982/83 and then, with the dazzling dribbling of Peter Beardsley added to the languid lurching of Chris Waddle, they sneaked back into the top flight the following year, finishing third in the final promotion place behind Chelsea and Sheffield Wednesday.

I was a little too young to fully appreciate the significance of Keegan's first spell, but I loved him dearly now. I suppose, looking back, I loved a lot of things when I was 15: Tudor crisps, sneaky pints of LCL, *Beadle's About,* the Stereo MCs' new album. But nothing with as much passion as Newcastle United and Kevin Keegan. I felt certain that his Second Coming was about to change my life immeasurably. The great man had returned, once again, to save us from the brink of disaster. Like Jesus, only with a mullet.

I can't remember how I first got into football. There was no major prodding or pushing by friends, no football strip under the tree at Christmas to ensure the bloodline of distinctly underwhelmed supporters lived on. It was kind of just … there. One minute I was going about my business, all dirty-faced and weirdly long arms, and the next thing I knew I'd inherited a lifelong obsession for a team that would go on to break my heart with way more regularity than any relationship would. There were other sports that kids were into at the time, of course. But they all came with obvious downsides. Cricket? Too boring. Athletics? Too much effort. Boxing? Fuck off! I spent most of my days in Sacriston trying to avoid being punched in the face. To choose a pastime where it was explicitly encouraged would have been ridiculous. Football had lain dormant inside of me, primed to activate at a certain age. I was like a Russian sleeper operative, only where they had the Cold War, I had the Canon League First Division. It's quite a commitment, I can tell you. A life in football isn't easy, and no two experiences are exactly the same – one man's Michael Ricketts (2001/02) is another man's Michael Ricketts (2003/04), as they say in Bolton.

Despite Newcastle's love for mediocrity, in 1992 the club already had a superstar in the manager's seat. Osvaldo Ardiles, midfield dynamo, Diego Maradona's mate, and the bloke who Escaped to Victory from the Nazis with Michael Caine and Pelé. In just two years, the Argentinian had made a promising start to his managerial career, too, winning promotion to the First Division with Swindon Town – beating Sunderland in the Second Division play-off final – only for the win to be chalked off due to irregular payments to players. In the fallout Ardiles came to Newcastle, taking over from 'Bald Eagle' Jim Smith, in what felt like a real coup for the club. A World Cup, UEFA Cup, and FA Cup winner, Ardiles had a reputation for building a team that played attractive and attacking football. Unfortunately, that was where the good vibes ended for him at St James' Park – the bit just before he actually started.

In truth it never really worked out anywhere for Ardiles as a manager, although he certainly gave it a good go. The former Spurs star held the position 14 times and with an eclectic roll call of clubs, from Deportivo Guadalajara in Mexico to Croatia Zagreb, Al-Ittihad in Saudi Arabia to Paraguayan powerhouse Cerro Porteño. But he never really spent more than a couple of years anywhere. I suppose, sometimes, great players just don't make great managers. Bobby Moore, Edgar Davids, Paul Scholes, Diego Maradona, Lothar Matthäus, they all came up short as gaffer. It's often said that when a football legend struggles in management it's because they simply cannot accept an inferior level of skill from a player under their charge. That's a pretty tough barometer. As players, they had few, if any, equals in the game. To expect to find one tucked away in the Oldham Athletic or Al Nasr squads seems unfair. But this level of ego didn't seem to be Ardiles's problem. In fact, any conversation about the Argentinian is almost always prefaced with just how darn likeable he was – presumably after giving a thought to the sheer madness of 'Ossie's Dream', his B-side single with Chas & Dave on Tottenham's 1981 FA Cup Final song. Unfortunately, the problem with Ardiles wasn't personality, it was performance. Barring the early blooding of some promising local talent – Lee Clark, Steve Howey, and Alan Thompson all started to feature more prominently under Ardiles, whereas Robbie Elliott and Alan Neilson were given debuts – Newcastle played nice patterns of football but failed at the fundamentals.

Ardiles arrived at Newcastle on 26 March 1991, and managed just two wins in the remaining 12 games of the season, with the club limping to a disappointing 11th-placed finish. In the following campaign things got even worse, and Ardiles presided over just six wins from 30 league games, including the St James' Park horror show against Charlton Athletic (3-0 up to 4-3 down and defeat). They took the sting out of that loss just one week later, gaining what many scholars have since described as the worst result in the club's history: a 5-2 battering in the fog at fellow relegation strugglers Oxford United. By early February Newcastle were second from bottom in the Second Division, and time was running out.

Sir John Hall – whose Magpie Group consortium was in the process of gaining control of the club – knew something that most people didn't. Newcastle were sitting with a debt of £6.5m and very little in the way of genuine assets. He also knew that relegation would likely mean bankruptcy, game over, the club spat out into football oblivion. Despite a reputation as a brusque, often ruthless businessman, Hall allegedly didn't know about the plan to oust Ardiles and deliver Kevin Keegan – at least initially – that was down to his son, Douglas. So, when he gave Ardiles a 'dreaded' vote of confidence after Oxford it was genuine. But once Keegan had shown a flicker of interest in the job, there was only one outcome. Legend has it that Freddie Fletcher, chief executive in Hall's new-look board and a man nicknamed 'the Rottweiler', was given the task of sacking the manager, but delivered the bad news at Ardiles's home with such care that he was invited to stay for breakfast. Hall has since said that making the final decision to fire Ardiles was one of the most difficult things he ever had to do. It was quite possibly the most important decision in the modern history of Newcastle United.

Perspective is a funny thing in football. Personally, I don't think it's always about winning when you're a young fan. It certainly wasn't for me. Yes, I was desperate for Newcastle to take home three points every time they played. I would pray for them, sweat over them, and obsess about them, and if we didn't get them – which was most of the time – I would be inconsolable for days. But I always approached the next fixture entirely without expectation. Following Newcastle felt just about as essential as breathing. Matchday was all about being part of this big collective effort. It was the build-up and the bus ride, singing songs as you walked to the ground. It was the bristle of danger if you saw an away fan outside the stadium; or a mocking wave to a player who'd been sent off. It was the floodlights coming on during winter, or awful burgers and reading your programme during half-time. It was misjudged first-minute tackles, magical last-minute winners, and everything in-between. But more than anything else it was the fact that, during those 90 minutes, none of the other problems in your life existed. The universe contained only this piece of grass in front of you and the 22 players on it.

The parameters of those feelings shift a little, of course, over time. To begin with, it was about going with my dad, and watching players I had only ever seen in football magazines play in real life. A few years later it was youthful independence, and heading off each week to the match with my friends, building rituals that would eventually make up my adult life. But the players were never auditioning for my attention. There was zero chance I would jump ship to Roker Park or Ayresome Park if Newcastle hit a losing streak, and I wasn't about to switch up my Saturday with a visit to the cinema or some ice skating should Wayne Fereday continue to hit the first man with his corner kicks. From the very first moment I set foot inside that ground, I was in it for life.

When Ossie Ardiles was relieved of his duties, the heartbroken Argentinian invited journalists into his home to discuss the situation, exuding the typical quiet dignity he had displayed during his short time in the job. There was precious little dignity on Barrack Road at St James' Park a few days later, however, as my friends and I jostled for position to get into the Gallowgate End for the return of Kevin Keegan. In the space of three days the home support had swelled from a beleaguered 15,663 at the Charlton match, to a staggering human mass of Newcastle Brown Ale, Fred Perry, and overconfidence. The Keegan effect had not only resulted in 3,000 new season ticket purchases, but also a further 15,000 on the gate, making it the first full house I had ever seen. On this hallowed day, every Newcastle fan in the city wanted to be there for the Second Coming. Fair play, most of them were pissed out of their heads and almost certain to forget the entire thing, but they were there, nevertheless. There to bear witness, and see the beginnings of a miracle.

It took 56 steps to reach the top of the Gallowgate End. I know this, because I counted them, and from the moment

I set foot inside St James' Park I became obsessed with standing on that piece of dilapidated, crumbling terrace. My first game had come around six and a half years earlier, a 2-1 win over Southampton in December 1985, with goals from Peter Beardsley and Glenn Roeder. But I remember sitting in the West Stand, keeping half an eye on the Gallowgate for the whole game. I was just fascinated by the songs and how everybody seemed to know exactly what they were doing, clapping, jumping, and singing at just the right time. Except when we scored, of course. Then it was chaos. At the time, every club had this type of famed terracing: the Kop at Liverpool, the Shed at Chelsea, the Stretford End at Manchester United. Somewhere that the hardcore support would congregate and, hopefully, inspire their team to greatness. At least, that was the idea. Historically at Newcastle it had been the Leazes End, a massive concrete space holding around 15,000 that, thanks to its yawning iron roof, created a cauldron of matchday noise. In 1978, however, the Leazes End was demolished to make way for something newer, safer, better, but it just never happened. The previous season's relegation meant that redevelopment money simply wasn't there, and the terrace was rebuilt as a shadow of its former self. As a result, Newcastle's more vocal support switched its allegiance to the opposite end of the pitch, and the Gallowgate.

It took me five years or so to finally get there, but as soon as I was able to go to the game with my pals, the Gallowgate Corner became my matchday home. You started at the front and, as your confidence built, slowly moved to the back where all the noise and mayhem began. But you had to do your utmost to avoid using the toilet. It was basically an open-air hate crime. Before booze became another essential part of the matchday mix, my main aim was always to be at the ground a good 90 minutes before kick-off. I've no idea why. In the pre-Keegan days you could have walked in at 2.55pm and pretty much picked your spot, but I wanted to spend as much time there as possible. It was imperative that I watched the warm-up, for example, just to see who was looking sharp and who was struggling. It also seemed vital to boo the opposition players both on and off the pitch during their own kickabout, just to let them know what they were dealing with. After a few months of inching up the terrace, I eventually settled on a position around ten metres from the very back of the corner, in front of a rough concrete barrier. You found that people almost always stood in the same place on these terraces, and you got to know the faces. The position in front of, rather than behind, the barrier was vital, too. It meant that you avoided being trampled in the melee after a goal, or during a rendition of 'Blaydon Races'. Once settled in place, and with a good few supporters in the ground, we sang songs with swear words in them, stuck two fingers up at the referee after a bad decision, and generally acted like we were hard for 90 minutes. With the opposition fans now tucked far away at the opposite end of the ground, you could sing that people were 'going home in a Geordie ambulance', or that they were about to get their 'fucking heads kicked in' and nobody would really check your credentials.

The last significant memory most Newcastle fans had of Kevin Keegan on the St James' Park turf came during his testimonial match eight years earlier. A night of high emotion, Keegan scored a penalty in a 2-2 draw against his former club Liverpool, took the adulation of a 36,722 crowd and then disappeared into the ink-black sky via helicopter like he was Bruce Springsteen or a Spice Girl. It was an act of showmanship that really hadn't been seen from a footballer in England before.

We were led to believe that Keegan had pretty much spent the years that followed on a Marbella golf course. At least, that's the phrase you'll find through any online search of his retirement. In reality, I'm sure that his time away from football had more to it than that. Dinners, shopping, playing cards, odd jobs around the house, sunbathing; loads of stuff. On being asked if he would ever return to the game, he had apparently once offered the following, 'If anyone ever hears that I'm coming back to football full-time, they can laugh as much as I will. It'll never happen. That's for certain.' So, the overriding message was this: Kevin Keegan was on easy street, with no desire or need for the hassle of professional football. Well now he had hassle, and he had it by the bucket load. There's a scene in the *Flash Gordon* movie of 1980, when Dale Arden tells Flash that she loves him, but that he only has 14 hours to save the Earth (controversially starting with the good news first). Well, this was a bit like that, only Keegan had 16 games to save Newcastle United. There were no women involved, at least not to my knowledge. If you're wondering about the rest of the analogy, I'm thinking Brian Kilcline as King Vultan, ruler of the Hawkmen, and Gavin Peacock as Prince Barin. Ming is probably the spectre of the Third Division itself, although I'm not really sure where his moustache fits into that. What can I tell you, it's a work in progress.

It didn't take long for the sold-out signs to appear around the ground ahead of kick-off that day. Something I had definitely never experienced before. I silently thanked my ridiculously early arrival policy for its service, as I found my spot and watched the spaces quickly fill up around me. I had never seen St James' Park like this. Not just full – although that was also true – but with such expectation and excitement, and songs bounced around the ground long before kick-off. By the time we hit 2.50pm, and Keegan walked out with his assistant Terry McDermott, the place was in a state of hysteria. 'Keegan! Keegan! Keegan!' We sang that day as if our lives depended on it, and the song cascaded down on to the pitch in waves, pounding at your head and occasionally taking your breath away. On the pitch, a pack of photographers jostled for position in front of the Newcastle dugout, elbows sharpened to get the best shot of Keegan's return. This wasn't just a huge day for Newcastle United – it was a moment for English football, too. The return of a legend. The new gaffer aimed a few claps at the crowd, but McDermott wasn't going to let him get away with that, and so nudged him forward once more towards the acclaim. Keegan duly ducked under the rope that had been set up to separate him from the snappers and aimed a more concerted clap of appreciation around the ground, focussing on the Gallowgate End in particular. I felt proud that he was doing it towards where I was standing. The same end he had rushed towards in celebration after his debut Newcastle goal against QPR in 1982.

Amid all the emotion it was easy to forget that a football match was taking place that day, and it would have been quite the pisser if Bristol City hadn't played along with the script and came away with a win. Considering the season of fuck-uppery we were having, I really wouldn't have put it past them. But this day felt different. From the very first whistle Newcastle pressed and pushed. They snapped into tackles and launched themselves at each and every ball into the box. Gavin Peacock was at the heart of everything good Newcastle did. Freshly back from injury, and chosen in place of Mick Quinn, he buzzed around the box tirelessly, harrying defenders and linking up play with David Kelly and Kevin Brock. Chances came and went, but the hoped-for early goal failed to materialise. Despite all the pressure, there was nothing to really trouble Andy Leaning in the Bristol City goal.

There are some moments in football that are so predictable that they move beyond cliché and into something else. Self-fulfilling prophecy, perhaps. A former player scoring against you, or the new manager bounce dragging a team of stragglers away from danger. Well chief among these phenomena is the classic goal-against-the-run-of-play, whereby the opposition soaks up all the pressure only to hit you on the break and, against all odds, take the lead. Suddenly, not only do you find yourself a goal down, but your fragile confidence is shot to shit. This was a concern that lay heavy on my mind during the half-time break. It felt very 'us'. But thankfully no such hammer blow came. After the break, Newcastle only increased their pressure on the away side, pushing harder and faster for the opening goal. There's a great TV clip, where local sports commentator Duncan Wood claims, 'Newcastle just needed some words of wisdom from the new gaffer to take the lead.' At which point the screen cuts to Keegan in the dugout shouting, 'Oi! Oi! Oi! Go on Ray!' in the direction of full-back Ray Ranson. I expect that this is where Jürgen Klopp got the idea for his revised version of the *gegenpress* tactic, because shortly after that Newcastle took the lead. The goal didn't look great, but it certainly felt it. A Kevin Brock Gallowgate End corner evaded everybody, only to be hooked back into the box by Steve Watson. The ball arced and dropped right on to the head of David Kelly, who nodded home from half a yard out. The crowd erupted, and was still busy erupting when the second goal came along two minutes later. The visitors again failed to deal with a ball into the box, leaving midfielder Liam O'Brien free to slide in and poke it home, sending the crowd, and Keegan, into raptures.

It was probably the adrenaline, but I remember feeling weirdly connected to everything, like the players and fans had suddenly become one. A giant Geordie organism. We shouted and Newcastle attacked, Newcastle attacked, and we shouted. Each entity was briefly in perfect synchronicity, possessed by the passion of the other. Six minutes later and, as 'Blaydon Races' boomed around the ground, it was game over. Newcastle scored a third and everybody went fucking mental. Brock played a lovely through ball to Peacock. The captain checked his run and laid the ball off for the on-rushing Kelly, who sent a fine, low shot into the back of the net. For the third time in quick succession, Keegan and McDermott sprang off the bench, leaping on to the pitch and embracing each other joyfully. My voice had almost fully disappeared at this point, save for a dangerously high-pitched squeak in moments of tension. Thankfully the remainder of the game played out in relative calm.

On a day when a miracle was needed, Keegan, the messiah, had delivered victory over Bristol City, a team described on the radio as 'sacrificial lambs'. Throw in some fatted calf and we were roughly 75 per cent biblical.

Whether a higher power was on our side that day or not, the job was far from over. There would be tough times ahead, moments when I felt sure we were doomed to relegation. But Keegan had brought with him the belief he had exhibited as a player. That utter defiance in the face of insurmountable odds. And while that was a new way of thinking for most battle-scarred Newcastle fans, at least when sober, it was something our new manager had been doing his whole life. As the rain fell over St James' Park, we pushed our way back down the 56 Gallowgate End steps and out towards the centre of town. Just for a moment, and for the first time in a long time, life at the football club felt good.

* * *

I've just thought of another football-sex reference: that fan who windmilled his cock in excitement after Allan Saint-Maximin scored the winner for us in the FA Cup down at Oxford in 2020. Maybe there's something in this after all.

2

The Tricky Third Coming

19 January 2008
Newcastle United 0 Bolton Wanderers 0

It is a truth held self-evident that almost any attempt to recreate former glories will fail miserably. All the episodes of *Only Fools and Horses* post-Del and Rodney becoming millionaires in 1996, for example, or the Stone Roses' short-lived resurrection in 2013. I dearly longed for both of those things, and they were well, fine, but I have long since had to consign them to a separate room in my mind, for fear of sullying the original greatness. People shouldn't always get what they want. What would you have to dream about if you did? So, when Mike Ashley brought Kevin Keegan back to Newcastle United in 2008 for his third spell at the club, you'll understand that I felt a little bit uneasy. I say uneasy, I was fucking delighted at first. But then came that feeling. The unshakeable one you get in the pit of your stomach when you know that something just isn't quite right.

I shall always love Kevin Keegan; I would like that placed on the record. Not that I fall for strangers in this way too often. John Lennon, David Bowie, Kevin Keegan, that's probably about it, really. But just as 'In My Life' by the Beatles, or 'Ashes to Ashes' by Bowie always makes me feel strangely emotional, seeing Keegan's face instantly brightens my day, even now. It's like he's some long-lost friend. At Newcastle, Keegan had a raw desperation to succeed that I have never seen in a top-flight football manager before or since. There was almost a naivety about him, at times, as he persisted with a joyful version of football in the mid-90s. It didn't feel solely about winning games, it was more than that, something purer. As cliché as it may sound I honestly think it was about making people happy. In a region that had suffered for decades at the sharp end of Margaret Thatcher's Conservative government, happiness was in short supply. Football in the north-east has always been a positive agent for change, and that goes for both Newcastle and Sunderland. Keegan wanted the supporters to have their week lifted by what they saw at St James' Park. As a result, the joy he gave as both player and manager is quite simply immeasurable. Call this the ramblings of a football fan who has never seen his side lift a major cup, but even if Newcastle United go on to win trophies and build dynasties, I cannot fathom how it will feel more special to me than his first five years of management between 1992 and 1997.

I do occasionally wonder why he returned 11 years later. In fairness he probably does, too. When he was interviewed in the throes of launching his Soccer Circus interactive football centre, Keegan emphasised a desire to stay out of football. Newcastle, Fulham, England, and Manchester City had all taken their toll on him. That was in October 2007. Just three months later he walked out of the St James' Park tunnel at around 6.10pm, pulled on a blue Newcastle United Adidas jacket, and took his place in the manager's seat of the dugout.

The role of the returning hero is one of the trickiest in the book. Beyond the romanticism and loud trumpeting of a favourite son coming home, it's just so fraught with danger.

Seriously, who has it worked for? Cristiano Ronaldo? Didier Drogba? Dirty Den? There's just too much reputation on the line, and all for one final stab at glory. In truth, few people ever come out of it looking good. If the returnee is a player, then the chances are that he probably left as a young, emerging talent. He has spent his peak years elsewhere, possibly winning trophies, before emotionally returning to the club where it all began. Shirts bearing his name will be sold by the bucket load but, the truth is, he will likely now be a spent force – the mind willing but the body unable. Age comes to us all. Except, perhaps, Peter Beardsley. In 1993 Beardsley was bafflingly considered surplus to requirements at Everton – the Toffees manager Howard Kendall then in search of his own glorious second coming – and was subsequently snapped up by Kevin Keegan's returning-to-the-top-flight Magpies. Although the Newcastle board had initially floundered over his age, Keegan's now infamous fib that Sunderland were also interested in the player swiftly got the deal done. The lad from Hexham was arguably even more impressive in his second spell at the club. He was 32 years of age – positively ancient in football terms – but in 129 games Beardsley scored 47 goals and, in a time just before Opta stats (they began the following season), he bagged a shed load of assists, too, developing an almost telepathic partnership with first Andy Cole, and then Les Ferdinand. As ever, Beardsley is the exception to the rule.

As a manager, however, it's a little different. Your fitness and physicality are not quite as important, and the returning gaffer can occasionally rustle up a bit of the old magic second time around. While Neil Lennon's second stint at Celtic saw them win the treble, Zinedine Zidane's double-back at Real Madrid, just eight months after leaving, helped deliver a La Liga title. Carlo Ancelotti's return to the Bernabéu has been arguably better than his initial stab at it – and he won the Champions League. But these examples are rare. The clubs involved dominate their respective leagues, more often than not, every single season. But this was Newcastle United.

When Keegan strolled back into St James' Park after accepting Mike Ashley's offer to return as manager, it was to take in the FA Cup third round replay against Stoke. News of his return and presence at the game had spread like wildfire, swiftly doubling the attendance. At the time, Newcastle were firmly entrenched in the Summer of Ashley, and the Sports Direct supremo was determined to enjoy the fruits that came with owning a top-flight football club, letting the juices drip down his chin. And by that, I mean he was buying drinks for everybody in the Bigg Market, wearing his Newcastle shirt to the match, and had just sacked Sam Allardyce.

Former Bolton manager Allardyce was something of a progressive coach at the time. He was an early adopter of player metrics and sports science, and attracted some wildly talented attacking players, such as Jay-Jay Okocha and Youri Djorkaeff, to the Reebok Stadium in his eight years as manager. In the 2003/04 season he guided Wanderers to a top-eight finish and a League Cup Final. The following year he took them to sixth and a UEFA Cup spot. The season after that, with blood in his nostrils and an unlikely Champions League spot in his sights, things hit the skids. His already strained relationship with owner Phil Gartside finally snapped over what was required to get his team into Europe's premier club competition, and Allardyce resigned with Bolton sitting in fifth spot.

Despite clear ability, old-school nous, and future-facing methods, his genuinely impressive CV did little to convince the majority of Newcastle fans, and his appointment by chairman Freddy Shepherd did not go down well. Despite the occasional splash of pizazz, Allardyce's teams came saddled with a reputation for muscular menace. For a toe punt and a long throw. This would not do. Warranted or not, there's a touch of romance in the soul of Newcastle supporters. Far from being the win-at-all-costs crowd many neutral observers take them for, St James' Park wants to be dazzled.

Not counting interim appointments, there had been five managers at St James' Park since Keegan had quit in 1997: Kenny Dalglish, Ruud Gullit, Bobby Robson, Graeme Souness, and Glenn Roeder. Yet even with the restoration of regional pride that came via the beguiling work of Robson, deep down a large majority of the crowd still secretly pined for Keegan. Allardyce was a victim of that sentiment, and of circumstance, too. Three months after being hired by Shepherd the club was sold to a brash new owner looking to make some noise. Allardyce would last just 22 games as manager of Newcastle (five wins, seven draws, ten defeats). A six-week run of five games stretching from December into January without a win was enough for Ashley to relieve the 53-year-old of his duties. For his next trick, he would deliver the messiah.

Allardyce eventually exacted revenge for his ruthlessly early dismissal at Newcastle, incidentally. Not surprising, really. He looks the type to hold a grudge. I'd be willing to bet that he has a whole host of last words ready for people on his deathbed, giving them zero chance of reply. In 2016, his 'new manager bounce' at Sunderland's Stadium of Light went some way to ensuring their Premier League survival at the expense of Newcastle's, with the Mackems finishing just two points above Alan Shearer's side in the final league table. Football's thirst for schadenfreude then, as now, is unquenchable.

I guess it's easy to use hindsight and say that Keegan's return to the club wasn't quite right; to see the whole story and pick away at the thread of its narrative arc. The game's ability to switch from irate despair to glorious victory in a matter of seconds is what makes it so truly compelling – just look at the daily chaos on NUFC Twitter. The reality was that his third coming briefly reignited the football fires of the region. For a moment, Newcastle fans dared to dream again. They were back in 1996, and the pieces were finally falling into place. A new billionaire owner, Keegan in the dugout, and some unfinished business with the Premier League title. The only problem, as far as I could see, was that I wasn't there to see it.

In January 2007 I left the north-east of England for Dubai. After completing a degree in journalism, I had wangled the position of editor at a football magazine in Gateshead titled *FC Business.* Forged in the utter drabness of the Baltic Business Centre, I toiled there for three years, working on a publication that focussed on grassroots clubs up and down the football pyramid. We had a kickabout in the car park every day during dinner ('lunch', for those of a southern persuasion) and, occasionally, the boss would just take us all down the pub for the day. But that, and the people who worked there, were the only highlights. It was my first real job in journalism and, to be honest, I didn't have a clue what I was doing. I'm sure this was all too evident in my performance, but then I was cheap labour and the deal probably worked out well for everybody concerned. My low-quality output wasn't just born out of a glaring lack of experience, though. I simply had zero interest in the job. I mean, it was football-related, sure, but I wanted to interview Ronaldo about the World Cup, not Ron at Gravesend about getting the finance together for a new stand.

At the time I was inspired by the Gonzo writings of Hunter S. Thompson, and dreamed of working somewhere like the *NME* or *Loaded* magazine in the early years of

James Brown's editorship. As farcical as it may sound, I wanted to go on adventures and have capers. Unfortunately, by 2007, the magazine 'for men who should know better' was a pale shadow of the one that had revolutionised the men's lifestyle market in the early 1990s. With weekly competitors such as *Zoo* and *Nuts* now in the market, the industry was mired in a depressing, big-breasted battle for readers – and the highest nipple count generally won. So, the plan was to move to London with my girlfriend, Alexandria, and hopefully get a staff job somewhere. That I was failing miserably to get even so much as a first interview made a mockery of my other role at the time: editor of a bi-monthly recruitment magazine called *Pathfinder*. Somehow, I was now telling people how to get jobs, change careers, and live the dream. It really was the blind leading the blind. Thankfully a reprieve came just a few months before we were to make our big leap to the capital, as Alexandria was offered a job as a features writer at *OK!* magazine in Dubai. A move to the Middle East with a frightening lack of research you say? It sounds like a caper to me.

Leaving home to live in a new country is an unfathomably large decision. So unfathomably large, in fact, that you can't really look directly at it. It's like when Belloq opens the ark in *Raiders of The Lost Ark*. You close your eyes, scrunch up your face, and hope for the best. But this time the ghosts swirling around your head are the things you'll miss – family, friends, football … Greggs. It's utterly discombobulating. Everything you know is gone; all the sights and sounds, the streets you've walked daily for more years than you care to remember, subconsciously aware of every pothole and broken brick. In those moments you cling to the familiar. The elements that anchor your days. But Newcastle's fixture list, for so long the metronomic background to my life, was now 3,507 miles away, replaced by the five-times-daily call to prayer that blasted out of the minarets perched on Dubai's jumble of mosques. Talk about a test of faith.

I think my absence was another reason why I met the news of Keegan's return with a tinge of apprehension, too. Don't get me wrong, I was genuinely thrilled, but I was removed from its reality. For me, there would be no boisterous queuing for the Gallowgate turnstiles with my friends, like on his return 16 years earlier. No slowly growled 'ey-man, ow-man, ey-man, ow-man' as we all bumped shoulders for position. There would be no thrill of walking out into the stadium to feel its hopeful vibrations reverberate around the ground and, perhaps most upsettingly of all, there would be no chanting of 'Keegan! Keegan! Keegan!' If a famed hero makes a glorious return to your football club but you're thousands of miles away, does it really even happen? I'm fairly sure that's a saying.

The match with Bolton would ultimately bear little resemblance to Keegan's managerial debut on the same ground almost two decades earlier. Part of me likes to think that this was due to my absence. That the club simply couldn't fathom the thought of me not being there if something life-changing was going to occur. Things were different, of course. Although Keegan had inherited a far better squad than the one he had in 1992, there was a chronic shortage of desire and confidence. As the game kicked off, and after the initial spark of Keegan's return faded, even the crowd seemed unable to rouse themselves, perhaps missing the sheer jeopardy that was present all those years ago in his first game in charge. The players struggled, too. The new manager had opted for a tried and tested 4-4-2 formation, but things just felt off. A central midfield pairing of David Rozehnal, a centre-half experimenting a little further forward, and Charles N'Zogbia, a precociously talented left-winger moved into a central role, looked uneasy. James Milner and Damien Duff rattled up and down the wings without much success, while the up-front pairing of Michael Owen and Shola Ameobi was left to feed off scraps. The game ended in a rather drab 0-0 draw, which was of no help to anyone, really. But it was a clean sheet. Keegan was back, and things would surely only get better from there on in, right?

Two weeks later, Mike Ashley hired the former Wimbledon and Chelsea midfielder/workie-ticket Dennis Wise as executive director of football. It would be the beginning of the end for Kevin Keegan at Newcastle United. This time for good.

3

The Little Chef Theory

4 March 1992
Newcastle United 3 Swindon Town 1
Kelly, Peacock, Quinn

It might surprise you to know that there are a number of similarities between Kevin Keegan and Diana Ross. Both are global superstars, both had glittering music careers (kind of), and both missed big chances at the World Cup (kind of). While for Keegan it was a vital header versus Spain in 1982, for Ross it was a penalty in the opening ceremony of USA 1994. Keegan could be excused his miss – the guy had just come back from injury and had only been on the pitch a matter of minutes. Ross, meanwhile, had no one to blame but herself. All that dancing about beforehand. Just hit the bloody thing!

Unusually, they have also both left a football pitch via helicopter. Keegan after his testimonial, and Ross from the Sun Devil Arena in Arizona, having become the first female artist to headline the Super Bowl half-time show in 1996. Finally both could, on occasion, be considered something of a diva. For Ross that included allegedly hitting airline staff with a hatbox while trying to smuggle her dog on a plane in 1966. For Keegan it was walking out on Newcastle United in 1992, just seven games after he had walked in.

Storming out is a fine art. It's usually the domain of the big personality, the showman, a person with heft. I'm not sure I've ever stormed out of anywhere, not really. I did once leave a job at Marks & Spencer because they wouldn't let me have time off for the Newcastle v Liverpool match in 1993 (Andy Cole hat-trick), but you can't really call that a walkout, I just didn't turn up for my shift. Then they sacked me. What I would say is this: if you're going to do it, the ideal scenario remains walking out while shouting, 'Good day, sir. I SAID GOOD DAY, SIR,' to your boss, or just whoever is in the room at the time, and then slamming the door behind you. Typically Keegan's dramatic departure, after only one month in charge, came just as Newcastle had started to turn a corner. His first six games in charge saw a healthy return of ten points from a possible 18, and suddenly our shitshow nosedive towards the Third Division wasn't quite the inevitability we had all taken it for.

Perhaps unusually for a side struggling at the arse end of the table, Newcastle had three rather decent strikers at the time in Gavin Peacock, David Kelly and Mick Quinn. It was a trio that had guile, craft, and the ability to smash a meat and potato pie in seconds – and they would go on to score 42 goals between them that season alone. But the team leaked goals for fun at the other end, conceding almost two, on average, in every single game. It was the worst defence in the league, and a problem that Keegan aimed to rectify with one of his very first signings. Because if you want someone to come in and save your team from disaster, make that person a man mountain who looks like he lives in the woods and could wrestle a lion.

Standing at 6ft 4in tall, with shoulder-length hair and a moustache that you could lose an otter in, Brian Kilcline was an FA Cup-winning thunderous bastard at the back. He looked like he was forged in Olympia alongside Hermes, Heracles, and any other Greek god that you care to mention. He was a leader, too, something that Keegan desperately needed after inheriting an incredibly youthful squad. It's impossible not to love signing a player like Brian Kilcline. A double-hard bugger who is prepared to go into war for you every single weekend. Suddenly the opposition looked at you a little differently, realising that you might not be the pushover they had taken you for. The man known to his friends – and certainly his enemies – as 'Killer' had a quick influence on the dressing room, too. It's said that in 1992 some of the younger players were almost too scared to run out at St James' Park for the pre-match warm-up. They just didn't fancy getting abuse from a home crowd that had grown weary at the club's plight. Kilcline became their protector. Keegan has since labelled him as the most important signing he made at the club.

Kilcline was joined on his debut by a shrewd free signing: Everton's Kevin Sheedy. A tidy, ball-playing midfielder, Sheedy had won the First Division, European Cup Winners' Cup and Charity Shield in his time at Goodison Park and his arrival felt significant. Well, he was a player we had actually heard of at least. Now 32, Sheedy had been brought to Newcastle primarily as a goal maker, but he was more than that. Not only had his ten years on Merseyside seen him average a very useful goal every four games, but he brought international experience and a match-winning mentality that was essential if you are to change the culture of a football club. While their debut ended in a disappointing 1-1 home draw with Barnsley, both players showed more than enough that day to tell you they would become difference makers.

Despite the mini-renaissance, all was not well at St James' Park, and the constant boardroom wrangling and fears of debt hampered any genuine progress made on the pitch. When Keegan joined he had been promised £1m to sign players who could help in the club's bid for survival, maybe even £2m if the right players became available. But after paying £250,000 to Oldham Athletic for Kilcline (following an initial loan period), Keegan's moves in the market suddenly hit the skids; when he tried to sign the scrappy Luton Town midfielder Darron McDonough for just £90,000 the deal was initially blocked. For an emotional manager such as Keegan, it amounted to treason.

Next up for Newcastle was Swindon Town, player-managed by Glenn Hoddle and featuring the former Spurs pass master Micky Hazard in midfield. A well-organised one-and-two-touch outfit, Swindon weren't far off a play-off spot when they came to St James' Park on an overcast Saturday in March 1992. But Newcastle made short work of them and their aspirations. Suddenly there was a confidence and a fluidity to the team, and they came away with a handsome 3-1 win. Although a nicely taken David Kelly goal had been cancelled out by a twisting and turning David Mitchell strike – the future Magpie skipping around Brian Kilcline to finish from a tight angle – the day was finished off by Mick Quinn bundling the ball over the line at the second attempt for Newcastle's third. But it was the goal in the middle, and the quality of its scorer Gavin Peacock, which really shone that day.

Signed from Harry Redknapp's Bournemouth by Jim Smith's Newcastle in 1990, Peacock was a £275,000 bargain buy. A busy and energetic midfielder/striker, with a playing style not too dissimilar to that of Keegan himself, Peacock was a tireless worker with a habit of scoring important goals. It came as no surprise when he eventually took home that season's Newcastle United Player of the Year award. Against Swindon, with the game stuck at 1-1 and Newcastle attacking the Gallowgate End, Peacock came into the orbit of a flicked ball over the top on 73 minutes. It was just a hopeful nod forward, really, and most players would have let it run on and then chased it down into the box, but not Peacock. Having first pulled it out of the sky with his right boot, he then teed the ball up with his left knee, allowing it to drop perfectly back on to his right and for him to stroke the sweetest of lobs over the now-stranded goalkeeper Fraser Digby. It was a goal of such beauty that birds in the nearby Leazes Park briefly stopped singing as a mark of respect. Around three hours after the ball had dropped into the Swindon net, however, Kevin Keegan was no longer the manager of Newcastle United.

It had been coming, of course, this whole debacle. Slowly simmering behind the scenes as financial and football tensions met on a collision course. For Keegan the problem was simple. He had been lied to or 'It wasn't what it said in the brochure', as he famously commented at the time. He had allegedly made the decision to quit prior to the Swindon game, to simply not turn up. Thankfully the councel of assistant manager Terry McDermott told him that the players deserved more than desertion. The fans did, too. He would see out the game, but after that Keegan and Newcastle were finished.

In moments of crisis it's important not to panic, that's what the Special Forces tell you. As a result I would like to think that I took the news of Keegan quitting upon hearing it on local radio with all the poise and control of a trained military man. Certainly for a good 30 seconds or so. After that I concluded that we would now be relegated and immediately went to pieces in the confines of my dad's bright red Sierra Sapphire car. That fear was swiftly followed by the type of sanguine resignation that befits a Newcastle fan from the 1970s onwards. We clearly didn't deserve nice things. Keegan had somehow worked this out already and had, quite rightly, cleared off. Now we were screwed. As an awkward 15-year-old boy I was used to rejection. But this wasn't rejection, it was abandonment. I shook my fist towards the gods, and wondered how we could rid ourselves of this terrible curse.

Back at St James' Park there was a press conference taking place. Standard procedure following a game, but this one was to be more explosive than most. As a gaggle of journalists waited in Newcastle's POW camp-style press room, the shocking news began to circulate. The newly installed gaffer had walked out of the ground, packed his bags, checked out of the Gosforth Park Hotel and was on his way back home. Suddenly club chairman Sir John Hall walked in, flanked by key members of the Newcastle board. He told journalists that all was well. Keegan remained manager 'to his knowledge', and that this was a 'tremendous win that would surely set us up for promotion next season'. It was all a bit 'North Korea', really. You couldn't argue with the thinking behind his appearance. Hall was attacking the problem the only way he knew how: head on. But his eyes told a different story. He was rattled, and pissed off, and rattled again. When asked if Keegan was expected back at the club on Monday he replied in the affirmative, adding – in something of a passive-aggressive shot across the bows – that 'the board is in agreement to move forward with the rescue plan for this club that we agreed on the 24th of January this year. There are no divisions between this board whatsoever.' The conference then came to a close as one Newcastle fan shouted from outside, 'Well divven't expect anybody else to come back after this frigging disaster.' He had a point.

Looking back at these moments more than 30 years later, it's difficult to get the story straight. Memories turn out to be completely incorrect. When you make shit up it gets even worse. There's a story I often told when discussing Keegan's post-Swindon meltdown. It goes along the lines of this: after his walkout, Terry McDermott pursued Keegan down the motorway (a bit like the O.J. Simpson chase) only for the pair to finally meet up at a service station Little Chef restaurant. There, over a fry-up, McDermott proceeded to talk his pal down from the ledge and back to St James' Park. During this exchange, the Little Chef's ubiquitous big tomato-shaped red sauce container sat awkwardly between them. Silently judging.

I'll level with you, I have no idea where this story came from. I think it possibly stemmed from a drunken chat in a pub, and somehow became the *actual* memory. Subsequently it was revarnished with new details (the tomato) over time and multiple retellings. The reality was that, after a long phone call with Sir John Hall the following day, Keegan was reassured that funds for the club's progress would indeed be forthcoming. Later that evening Keegan read a statement to the press decked out in a purple shell suit (the 90s really were wild) confirming that he would be staying on.

Although it was devastating when Keegan briefly packed up and quit, it was – along with being a useful dress rehearsal for his real departure five years later – necessary for the club's development. Over the course of his managerial career Keegan would develop something of a habit of leaving clubs – and the national team job – rather abruptly. Legendary Newcastle United journalist John Gibson always felt that there was a piece of his heart missing in every role he took after leaving St James' Park, but this first walkout was no bout of petulance. It was a vital act of defiance that a lesser manager likely would not, and could not, have performed. Keegan mattered to the city of Newcastle, and both he and the board knew it. A serial achiever, he had never failed at anything in his football career. But Keegan was smart, too. This was a test for Sir John Hall and the board. Like when you have to punch the hardest-looking bloke in your wing on the first day in prison. Keegan had publicly called out the club's new owner and fired a warning shot of his own. He had not come out of retirement for anything less than success. And success for a club that had fallen as far from grace as the Magpies would not be cheap or easy.

After years of successive Newcastle managers losing their way thanks to a board intent on cutting corners, the club now had a manager who possessed the power to hit back and, perhaps, change the future. No more lies, no more broken promises. After decades of false promises it felt like something good was finally happening. The sleeping giant was rising from its slumber, whether it liked it or not.

4

An Ignacio González Vortex

13 September 2008
Newcastle United 1 Hull City 2
Xisco

St James' Park was like a nest of vipers by the time Hull City came to visit on 13 September 2008, and not in a good way. The skies had been slate grey across the city all afternoon, heavy with passion, discord, and well, rain. Kevin Keegan had just left Newcastle United, and the football gods were showing their fury. The vast majority of Tyneside wasn't best pleased either.

After an earth-shattering development at your club, you normally let your anger simmer for a few days before having the chance to vent your spleen at the match. However, on this occasion, an awkwardly placed international break meant that the city had been given some extra time to fume. It did not need it.

This was, of course, not our first Keegan departure. Let me evoke the dark spirits of 8 January 1997, and the great man quitting on the basis that he had 'taken the club as far as he could', even though we had recently signed Alan Shearer, were sitting nicely in fourth position, and had whacked Tottenham 7-1 and Leeds 3-0 in our last two games. Worlds collapsed that day my friends, as we all went through the six stages of Geordie grief: denial, anger, bargaining, depression, acceptance, and eight pints of lager in the Black Garter. But when it happened again 11 years later, and Phil Brown's not-won-away-all-season Hull came to town, people were fucking apoplectic. Betfred was trundling vans back and forth on Barrack Road plastered with the words 'Bring Back King Kev', while fans marched to the ground singing impassioned versions of 'Walking in a Keegan Wonderland'. Meanwhile, outside the St James' Park players' entrance, PTSD was freely available to supporters of a certain age, as fans gathered in big numbers to chant 'Sack the Board'.

Up in the rarefied heights of the directors' box, meanwhile, senior staff numbers were unsurprisingly thin on the ground. Mike Ashley and Dennis Wise were nowhere to be seen, with only managing director Derek Llambias brave enough to take his seat (either that or he was just shit at Rock, Paper, Scissors). Llambias built an empire based around the entertainment, bread, and leisure industries, according to his bio. I mean, fair play, but that's a curious hat-trick. I suppose if nothing else, it gives me hope that my footwear, sausages, and athletic equipment dream could be more than the mere fantasy I first took it for.

Regardless of their absence that day at St James' Park, Ashley's recently christened Cockney Mafia was subtly growing by the week, spreading throughout the club like a virus. There was Ashley, Wise, Llambias and Tony Jimenez (vice-president of player recruitment, Spanish but also Cockney). Who would be next, the Mitchell brothers? They probably could have done a job, actually. But Rolly, running about the training pitch and digging up the goalmouth? Dot Cotton buzzing around in the tearoom, banging on about 'her Nick' and her varicose veins while Geremi's waiting for his pre-match pasta? No thanks, mate. Cockney Mafia out, as the banner soon to be unfurled in the West Stand would demand.

It all feels vaguely comical now. Unless Ashley's grand plan to ruin Newcastle really did involve jellied eels and a strict in-house Lambeth Walk policy. Most of them weren't even Cockneys anyway, at least not in the strictest sense of the word. Unfortunately that definition – born in east London and within earshot of Bow Bells – came into direct conflict with the opinion of the north, stating that anybody living in the Greater London area was a Cockney. In fact anybody from down south full stop. And by down south we mean the Midlands and beyond. This was not northerners blindly hating southerners, but a way of pointing out that Ashley and his cronies did not understand our city, club or people. Newcastle fans don't care where a player, manager, or owner comes from. Supermac, Paul Goddard, Glenn Roeder, Rob Lee, and Les Ferdinand all hailed from the south and are beloved Newcastle legends. When it comes down to it, we just want somebody who gives a fuck.

I'm a firm believer that if a player gives their all for the club then our fans will show them love like nowhere else. A 'Go on, son, let's beat the bastards this weekend, you can even shag my wife' type of affection. This has little to do with being an elite talent, and our recent history is littered with players who became terrace favourites without being what you might call a world-beater. The likes of James Perch, Ryan Taylor, Leon Best, Antoine Sibierski. Players like these ran themselves into the ground for the shirt, and were proud to represent the club. For that they will always hold a special place in the heart of Newcastle supporters everywhere.

The opposite is true of the likes of Michael Owen. The former England striker is heavily criticised for his time at the club, and sometimes even added to lists of worst-ever NUFC signings, but I don't think that last part is accurate. Even though his best years were behind him when he came to St James' Park, you could see Owen's ability the minute he stepped on the pitch. His movement and quality on the ball immediately elevated the team, and, considering he had a pretty horrendous time with injuries, his goal record of 30 in 79 wasn't bad. The problem with Owen was his attitude. The guy just didn't want to be there, and was pining for a move back to Liverpool long before he put pen to paper on a £16m deal to join Graeme Souness's Magpies. I've never had an issue with a player's personal ambition – to go to Barcelona or Real Madrid one day, perhaps. Owen wanted an emotional Anfield return, and that's OK. But if it doesn't happen, then why not put everything into the club you're at, the place where you're adored by thousands? As Stephen Stills (of Crosby, Stills & Nash fame) quite rightly said, 'If you can't be with the one you love, love the one you're with.' While Owen was undoubtedly a world-class footballer, part of him will always be that young shithouse striker, laughing as he smashes volley after volley past a bewildered 13-year-old goalkeeper in his *Michael Owen Soccer Skills* TV series.

In times of trouble, creativity comes to the fore. Long before the collective brilliance of Wor Flags, the fine people behind the club's current *tifo* game, it was all about the ingenuity of the homemade effort. 'BMX For Sale' at Monaco for the 1997 UEFA Cup clash is a modern-day work of art in that respect. But I shall always hold a cherished memory for the banner paraded on Barrack Road before and after the Hull game. 'Wanted: Mike 'Fatboy' Ashley and Dennis 'Ratface' Wise, for crimes against Newcastle United. Last seen being clueless and interfering in the vicinity of St James''. The banner epitomised the wit and brilliance of football fans, even when they are absolutely livid. What can I say, it was the worst of times, it was the best of times.

Unlike his first departure as manager, Keegan's second disappearance wasn't exactly out of the blue. There had been rumblings of discontent from the moment that Ashley installed Dennis Wise as executive director of football, roughly two weeks after Keegan's return. It was a move that effectively hobbled the manager from doing what he did best: player recruitment. In his Entertainers heyday, Keegan was an essential part of the transfer mix, and would watch a potential target play live three or four times before making an offer (or not; one player unwittingly ruled himself out of a transfer once, thanks to an alleged lacklustre warm-up). Keegan then sat down with the player and agent to discuss the move. In that respect he was the wow factor, the eye candy, the finisher. A plethora of players – including Les Ferdinand, Alan Shearer, and David Ginola – have since cited Keegan as the defining factor in their signing for Newcastle, even in the face of higher salaries or interest from bigger clubs.

Unfortunately for Keegan, football was a different animal in 2008, and any Premier League club worth its 'long-term project' was looking to hire a sporting director. It was a role that encompassed player recruitment, negotiation, data, and more. These are blokes with files, and stats, and a scouting network that operates with KGB-like diligence. You know the type, they've got a haircut. While Newcastle's high-profile fallout with avid gardener and, now former, Manchester United sporting director Dan Ashworth is a sign of how vital that role has become, Frank Arnesen at PSV was probably the standard-bearer, forging the position at the Philips Stadion for a decade before taking what he had learned to Tottenham Hotspur in 2004. Other clubs quickly followed suit with similar appointments as the model for club management evolved beyond all recognition. Whether Dennis Wise banging over some YouTube clips of a player to his manager is really the benchmark for this role, too, I'm not so sure, but it's allegedly what happened anyway.

It took Keegan nine games to achieve a first win in his second spell as manager – he had picked up five wins in that same period the first time around – but by the end of the season there was a visible improvement in form. Keegan's natural affinity for attacking football saw him utilise a front three of Owen, Obafemi Martins and Mark Viduka to great effect, as Newcastle went seven games unbeaten, a run that had four wins and included a derby-day victory over Sunderland – but then Keegan *always* beat Sunderland. However, as championship hopefuls Chelsea picked up a comfortable 2-0 win at St James' Park on the penultimate day of the season, Keegan couldn't resist a post-match dig at the club, claiming that Newcastle would never be able to get near the top four again. Unfortunately this wasn't the Newcastle United of 16 years ago, and while Keegan's walkout after the Swindon game in 1992 proved a pivotal power move, his words fell on deaf ears this time around. Ashley was suitably irked and boardroom discussions were had. Eventually, they shook hands and the crisis was averted, but Keegan arguably had one foot out the door from that moment onwards.

While losing James Milner to Aston Villa ahead of the 2008/09 season was a blow that Keegan shouldered manfully ('we received a bid I thought was fair'), it was the signings of Spanish centre-forward Xisco and Uruguayan mystery man Ignacio González that took the biscuit. According to Keegan's biography, *My Life in Football*, Wise had sent clips of both players to the manager, who felt that neither were quite right for the Premier League. Yet both players arrived regardless, Xisco from Deportivo for £5.7m and a £60,000-a-week salary, and González on a season's loan from Valencia on £26,000 per week. The whole thing was allegedly a favour to the agents who had helped bring the much more highly rated Jonás Gutiérrez and Fabricio Coloccini to the club that same month. If that wasn't bad enough, Keegan was simply told to 'park them'. González played a grand total of 38 minutes in two substitute appearances before a serious achilles injury sent him back to Spain. It's rumoured that in that time he earned a salary of close to £1m.

There were other problems too, of course. Tony Jimenez allegedly waded into a deal to sign Luka Modrić, telling the player's agent that the Croatian – and future Ballon d'Or winner – wasn't quite strong enough for the Premier League, and the club offering a risible £5m for Bayern Munich's Bastian Schweinsteiger seemed another nail in its international credibility (Germany legend and Bayern board member Karl-Heinz Rummenigge simply laughed down the phone at this one). These claims have been refuted by the parties involved. In a 2018 interview in *The Times*, Jimenez claimed it was actually Ashley who vetoed the Modrić transfer, and that Keegan had turned down moves for the likes of Karim Benzema and Samir Nasri, instead handing out a wish list that included names such as David Beckham. When the transfer window slammed shut on 1 September, rumours abounded that Keegan had resigned. Three days later he made it official, stating, 'A manager must have the right to manage, and clubs should not impose upon any manager any player that he does not want.' King Kev's final reign at the club lasted just eight months. While at the time Newcastle claimed he had simply quit, he promptly took them to court, eventually winning a £2m payout for constructive dismissal in 2009. His situation had simply become untenable.

I always wonder how much of Keegan's heart was in the job by the time things came to an end at Newcastle. The only style of management he knew dictated everything had to be done with a certain passion, but that surely takes its toll eventually. His heart was both his biggest strength and greatest weakness. Did Alex Ferguson exploit that in 1996? Maybe, maybe not. But regardless, there was a school of thought that believed Keegan was never quite the same after the title capitulation that season. There did look to be a certain weariness about him the second time around; the trademark bravado had all but gone.

In the absence of Keegan it was left to the former Spurs full-back and experienced defensive coach Chris Hughton to try and get something (anything) out of the game against Hull. His line-up was certainly an interesting one. Because if I really needed a win I would stick Michael Owen, one of England's most prolific strikers, in the hole behind Shola Ameobi and Xisco, too. Part of me wonders whether he was forced to play the Spanish striker just so the club could make a point to the now-departed Keegan. The guy had scored for Spain's under-21 side a week earlier, but you had to feel for him. Imagine not only walking into this shitshow at a new club, and a new country, but also knowing that your signing had partly caused it all in the first place. Hull wore Newcastle away shorts that day, after the referee had vetoed their grey strip. It would not be the only gift they left with.

Once the banners, boos, and renditions of 'get out of our club, get out of our *cluu-uuub*' had died down, Newcastle started the game reasonably well. Guthrie bobbled an effort past the Leazes End post, before Owen missed with a header from close range. Any of those go in and perhaps you have a different story. Goals can change not just games, but career paths and clubs, too. Jon Dahl Tomasson's opening-day chance against Sheffield Wednesday in 1997 comes to mind. He sticks that one-on-one away and maybe goes on to become a Newcastle legend. He didn't, we sold him off rather quickly, and he became an AC Milan legend instead.

Midway through the first half, Xisco gave the ball away cheaply in midfield. Before there was even time to exclaim 'for fuck's sake', Nicky Butt had upended Péter Halmosi for a penalty, and Marlon King did the business from 12 yards. The on-loan striker would kill the game off midway through the second half after a through ball left him with the time and space that saw Kenny Wharton sit on the ball on this very pitch 20 years earlier. King cut inside Charles N'Zogbia before dispatching a smart shot inside Shay Given's right-hand post. To their credit, Newcastle still toiled. Guthrie's cross/shot smacked off the bar, before an N'Zogbia effort also came back off the woodwork, leaving Xisco to follow up and tap home for a debut goal. His first and last strike for Newcastle. The real entertainment that day came from Danny Guthrie's late sending off: a genuinely wild tackle on Craig Fagan by the Leazes End corner flag, clearly motivated by something that had occurred off the ball. But it wasn't the challenge, or the subsequent pushing and shoving that tickled me. It was the fan you can see in the background running all the way down from his seat in the stand and towards the pitch, seemingly convinced that he can get on and get involved in the dust-up.

Turbulent games like the one against Hull always upset me. My instincts are to support the club no matter what. Perhaps a little naive, but there you have it. At some clubs, protest is the standard route to change. Supporters of Spanish sides, most famously Real and Barcelona, will wave white handkerchiefs when they've had enough of a manager, a symbolic gesture to show their displeasure. It often happens painfully quickly, too (as Rafa Benítez found out in 2015). Maybe that high-pressure environment is what's required for consistent success. But it's just not for me. Never leave early and don't boo your own players. What can I say, I'm no revolutionary. That said, dissent on this particular day was vital. The fans owed it to themselves, to Keegan, and to the history of the club to voice their displeasure. Had we won, it would have simply papered over the cracks, offering a win for Ashley more than anybody else. On these dark days, you know it's only a matter of time before the angry fog drifts from the terraces and down on to the pitch, ready to sap energy and break spirits. Suddenly second touches are tackles, and cows' arses are missed by banjos. Defeat is almost inevitable.

Perhaps catastrophe is what you need if you are to eventually rid your club of a malevolent force. Maybe defeat and disaster are the football equivalents of an exorcism, and the only way to grow is by blowing the whole thing up and starting all over again? Unbeknownst to us, a long and torturous season stretched out ahead, involving the return of Alan Shearer, some top-level swearing, and a number of botched attempts to sell the club. Kevin Keegan was gone for good, but the madness at St James' Park was only just warming up.

5

Staying Up

25 April 1992
Newcastle 1 Portsmouth 0
Kelly

You could say that arguing with a disabled group of supporters from Portsmouth wasn't exactly a good look as Newcastle United's date with destiny rolled around. It's just bad karma really, isn't it, and at this point we needed all the help that we could get.

When you look back on Kevin Keegan's rescue mission, it's easy to assume that everything was golden from the minute that he walked back through the door. But nothing was further from the truth. Although he took 15 points from his first nine games, the effervescence of the great man's influence temporarily plateaued after that, leaving real panic to spread through the team, boardroom and city itself. After battling their way to five places clear of the drop, Newcastle suddenly had a change of heart and decided to jump back on their original suicide mission. They promptly lost the next five games in a row, found themselves stuck in 22nd position and looked in some real trouble. To avoid relegation, Newcastle technically needed to win both of their remaining matches – at home to Portsmouth and away to promotion-chasing Leicester City – and even that might not be enough to stay up. Understandably, tensions were running high.

To make the 15-mile journey from Sacriston to Newcastle, I had to catch a battered old red double-decker bus that had the number 726 on the front. Every other Saturday I jumped on board with a small gang of Newcastle-supporting friends from my estate and headed upstairs. They were a good bunch, really. All of us outliers in a predominantly Sunderland-supporting village. We had some decent footballers in that group. There was also a lad who would be your best mate one day then shoot you from a distance with a catapult the next, another who always seemed to have a bit of a dirty face, and one who was fairly quiet unless you drank a bit too much of his Capri-Sun, at which point he would go absolutely ballistic. Catching the bus had its pros and cons, too. The route was direct, but even a bus stop could be a little bit edgy in Sacriston. Many years ago, I was standing there with three other people as a bloke sped past on a scooter. Roughly 20 yards down the road he suddenly hit the brakes and screeched to a halt. He got off his Vespa and walked towards us, angrily enquiring what we were 'all fucking looking at?' Terrifying, really.

The journey was only one hour, but it always felt longer, as we stopped at every town and village en route to the city's Worswick Street station. The only exception to this tedium was on a matchday, when a sort of magic occurred. These journeys flew by and were usually a cacophony of raucous laughter, Newcastle songs, and inane conversation – and that was just the driver. Except on this occasion, of course, as we travelled to a game that could very well decide the fate of our football club. You could have cut the atmosphere with a knife as we sank into the worn fabric of the bus's tired back seats. Even the usual little pleasures felt awkward and off the mark. After noticing some Portsmouth fans who had stopped off at a service station, the youngest of our group jumped up, stuck his head through the small rectangular-framed gap in the window and shouted, in no uncertain terms, that they were going to get beat. In fact they probably shouldn't even bother with the game at all. He then closed the window looking pretty pleased with himself. At least until he realised that he had accidentally been directing his abuse towards the opposition's disabled fans. Things got even worse (or better, depending on your perspective) when three lads in wheelchairs, all decked out in bright Pompey blue, gave him a furious v-sign right back.

In the build-up to the game, I had been chain-dialling Newcastle United Clubcall like an absolute maniac, desperate for some information that might give me a glimmer of hope in our quest to beat the drop. I called it so many times that I can still remember the number now: 0898 121190. At 38p per minute it's fair to say that my dad knew that number pretty well, too, at least once the phone bill dropped through the letterbox.

For the uninitiated, Clubcall was a team-by-team telephone information service rolled out by British Telecom in 1986, and it was the only way to get up-to-date information about your club. To reiterate, we called a telephone number and listened to somebody telling us who was fit, who we were signing, and how the manager was dealing with whatever current crisis we were in. It sounds archaic now, in a time of 24-hour rolling news, social media rumour, analysis, player threads, and 'in the know' crankery. But when discovering even the most cursory of information about your team was an absolute mission, Clubcall was a godsend. The football teams loved it, too, as it was making them so much cash. Eventually they just saved up their prized content, such as player announcements and major interviews, for Clubcall. The whole thing peaked when Ian Wright, in a Clubcall exclusive, called the referee David Elleray a 'little Hitler'. They were truly great times.

When even the simplest innovation felt staggeringly futuristic, Ceefax was another grail hit when in search of football gossip and transfer rumour. Picture the scene: bored out of your mind watching *Neighbours* or *Home and Away*, you flick idly on to page 302 of the television news and information service, only to find your club linked with the Romanian powerhouse Gheorghe Hagi. What a time to be alive.

Those who preferred to keep things ruthlessly analogue maintained newspapers as their primary source of football information, reading the paper from back to front as a result of their skewed priorities. 'Nelson Mandela's been elected president of South Africa, you say? That's amazing, but let me just get through this story about Rob Lee's England ambitions first, yeah?' I was 15 at the time, so would also inhale football magazines such as *Match* and *Shoot!* too. The only problem was that they didn't so much offer breaking news as a Q&A with Bryan Robson, explaining how he loved Phil Collins, took holidays in the Canary Islands, and drove a Sierra Cosworth.

For the obsessive fan there was also *The Pink*, a football paper formerly known as the *Evening Chronicle Football Final*. This no longer exists unfortunately, strangled by TV and the internet in 2005, but it was absolutely essential in its day. If you weren't at the match, or listening to it on the radio, the only way you could find out about the game in any great detail was by rushing to the newsagents 60 minutes after the final whistle had gone, and buying this hastily put-together paper. It often came out so quickly that the ink still appeared a little wet, and was literally hot off the press. My friend Baz also worked out he could use *The Pink* to steal porn mags. The counter was chaotic when they arrived, so Baz used the commotion to stick the magazine of his choice between the warm pages of *The Pink*. He would show it to the man behind the counter, pay, and walk out with confidence. As with all grifts it was great until it wasn't, and he was eventually collared for his bongo magazine caper.

Not even Clubcall or Ceefax had prepared me for the carnage of Newcastle's fifth game in their terrible March-April losing streak in 1992, however. An absolute car crash against Derby County appeared to hammer the final nail in our relegation coffin. The game has since become known as the Battle of the Baseball Ground.

Things started off well enough. I mean, we got through the warm-up in one piece, and then walked out of the dressing rooms with the score still level, so that was something. It was only *after* kick-off that things went to shit. Within the first three minutes Kevin Brock had been sent off, we'd given away a penalty, and were 1-0 down. It only got worse from there. Future Newcastle striker Paul Kitson quickly added a second, before Newcastle's Kevin Scott saw red for a tackle on the former Sunderland striker Marco Gabbiadini that was basically GBH. Gavin Peacock somehow got the nine men of Newcastle back in the game with a goal early in the second half, but Derby added a third on 70 minutes. After that? Pure fantasy. The clock had just hit 73 minutes when Liam O'Brien set off on a mazy run to nowhere. By the 74th minute, he had lost possession and decided to chase after the Derby striker – and Newcastle United fan – Tommy Johnson, trying, and failing, to kick him up the arse. It was kind of brilliant. The Irishman quite rightly got his marching orders and Newcastle conceded a fourth just a few minutes later. Somewhere in the middle of all that Terry McDermott was sent off from the dugout by the card-happy ref, Brian Coddington.

Weirdly, that game galvanised the fanbase for the rest of the season. It was like a 'fuck it' switch had been flicked. Ask any number of Newcastle's travelling support about their favourite away day that year, and I would wager that the majority say Derby. It's that weird football phenomenon when you relinquish all care over the result and just wholeheartedly support your team. Around 4,000 fans were crammed behind the goal that day, and simply refused to stop singing. If we learned one thing it was this: if Newcastle were going to survive, the 12th man of the crowd was going to be vital.

Back at our date with destiny, now fresh from accidentally insulting some disabled football fans, it was all about the victory. I don't think I had ever wanted anything more in my life than a win against Portsmouth that day. A Raleigh Super Tuff Burner BMX, the Millennium Falcon from *Star Wars*, Bigg Traxx (the robot truck that, looking back, did very little); they were all just a precursor to this game. The big difference was that these three points weren't a possession. They weren't something shiny that I could show off with and make friends jealous, this was for the greater good. Not just for me, but for thousands of others, too. Football had made me temporarily altruistic.

There were only 26,000 fans in the ground that day, around 4,500 shy of capacity for a game that was so important. But I can honestly say that I have never experienced a football atmosphere like it. Not the Tyne-Wear derby, not the 5-0 battering of Manchester United or the legendary Champions League win over Barcelona yet to come. Nothing has come close to the noise inside a nerve-shredded St James' Park with survival on the line. These weren't football songs; they were howls of desperation.

Every attack was pushed gutturally forward by the crowd, and every ball slung into our own half temporarily stopped hearts. I'm not convinced that I enjoy these games, certainly not in the traditional sense of the word. I endure them. If we win they become great memories. Lose and they are cautionary tales.

I think that one of the great disappointments with the modern game is that fans behind the goal have lost their edge. On the Gallowgate End, we had a host of ways to intimidate the opposition, a favourite being how we welcomed their goalkeeper. It was a rather simple routine, where we waited for him to jog towards us and offered him a respectful round of applause. Taken aback by such generosity, the goalie likely reciprocated with a few claps back of his own, at which point we had him. He had fallen for the trap, the fool, and we immediately unleashed an almighty 'aaaaah' in his direction, along with a few casual 'fuck offs'. It really was brilliant and the goalkeepers thought it was pretty funny, too. This happened on 25 April 1992, albeit without the clapping bit. It was a game that would define not just our season, but perhaps our whole future as a football club. Win and we took one step towards safety, lose and it could be a collision course with oblivion. So, as the Portsmouth goalkeeper Alan Knight approached our goal to take his position for the first half, we basically just told him to fuck off en masse.

Despite coming off the back of a truly horrendous run of results, I could see the fight from the terraces mirrored in the players from the get-go that day, and Newcastle attacked the Leazes End with absolute menace. Kevin Sheedy bent a couple of curling efforts narrowly wide, while Kevin Brock fired one over the bar from distance. But as the game moved into the second half, things began to simmer. We were one goal away from heaven and one goal away from hell.

In the rare moments of downtime, the Gallowgate Corner and Scoreboard sections would look inwards, teasing and pushing each other into louder, more vociferous outputs. I always liked it when a younger fan aimed some abuse at your part of the ground, only to be met with the chant, 'Back to school on Monday!' I found it particularly useful as, unlike the majority of people around me, I was back to school on Monday, so it often also served as a handy reminder.

Then, in the 85th minute, it happened. Quite possibly the most important goal in Newcastle United's modern history. It wasn't until the following weekend's game against Leicester that the club ensured safety, but for me it will always be this game, this Saturday, and this goal that did it. After taking a clean catch, goalkeeper Tommy Wright bowled the ball out to full-back Ray Ranson, who lofted it downfield. The high, hopeful ball was flicked on by David Kelly to Mick Quinn, who somehow bent time and space to smartly return it to Kelly from an awkward position. After that it was like an out-of-body experience. Kelly ghosted into the box and, without taking a first touch, arrowed the ball towards the far corner of the Gallowgate goal. In the distance an eagle cried out and, somewhere, I think a nun cried a single tear of joy. The next thing I knew the ball was nestled in the Pompey net and pandemonium had broken out. For what seemed an eternity I was jumping, shouting, and grabbing anybody I could get my hands on. It was a moment of utter release and, although somebody nicked my hat in the melee, I came to terms with it. There are always casualties in war.

As the full-time whistle blew, some of the crowd raced on to the pitch and I remember Kelly being hoisted shoulder-high, like we had won the league as opposed to simply giving ourselves a better chance of staying in it. But that's what it felt like. Even now just thinking about that game gives me goosebumps.

A week later, Newcastle travelled to Leicester with the spectre of relegation still hanging over them, playing a side that had an outside chance of automatic promotion to the soon-to-be Premier League. In typical Newcastle fashion it wouldn't be easy. Gavin Peacock's opener – a lovely little dink after a poor Steve Thompson backpass – was met with sheer joy in the Newcastle end, and feral scrapping in the Leicester sections, after scores of away fans had bought tickets from touts ahead of the game. But just when you thought we had done it, won and survived, the Leicester captain Steve Walsh weighed in with an 89th-minute equaliser, a goal eerily similar to David Kelly's first against Bristol City on Keegan's managerial debut. As the Leicester fans streamed on to the pitch in celebration, Newcastle's were busy trying to discover what the other relevant scores were at the bottom of the Second Division, and whether this late goal had, in fact, sent the club down. But there was no need to worry. As the fans were cleared from the pitch, a Newcastle ball over the top led to confusion in the Leicester box with Walsh, the man who had just scored the home side's equaliser, putting it past his own goalie. Newcastle won 2-1 and were safe. As it turned out the win hadn't been necessary. The club would have avoided relegation even in defeat, but the team hadn't known that. They showed heart and fight, and earned the right to stay up on their own terms that day.

In the post-match interview Keegan didn't waste any time in shining the spotlight firmly on the Newcastle board, calling for action. 'It's up to the chairman and the board now to ensure that this doesn't happen again,' he told a pack of photographers and sports writers in a not-so-subtle application of pressure. 'It's just not on for a club of this size,' he continued. 'I've told them what I need to turn the club around. If they do that then I will certainly be Newcastle manager for the next three years.'

I experienced a strange mix of emotions that day, as we avoided relegation in the last game of the season. Like a near-death experience, it was confusingly joyful. I didn't care if we had endured a god-awful season or not, all that mattered was that we had survived. But now that we had done it, nobody knew what was going to happen next. Maybe Keegan would stay? Maybe he would clear off again? Maybe there was a third option where he became some sort of hot-shot private investigator? All I knew was that it felt strangely exciting. I was about to discover that there's a difference between excitement at not being shit, and excitement that comes following a team that actually wins games.

6

Going Down

24 May 2009
Aston Villa 1 Newcastle United 0

What's the strangest thing that you've ever left a pub with? I only ask as one night, somewhere around 1996, I woke up at 2am behind the bar of a Durham City establishment with a bottle of Blue WKD gaffer-taped to my arm. I have zero recollection of the events which brought me to that point – I have never even drank the stuff – yet I walked out of the place with it attached to my forearm like some sort of alcohol-powered body armour, and taking the whole thing as a minor victory.

If the rumours are to be believed, in 2008 Joe Kinnear left the Orange Tree pub in Totteridge Village with the Newcastle United manager's job. I mean, I've massively simplified and condensed that story, but this London boozer is the alleged spot of Kinnear and Ashley's first meeting, the latter being so impressed that he offered the former the job at St James' Park around seven years later. Kinnear, true to obstinate form, denies ever setting foot in the place.

In a parallel universe Kinnear and Newcastle are a successful combination. Seriously, I've put some thought into this. Look at it this way: to upset football's elite, why not install a manager who will throw two fingers up to the establishment, wear a sheepskin coat, and have a twinkle in his eye? Often foul-mouthed, always utterly unrepentant, a total loose cannon, but Joe Kinnear could have been *our* loose cannon.

This might have been exactly what was required in 2008. Or a toned-down version of it at least. Someone who, in lieu of big spending, could have bloodied a few noses, ruffled a few feathers, and got the club back up the table. I'm not saying that the former Wimbledon gaffer should have gone full Crazy Gang, but when you're unable to compete with the resources elsewhere, a one-for-all-and-sod-the-rest siege mentality can go far – and geography dictated that we had something to offer in that respect.

Whether you lay the blame for the north-south divide at the door of Danelaw and Viking warriors, William the Conqueror's 'harrying of the north', or industrial decline and the machinations of Margaret Thatcher, the old rivalry could have been useful motivation. It's certainly a factor for the supporters – hence the Cockney Mafia jibes aimed at Ashley's administration. Newcastle United is English football's northernmost club, and has often lived in top-flight isolation. That's not a dig at Sunderland or Middlesbrough (ahem), but the historic disparity in finance and opportunity between the north and south could have been prime fodder for big-match inspiration. And who better than Kinnear to whip that fervour into a match-winning frenzy? I know what you're thinking, the guy was brought up in Watford, so was a southerner himself. Well that only amplifies the beauty of it all. Just imagine, for the love of the Magpies he turns against his own people. Honorary Geordie status achieved.

But of course this is all just cosmic chat. In the real world, Kinnear and Newcastle were an absolute car crash, even if his first official duty as manager did give us the finest press conference exchange of all time, ahead of the game with Everton.

> Joe Kinnear, 'Which one is [the *Daily Mirror* journalist] Simon Bird?'
> Simon Bird, 'Me.'
> Kinnear, 'You're a cunt.'
> Bird, 'Thank you.'

Regional and national press understandably went to town on Kinnear after this outburst – with splashes across the front *and* back pages – while Newcastle fans were left bemused by the whole thing. But, going back to our parallel universe for a second, what if Joe had the team coming out swinging and results picked up? Maybe he gets a derby win, and a couple of big scalps? After that he drops an f-bomb at a press conference and everything has changed. Now we're all, 'Awww, *that guy*, what's he like, eh? Go on, Joe, now call the ref an absolute bellend.'

Away from the outrage of Kinnear's appointment (he was not a popular choice by the fanbase), the guy wasn't a bad manager in his day. During seven years at the helm of Wimbledon, when being a motivator of men was prized above the more cerebral tactician, the former Tottenham and Republic of Ireland full-back delivered success with a fine us-against-them mentality.

Arriving after the FA Cup Final victory over Liverpool and the early Crazy Gang years, Kinnear was given the job in 1992, steadying the ship just as Wimbledon looked susceptible to the drop. In his first full season he was named Manager of the Month three times, helping establish the

Dons as a bonafide Premier League outfit. A sixth-placed finish came in 1993/94 and was followed by two top-ten spots, with semi-finals of both the FA Cup and League Cup reached in 1997. There was another League Cup semi-final in 1999, but it papered over the cracks of their league form. That struggle took its toll in more ways than one and, ahead of a league game at Hillsborough on 3 March 1999, Kinnear suffered a heart attack. The subsequent 2-1 victory his side picked up that day would be the club's last win of the season. Kinnear officially retired three months later, and the following year Wimbledon were relegated from the Premier League.

Prior to Kinnear's arrival, people often forget that this most dark of seasons had begun pretty well. Keegan's side enjoyed a rare draw at Old Trafford which was followed by a 1-0 home win over Bolton and fourth spot in the table. Experts will tell you that the early season table counts for nothing, and that you don't win the title in August, but it's still nice to look at it dreamily. At least until football reality resumes. The following week we were humped 3-0 at the Emirates, Ashley downed a pint in the away end wearing a Newcastle shirt bearing the number one and 'King Kev' on the back. Five days later, Keegan left St James' Park.

Caretaker manager always sounds like a confusing job title to me. It's like we've said, 'Well, for a short period of time this man will pick our first XI. But he'll also sweep up and take the bins out.' But you could say that the job is also something of a free hit. Nobody's expecting anything from the caretaker. So, after Keegan's third departure, defensive coach Chris Hughton stepped up to the plate. Who else but the affable Irishman to help heal wounds on a distraught Tyneside? Unfortunately he was powerless to prevent either the clusterfuck defeat to Hull (expertly dissected in chapter four), or the new manager bounce of Gianfranco Zola at Upton Park, as Newcastle fell to a 3-1 defeat against West Ham – a first loss against the Hammers in nine games.

The king of the caretakers, in my opinion, is our own John Carver, former assistant manager to both Sir Bobby Robson and Alan Pardew. In a sport where these unsung guardians generally operate in the shadows, Carver's time as caretaker manager – sandwiched between the tenures of Pardew and Steve McClaren – involved a wild, 19-game ride in 2015. He ended up with just three wins, a 15 per cent ratio, before exclaiming, 'I still think I'm the best coach in the Premier League.' I wish we all had Carver's confidence. It's the conviction that says 'yes, I will have a crack at disarming this bomb' or, 'of course I can fly the plane if the pilot has suddenly fallen ill'. It's pure hero stuff. Bollocks to the fact that he didn't win many games. John Carver loves Newcastle United, and he added a much-needed touch of bravado to the role of caretaker manager. We should all respect him for that.

Joe Kinnear was announced as interim manager on 26 September 2008. I'm not sure what the difference between interim manager and caretaker manager is, the whole thing has lost all meaning. I do know that he hadn't managed in the top flight since 1999, and not managed anywhere since 2004 – a one-year stint in charge at Nottingham Forest that was as successful as that timeframe suggests. Not that he was expecting a crack at the full-time Newcastle job anytime soon.

Back at the press conference from Hell, and in-between calling people a cunt, Kinnear had explained, 'I think the club is going to be sold at the beginning of October – so I'm informed by Mike Ashley – and Chris Hughton needs all the help that he can get. So I can get in there and get a few results together until the two main people that they are naming – I assume from the people coming in that those will be Kevin Keegan and Alan Shearer – arrive.'

Quite where Kinnear pulled those two names from is anybody's guess. Perhaps he was just looking to buy a little time with a fanbase unhappy at Keegan's departure and his own arrival. In that case why not go the whole hog? Name Ant and Dec as backroom staff and Jimmy Nail defensive coach. Maybe Cheryl Cole can come in as physio, and let's have Sting managing the club shop. Go full Geordie.

It certainly didn't help that, after two creditable draws (away to Everton and at home to Manchester City) Kinnear's third game in charge saw Newcastle lose at Sunderland for the first time in 28 years. A real punch to the gut. I watched that derby in a bar in Dubai, with Kieron Richardson's walloping free-kick winner still fresh in my mind as a fight broke out in the toilets. The main point of contention wasn't the result, however, it was that Sunderland were still shit because their city didn't have a cathedral. Religion being, as ever, a catalyst for war.

Kinnear remained in charge for 18 games, presiding over five wins, nine draws and seven losses, leaving the club 13th in the table before another heart attack forced him into a second retirement. He was hampered by the January sales of Shay Given and Charles N'Zogbia (or 'Charles Insomnia' as Kinnear would call him in a 2009 press conference. See also 'Yohan Kebab' instead of Yohan Cabaye in 2014, after he had briefly returned to Newcastle as director of football). The sale of Given in particular was a huge blow to the club's hopes of survival. Although they had an admirable deputy in Steve Harper, Given was a world-class goalkeeper who had saved Newcastle more times than I care to remember. His shock move to Manchester City seemed inevitable to many, and that he had simply had enough of playing behind a leaky backline. However the Irishman later claimed that he had no wish to leave at all. Sadly, when it came time to renegotiate his contract, the club came back with the same terms he was already on, take it or leave it. His own self-respect told him that he had to leave.

In the aftermath of Kinnear's second heart attack, Ashley did what Ashley does: a shit thing, a shit thing, a *shitter* thing, AN AMAZING THING. As a fan you just never knew where you were with the bloke, and it was basically an abusive relationship at this point. But I was 100 per cent sure that, when Alan Shearer walked back into the club, we were as good as safe. 'This guy wouldn't come back without assurances,' I explained to anybody willing to listen. 'Ashley has given him carte blanche.'

'Keep us up, Alan,' he probably said. 'Next season we'll have a real pop at the title,' that sort of thing. Of course it didn't quite turn out that way.

I feel massive amounts of sympathy for Alan Shearer in this whole debacle. I know he doesn't want our pity, but it really must sting. He was on a hiding to nothing with the situation he inherited at Newcastle. Eight games to go – including matches against Chelsea, Tottenham, and Liverpool – and a side devoid of confidence, desire and gumption. I'm sure that his financial compensation was befitting the role and situation but, let's be honest, the only pull for a man like Shearer was the chance to save Newcastle from the abyss. As it turned out, even the new-manager-who's-also-local-hero bounce wasn't quite enough.

Shearer certainly wasn't helped by an underperforming squad. Featuring players such as Michael Owen, Joey Barton, Kevin Nolan, Obafemi Martins, Mark Viduka, Alan Smith, Nicky Butt, José Enrique, and Fabricio Coloccini, the Newcastle side of 2008/09 feels nailed on for the 'too good to go down' category. But they went down regardless.

By the time Newcastle arrived at Villa Park for the final day of the season, they had won only once under Shearer, 3-1 at home to Middlesbrough, a team that would also end up facing the ignominy of relegation. Everything about the game felt wrong that day. It was the polar opposite of the guts and glory atmosphere that had powered us away from relegation 17 years previously. This time around, Newcastle started lethargically and pretty much peaked there. There were a couple of half-chances, Villa goalie Brad Friedel pushed a Damien Duff shot away with his knees, but that was about as good as it got. In the end, all I remember is Gareth Barry's heart-sinking shot deflecting off Duff and into the corner of Steve Harper's Holte End net. Young centre-back David Edgar was sent off in injury time for a second yellow card, but it didn't really matter. Cue Aston Villa fans' now infamous 'Sob on The Tyne' banner and a half-hearted 15-year rivalry. After the match, BBC football writer Phil McNulty summed things up best, 'No fight. No urgency. No desire. No willingness to put limbs on the line to get the desired result.'

Looking back, it's hard to imagine how a season that saw both Kevin Keegan and Alan Shearer as Newcastle manager could have ended so badly. Supporters dream about legends returning to their club, and that collective joy should be enough to power success. But the club needs to be pointed in the right direction, too, as it was in 1995/96. Ultimately, Keegan and Shearer in 2008 felt like performative signings. Something to appease the fans and make a noise – handily offering Sports Direct some global reputation in the process. But after doing the hard work and tempting them back into football, the club were unable, or unwilling, to offer both men what they required to thrive. Whether that's Keegan's need to have a final say on transfers or how, following a post-season meeting between

Ashley and Shearer that was essentially an interview for the permanent manager's job, the board subsequently blanked the club's greatest goalscorer of all time. The whole thing just felt rotten to the core.

In a season packed with dizzying highs and gut-wrenching lows, Newcastle had been relegated to the Championship. They had a squad packed with highly paid players who didn't want to be there, had no manager, no direction, and an owner capable of anything. I appreciated my distant location more than ever. Being in Dubai meant that I had fewer reminders of our plight each day. There was little chance of seeing a Newcastle top, or bumping into a gleeful Sunderland fan in Dubai's Mall of Emirates, so I could put the heartbreak out of my mind for a little while longer. I felt guilty about my reprieve, and that I was avoiding my fair share of the pain, but I had never felt so pleased to be thousands of miles away from St James' Park in all of my life.

7

Greatness in Grimsby

4 May 1993
Grimsby Town 0 Newcastle United 2
Cole, Kelly

Before men talked openly about their mental health, I was quietly concerned about my own emotional capacity in relation to the goings-on at Barrack Road. Don't get me wrong. I was a pretty happy kid at the time. I was 16 and my days revolved around playing football, listening to music, doing a very small amount of school work, and going to the match. *Reservoir Dogs* was at the cinema, Primal Scream were about to take *Screamadelica* to Glastonbury, and Newcastle United were suddenly shit-hot. What's not to like? But that was actually part of the problem. I couldn't escape the fact that no feeling I ever had in my day-to-day life came close to the heightened emotion after a Newcastle goal. I didn't discriminate. All goals were equal as far as I was concerned, and I celebrated Frank Pingel scoring with the back of his head in 1989 against Liverpool in much the same way that I celebrated Andy Cole's slick first Newcastle goal in 1993, namely: jumping, shouting, and grabbing anybody in the vicinity. Limbs they call it now. Back then it was just *gannin' radge*. I almost never went *radge* outside of football. You don't want to be the bloke hugging everybody just because he's excited to be at Alton Towers, or who loudly whoops if he gets hold of *(What's the Story) Morning Glory?* before his mates, do you.

My even keel was a good line to tread as a teenager – the lows never too low, the highs never too high – but it confused me. I even tentatively broached the subject with my sister. I don't know why, she'd never been to the match, let alone experienced Mark McGhee beating three men and scoring a last-minute winner against Bradford. However, she sat and listened, like some sort of footballing Dr Hilary Jones, as I tried in vain to describe my feelings. After a moment of quiet contemplation she looked at me with a mixture of care and confusion, and told me that it would all probably be OK. Ah, *probably*. The least reassuring word in the English language. I mention all this because the 1992/93 season brought emotions that I had never experienced before as a football fan, largely because they were associated with success.

Kevin Keegan had spent much of the summer following our dogged survival tangling with the club over the thorny issue of ambition – the sticking point appearing to be that he had some. Newcastle, however, preferred the role of plucky underachiever. At the time, the short-term deal Keegan had suggested and signed in February felt right for all concerned. Should the worst happen and Newcastle disappear down a third tier-shaped hole, then the club wouldn't be saddled with a big-money contract. Keegan, meanwhile, could avoid the ignominy and get back to Marbella, putting the whole sorry mess behind him. But now things were different.

Free from the spectre of relegation – at least until the following May – Keegan was keen to see whether the club's ambitions matched his own. How badly did they want success, and how invested were they in creating something special? Not much if the first contract was anything to go by, stating that he must raise £1.5m via player sales, of which only half would filter back to him for team improvements. No dice. In fact so little dice that the press claimed Keegan had quit again – which would have been pretty impressive considering he wasn't even officially in the job at the time. Eventually a new dynamic board, featuring the key figures of Sir John Hall, local businessman Freddy Shepherd as vice-chairman, Hall's son Douglas, and Freddie Fletcher – who had been commercial director at Glasgow Rangers – decided that they were serious, and this was the dawn of a new age for Newcastle United after all. So, £1.15m was released for the purchase of three players who would prove crucial in the club's miraculous 12-month turnaround: Paul Bracewell from Sunderland, John Beresford from Portsmouth, and Barry Venison, a former Sunderland captain who was now a Liverpool utility player. I know what you're thinking. A little too much Sunderland in there. But just like when they decked out the Stadium of Light in black and white for our 2023/24 FA Cup win, we must thank the club for its service. Both ex-Mackems, Venison in particular, were immense at St James' Park.

Following a football team that wins regularly takes some getting used to, and requires a real change of mindset. Rather than approaching matches with apprehension, I was gung-ho and rather annoying about it all, predicting two- or three-goal victory margins like they were going out of fashion. The whole thing was utterly surreal, and it didn't matter to me that we were in the second tier. While subsequent promotions under Mike Ashley were enjoyable, this one felt special. I don't think I could have enjoyed it more if it had been the top-flight title we were steaming towards. With no social media, I had to content myself with trash-talking around the house. 'Tranmere away?

Seriously mate, we could play our reserves and still win by three down there.' It worked best if I looked in the mirror, maybe drawing a pencil moustache on one half of my face to turn it into a 'real' conversation. The only restriction was my imagination, that and my mam shouting upstairs to keep it down.

Newcastle won the first 11 games of the season in 1992/93. Eleven games! That's 33 points. It had taken us until February to reach that total in the previous campaign (27,670 turning out in Keegan's third game to catch a 1-1 draw with Barnsley), and this season we had done it by October. Not only that, but we had done it at Roker Park, Sunderland. And even better than all that, I was there.

Up until this season I had only seen Newcastle play away from the north-east on one occasion. It was in 1987 and during the school summer holidays. My mam and sister had gone away, leaving the lads – me and Dad – at home. Dad wasn't great at these things, but fair play, he made an effort. We had been to Hadrian's Wall, and were planning on watching a Newcastle friendly too, with a game scheduled at Gateshead Stadium for some late-July Saturday afternoon. I had been pining for Newcastle ever since the last game of the season, so this was the highlight of my entire six-week holiday. At least until we got wind that this local game would feature a collection of youth and reserve players, and that the first team was actually set for a friendly two and a half hours away at Scarborough's Seamer Road.

The news came from the radio like a boot to the head, but then something magical happened. On seeing my distress, Dad displayed what I'm fairly sure was the first instance of spontaneity I had ever seen from him. 'Shall we go down to Scarborough then?' he said quite matter-of-factly. I was absolutely gobsmacked. 'We should probably be there to cheer them on, shouldn't we?' he concluded. It remains one of my absolute favourite memories of him.

Newcastle fans took over the seaside town that day. Cars honked their horns as they drove along the front, while fans hung out of windows with a can in hand, singing, 'hello, hello, we are the Geordie boys!' I had never seen anything like it in my life, and it felt like I had suddenly been promoted to a higher level of supporter. After wandering around the town – and a few rounds on *Double Dragon* in the arcade – we had beans on toast at a small cafe and made our way to the ground. The game itself was poor, and Newcastle were 2-0 down to the Football League's newest side by half-time. A semblance of pride was restored in the second 45 minutes thanks to goals from Neil McDonald and Paul Gascoigne, but none of that mattered to me. I sat on a barrier not far from the main group of rowdy Newcastle fans and tried, for the first time ever, singing some of the songs along with them. For a brief moment I was part of the crowd that I had obsessed over for years in the Gallowgate End. As the game came to a close, and Newcastle fans invaded the pitch, one of them nicked the corner flag. I was suitably impressed.

Scarborough gave me the away bug, but it took five more years before my dad took me to another away match. In my defence it was hard enough getting the guy to St James' Park every other week. Convincing him that we should drive around the country following Newcastle required the type of conversational wizardry that is challenging at the age of 15. Eventually we went to Derby's Baseball Ground on 22 August 1992 for a game that felt like an early-season title fight. A win, following our 3-2 opening-day victory against Southend, would send out a message to the rest of the division. I was also there for revenge for the previous season's Battle of the Baseball Ground, a debacle that saw us ship four goals, three players and an assistant manager. As it turned out, a convincing 2-1 win – courtesy of goals in quick succession by Gavin Peacock and Lee Clark – proved to be all of those things and one more: Namely that it was far better going to away games than it was watching them at St James' Park.

Following Newcastle away from home was magical. It made me feel like a real fan, as stupid as that sounds – one of the hardcore. From trying to get a ticket in the first place, to booking travel at the old NUFC supporters' club, found in a shack behind the city's Eldon Square shopping centre. Being part of the convoy driving out of Newcastle, to the service station stop-offs which we briefly turned black and white, hoping that we'd see some rival fans and add some spice to the journey. My favourite moment was always when we hooked off the motorway and drove into the city centre of our opponent. We were an invading army, crossing the border and ready for war. People stopped and stared as the buses slowly rolled by, giving v-signs or kissing the badge of their own shirts as they walked to the game. It sounds incredibly arrogant, but it felt like people were looking at you with just a hint of awe. It was a hell of a buzz.

After the Derby match there was no stopping me. Chelsea in the League Cup was the first away game I attended without my dad. A few parenting thoughts: first off, cheers for letting me go. Secondly, allowing your child to attend their first unsupervised away game midweek in London, at Stamford Bridge, is questionable. They even allowed me to bunk off school for the afternoon just to catch the bus with a mate. We arrived late, and as we slowly inched through the crowd, the Chelsea supporters began to bang on the windows and shake the bus. It was my first game away from home without Dad, and I was going to see some trouble. Typical. I scanned the bus looking for potential weapons (all hooliganism films expect you to be tooled up), but found nothing. So, we decided to take the psychological approach, and basically just shouted at the baying mob from our seats on the bus, as if we were trying to scare off a bear. Thankfully they got bored and wandered off, which was a relief as I was in no position to deal with things getting tasty.

Not only did we get there late, but we ended up losing the game 2-1 to a Mick Harford winner. I did manage to catch Robert Lee's first Newcastle goal, a stooping header in the box to level the scores at 1-1 in the 77th minute. Lee was the fourth of five signings that season who went on to help change the club (Andy Cole was the fifth, and would arrive six months later to score goals like a robot centre-forward from the future). After Bracewell, Beresford and Venison, Lee – signed on 22 September after seven straight wins – was Keegan's first attacking signing, and was purchased from a position of strength as he loved to do. Twelve games in and Keegan was already buying players that would help the club in the Premier League. It was the direct opposite of Mike Ashley's transfer strategy.

Lee was signed as a right-winger, but Keegan had spotted something else in the 26-year-old Charlton Athletic midfielder. He had gut-busting energy, drive, and football intelligence, and became one of the best English midfielders of the decade – recognised by Geordies more than it was by England. He played with his shirt untucked at the front, a size too big, and scored goals from distance that contained sneaky levels of power. These shots looked like he had barely touched them, but from the minute they left his Puma King they increased in speed, eventually crashing past the goalkeeper and into the net like an Exocet missile. For ten years and 303 games Robert Lee was an absolute revelation in black and white.

A tight defeat at Chelsea showed how far we had come in a short space of time. Victory at Sunderland – our 11th straight league win of the season – made us feel invincible. The song of choice on the terraces was 'Newcastle United will never be defeated', inspired by the famous miners' slogan of 1984/85 (the miners united will never be defeated). Our run was so impressive that I genuinely wondered if the song might be true. What if it went on for years and we won everything, and eventually were expelled from the league because we were just too good and everybody was sick of it? That would be so typical of Newcastle. We'd just escaped relegation and possible bankruptcy, only to get kicked out because we were now class. I was getting ahead of myself, and of course we would lose again. But it wouldn't be on this day, and it wouldn't be at Roker Park.

There are times in 2025 when I'm almost grateful that I'm no longer trying to follow Newcastle home and away. Getting hold of a ticket seems utterly exhausting. Whether it's about ballots, draws, or arguing on Twitter over who has the right points, it feels like a minor miracle that anybody gets to see the game at all. In 1992 it was far easier, but I was still impressed when my dad came back from Witton Gilbert WMC one afternoon holding two tickets for the Wear-Tyne derby, a game that was obsessed over in the region no matter how badly the respective sides were doing. He had previous form in this pub-based mystery ticketing bonanza, and had also come up trumps for the game at Roker Park the year before, a game that saw Liam O'Brien's audacious lob get Newcastle back on level terms for a 1-1 draw. It's a very underrated goal, but that's largely because of what happened next.

We were top of the league, playing at our biggest rivals – who were struggling – and life couldn't have felt any better. At least until Gary Owers turned the ball into his own net after 16 minutes, giving Newcastle the lead. Suddenly fights broke out everywhere as Geordies scattered from their hiding places among the home sections, unable to contain their joy. These scraps were chaotic and messy, like fights in *The Beano* or *The Dandy*, where clouds of mayhem would obscure the detail save for the occasional boot or fist. If I close my eyes I can still remember two freshly liberated Newcastle fans being marched around the touchline from their position in the Fulwell End. They received the acclaim of the away support like conquering heroes, only for a Sunderland fan to suddenly launch himself at them from the Clock Stand Paddocks. He shot out like a pissed-up gazelle, propelled by a combination of Double Maxim and fury. It was thrilling. So much so that the players struggled to regain people's attention. Thankfully O'Brien scored a stunning free-kick winner, six minutes after Sunderland found parity via a 70th-minute Gordon Armstrong goal. From my position crammed into the Roker End I found myself right behind the flight of the ball. O'Brien struck it so cleanly, and it seemed to curl over the wall at a leisurely pace. Tim Carter in the Sunderland goal simply turned to watch it whistle past him, unable to make his limbs work. There was a split second of silence, and then 6,000 Geordies went absolutely mental!

At home we were imperious that year. In fact home games had to be made season ticket-only for safety reasons, as so many people were turning up each weekend. That meant I had to move from the Gallowgate Corner to its neighbouring Scoreboard section, but I was just happy to be there. We lost only once in 23 games at St James' Park, and that solitary reverse came against Grimsby Town just six days after we had beaten Sunderland on Wearside. Defeat finally came via an absolute thunderbolt by Jim Dobbin from 30 yards in the 89th minute for a 1-0 win. It was a great goal that was met with a horrified gasp from the home fans. After 11 wins in a row we had changed as a people, and weren't used to losing. I honestly don't think the crowd would have been more surprised if Dobbin had taken out a revolver and shot Keegan up the arse, rather than lashing a shot past Pavel Srníček. People were already huffing and puffing over the potential draw, so when that draw turned into a defeat it pushed them towards insanity, with some confused booing ringing out as the full-time whistle went.

The records will tell you that Newcastle took top spot in the First Division – as the second tier was now called after the initiation of the new Premier League – after game six that year, a 3-1 home win over Portsmouth, and that they stayed there for the rest of the season. But that wasn't the full story. While home was indeed full of comfort, significant moments happened away from St James' Park. From the win at Roker Park (a first there since 1956) to beating Premier League Middlesbrough in the League Cup 3-1, to ending our only real bad patch of the season – a six-game spell in January and February that served up five draws and a defeat – with a resounding 3-0 win at fellow promotion chasers Tranmere Rovers. This was the first time I remember us being a force away from the north-east. Then there was the FA Cup fifth round tie at Blackburn Rovers that was pitted as the battle of the former Liverpool number sevens: Kenny Dalglish v Kevin Keegan. The game ultimately ended in a tight 1-0 win to Blackburn, Roy Wegerle with an 89th-minute winner for a team that would go on to finish fourth, second, and then win the Premier League in the course of the next two and a half seasons. I was forced to listen to that one at home when, after getting into Newcastle at 6am to queue for a ticket, I discovered that so many people had headed there after the pubs had shut the previous night that they had been forced to open the ticket office early, and our allocation sold out in minutes. All that remained were discarded cans of lager, packets of crisps and, weirdly, some deckchairs and a beach ball. But all of those days were simply the precursors to the biggest away game of the season. Actually scratch that. The biggest away game of my life.

You might think that great moments in life rarely happen in the Lincolnshire port town of Grimsby. But I went there in 1993 with my mate John and we had a great time. We sang, we danced, we drank Skol – the pubs were rammed and that was all that was left in the off licence – and we won the league. Perhaps it was fated that the team who inflicted our first defeat of the season would also be the one we beat to clinch the title? Football is serendipitous like that. Seven months earlier we had laboured against this team but on a warm May evening at Blundell Park we pinged the ball around like nobody's business. Clad in the now classic yellow and green Umbro away strip, Keegan's men simply swarmed all over the home side from the word go. Lee Clark fizzed shots in from the edge of the box, linking up play with swift one- and-two touch passing moves. Andy Cole twisted and turned in the box like an electric eel in a pair of Reebok boots – the classic defender's nightmare – and Robert Lee ended the half by striking a decent shot off the foot of the Grimsby post. Lee was quickly back in the groove at the beginning of the second half, powering past two challenges to play a through ball to Cole, who neatly dispatched his shot past the Grimsby goalie Rhys Wilmot. At this point I was close to meltdown, fuelled by eight cans of Skol and a dream. If you check the YouTube footage I'm fairly sure that you can see me there, clad in a black and white Umbro training jacket and shaking the fence like a frenzied lifer welcoming the 'fresh fish' at Shawshank.

I don't recall much of the action from the second half. The away end was mayhem, and from Cole's goal on 46 minutes we joyfully went through our repertoire of songs, along with the season's new additions of 'We are top of the league', and 'Championeeees'. Both of those songs felt unusual to sing, generally the reserve of Liverpool, Arsenal or Manchester United. Trophy winners. But tonight, for the first time in my life, they belonged to Newcastle United, too.

My favourite Newcastle terrace anthem is 'Blaydon Races', a song that doesn't seem to get much air time at St James' Park these days. My heart aches at the thought it might eventually be lost for ever to the Newcastle crowd, and in its place a templated ditty also sang by eight other teams, where each fanbase simply inserts the name of their own player into some soulless Dua Lipa track. 'Blaydon Races' is the perfect football song. Strong local roots and a rambling verse that speeds up until reaching a mayhem-inducing chorus. What more could you want? On the Gallowgate End you had to start preparing the minute it began. The slow staccato intro of 'We. Went. To. Blay-don Ra-ces…' was a sign to push back and get some purchase. Observers from the Leazes End, East or West Stands would notice the terrace vacuum phenomenon, whereby a gaping hole suddenly appeared on the Gallowgate. This was self-preservation.

As the song continued I would push myself ever further back, until I was almost on top of the person behind as we sang, '18 hundred and 62 on a summer's afternoon'. A few lines later the chorus hit, releasing us forward in joyful propulsion, as we jumped, pushed, and danced our way down the stone terrace with an, 'Ohhhhhh me lads …' By the end of the first chorus – the song rarely got further than that – I often found myself ten yards away from where I had started, and would have to fight my way back up into position, possibly having to look for a lost shoe in the process. It was never anything less than brilliant.

As the game at Grimsby came to a close, there was one last push from Newcastle, and a tired clearance somehow found David Kelly in on goal, with Andy Cole free to his right. I remember praying for him to just square it to Cole – I was obsessed with him scoring as many as possible – but he took it around Wilmot, with the goalkeeper catching his leg ... it buckled and bent, but amazingly Kelly stayed on his feet long enough to steer a shot into the back of the net from a wide angle. We had done it. Newcastle United were champions!

With two games left in the season, it would have been easy for the team to have taken their foot off the gas, or for Keegan to have experimented with some youth players. After all, we already had the title in the bag. But that was never going to happen. We beat Oxford United 2-1 at home two days later – a game that most people (including me) pretty much forget about – before beating Leicester City on the last day of the season, as we had done one year previously to avoid relegation.

The Foxes were once again in the play-off mix but Keegan's side, sporting a new Asics home kit, tore Brian Little's men to shreds. It was 6-0 at half-time, with a hat-trick from David Kelly, two from Andy Cole, and one from Robert Lee. Cole completed his own hat-trick (a 12th goal in 13 games) in the second half, while Leicester's Steve Walsh grabbed a consolation goal, just as he had done 12 months previously.

In just one year, Kevin Keegan and Sir John Hall had turned Newcastle from relegation certainties into all-conquering champions. It was nothing short of a miracle, and largely testament to the persuasive powers of Keegan. Not that he was content with promotion, of course. After they had clinched the title at Grimsby, he was interviewed in a chaotic dressing room. Far from being happy to take the praise, he was already setting out a new challenge. 'We're after Man United now, you can tell Alex Ferguson,' he said with a mischievous grin. It was classic Keegan, offering the fantastical and impossible. But here's the thing: deep down, he meant every single word of it.

8

A Party in Plymouth

19 April 2010
Plymouth Argyle 0 Newcastle United 2
Carroll, Routledge

Newcastle United were relegated from the Premier League in 2009. A team boasting the talents of Michael Owen, Mark Viduka, Obafemi Martins, and Damien Duff managed to finish 18th in the table, and only picked up seven wins all season. My pals and I chose Nelson's bar in Dubai to watch the crucial decider against Aston Villa. I've no idea why. It was packed with so many Chesterfield sofas and wooden cabinets that it resembled my nan's house. Maybe subconsciously I was looking for the kindness and comfort of a grandparent. When defeat condemned us to the Championship, I was actually consoled by a Sunderland fan. Not in jest, or mockery. He didn't wait for me to react and then go 'Aaaaah!' in my face, or whip out a trombone and make that buuuuurrrruuuup! noise. It was genuine empathy. Up was down, down was up. Maybe one of those wooden cabinets would look good in my apartment? Things had gotten weird.

Newcastle were in a right old mess as they slipped out of top-flight football for the fifth time in their history. No relegated club has their shit together, but as May trickled into June, Newcastle were crumpled and directionless. Largely because the owner couldn't decide whether he wanted to keep the club or not.

Mike Ashley first put Newcastle up for sale in 2008. It felt motivated by petulance, after the fans protested the Kevin Keegan debacle. He took it off the market again in December 2008, shortly after hiring Joe Kinnear as interim manager and stating, 'Joe's the man to do the job. He's my hero. Is he better than Fabio Capello? Definitely. We are going to be in Europe by the end of the season!' So, when Newcastle were duly relegated, the erratic owner let it be known that the club was, once again, up for sale. Only this time the hoped-for £400m asking price had been slashed to £100m … and then £80m … Everything Must Go! It was all very Sports Direct.

Tony Jimenez, Ashley's former vice-president of player transfers, claimed the owner had ruined a potential Middle Eastern takeover by causing a disturbance in Dubai's Bahri Bar. A further claim was that Ashley refused to meet with representatives of the Abu Dhabi United Group, a private equity company owned by Sheikh Mansour bin Zayed Al Nahyan, that would go on to become the majority owners of Manchester City. So, yeah, things were messy at the top. But Newcastle United under Ashley was nothing if not surprising. Just when you felt things couldn't get any more nightmarish they suddenly got a shite-sight worse, as a strong side was thumped 6-1 in a friendly at League One Leyton Orient. It was a defeat that quite possibly saved the Magpies' season.

Friendlies are ostensibly about fitness and formation. At least that's what everybody says when you lose them. But this pre-season kickabout wasn't just a defeat, it was a catastrophe, the clusterfuck at the club in 90-minutes-of-football form. All the bile and apathy that had allowed this genuinely talented bunch of footballers to be relegated seeped out at Brisbane Road. But as the historian Thomas Fuller said in 1650, 'It's always darkest before the dawn,' and defeat proved something of a tipping point for the club. A players' group led by Kevin Nolan, Steve Harper and Joey Barton drew a line in the sand in its aftermath. Who wants to be here and who doesn't?

Suddenly the clouds broke over St James' Park. High-profile underachievers such as Owen, Viduka, Martins, and Duff were shipped out, and few fans maligned their departure. Personally I was a little more downbeat over the sales of Sébastien Bassong and Habib Beye. Despite relegation, the 21-year-old Bassong had enjoyed a decent first season at the heart of the defence after signing from Metz. I could see him blossoming had he remained at St James' Park. Instead he chose a move to Spurs and his star in English football quickly faded. Senegal international Beye, meanwhile, had been a bargain £2m signing from Marseille in 2007. Thanks to some all-action displays and a terrace song to the tune of the *Happy Days* theme ('Monday, Tuesday, Habib Beye') he had become a fan favourite, exuding passion that made me certain he would stay at the club. So, yeah, his subsequent move to Aston Villa (of all places) was a real kick in the balls.

When a club gets relegated, from any division, a bizarre phenomenon often overcomes its fanbase. After the pain and embarrassment heals, supporters suddenly become super-confident. Like they're far too good for the division and will certainly make short work of getting promoted. That's certainly how I felt upon experiencing relegation for the first time as a young, foolish Newcastle fan in 1989.

One year previously I had been optimistic about Newcastle's chances in the First Division, too. We had sold Paul Gascoigne to Tottenham Hotspur, at which I was utterly crestfallen, but manager Willie McFaul had been allowed to spend. In came the Wimbledon goalkeeper (and FA Cup Final hero) Dave Beasant, their centre-half Andy Thorn, prolific Hearts striker John Robertson, and the barrel-chested winger John Hendrie from Bradford. They all looked like solid signings. Sadly almost all of them, to a man, failed at the club. The 4-0 battering at Everton on the opening day didn't help. So, after finishing the previous season in eighth position Newcastle were relegated, coming in dead last, and nine points adrift of safety.

Regardless of the previous season's disaster, within three months I was once again desperate to watch football at St James' Park. The fact that we were in the Second Division didn't really bother me too much, I just wanted to go to the match. The only problem was that my dad had frustratingly planned a four-week holiday back to his hometown of Szombathely in Hungary which coincided with the start of the football season. The decision quite frankly staggered me in its insensitivity. I mean, yes, this was to be the first time that he would return to his childhood home since running away as a 17-year-old boy, fearing for his life amid the Hungarian Revolution. And *OK*, he had been away for roughly 33 years, with only the falling Iron Curtain and declining Soviet influence making him feel comfortable enough to return. But still. It was the football season! He was taking us to his home, proudly showing off his family and the life he had built against all the odds, and I was furious.

We returned from Hungary one day after Mick Quinn's four-goal debut as Newcastle smashed promotion favourites Leeds United 5-2 at St James' Park. I mean, one day. Fair enough missing pre-season, but he could have easily come back a day earlier for the match. As it was I had to read about it in the paper after demanding we head to the newsagents before going home (after two days of travelling). Being an impatient little arsehole aside, I felt sure after such an opening-day win that we were going to storm the league, and probably have the whole thing put to bed around March. Of course it didn't quite work out that way, and we languished in the second tier for another three seasons until the Miracle of Kevin. Should have probably called the book that, actually.

Fast forward 20 years, and with a hatred of Ashley running through the support like a stick of Blackpool rock, there was precious little optimism. If that wasn't bad enough, Sir Bobby Robson passed away on 31 July 2009 following a long battle with cancer. Thankfully that Orient result wasn't the last one he had to see, as Newcastle drew 0-0 with Leeds just a few days later. But the former manager's death was another hammer blow to the soul of the Magpies. Despite his poor treatment by those in charge in 2004, and although small pockets of Newcastle fans had questioned his control over a squad that included firebrands such as Craig Bellamy and Kieron Dyer, Robson was guardian of not just the club, but a purer version of football. He and Keegan were rather similar in that respect – they both operated with hearts firmly on sleeves, and people quite rightly adored them for it.

While Newcastle were looking for some heart in 2009/10, they were also short of a manager, too. Ashley and his cronies were busy blanking Alan Shearer, following a meeting whereby he laid out a plan to get the club straight back into the Premier League. I've been ghosted a lot when it comes to job interviews, but can you imagine doing it to Shearer? 'Shall we at least get back to him, Mike, send him the old "thanks for your time" email? Or shall we just fuck off this living legend and crack on into the season without any manager at all?' Ever the maverick, Ashley opted for the latter, and Newcastle opened the 2009/10 season away to West Bromwich Albion with Chris Hughton continuing in his now-legendary caretaker role.

Being in Dubai meant that relegation gave me more problems than most when it came to following Newcastle. Now that they were in the Championship I couldn't watch the games. From being able to follow the club home and away in the Premier League, even from the Middle East, I was left with just the occasional big game on TV, and maybe some highlights if I was lucky. I could have listened to it on the radio, but I had done that loads as a kid and would spend entire games thinking that the opposition was basically on the edge of our box – it's 90 minutes of pure angst. Twitter wasn't the beast it is today, either. Back then, before PR and marketing teams got to grips with the platform, it was the Wild West. Some clubs, like Manchester City, posted with a healthy dose of very unofficial sarcasm, while others failed to offer much in the way of updates at all. The players themselves, meanwhile, treated it as a private messaging service, seemingly unaware that every post was beamed out to the world. Whether it was Andy Robertson wondering aloud on how to get a retweet by the Pope, Michael Owen posting his devastation at running over a rabbit, or Wayne Rooney offering himself out for a fight, it was a golden era of sporting social media. Unfortunately not when it came to a matchday. So, in 2009/10 I followed our season via the BBC Football app and its scrolling live-match commentary. Featuring regular updates such as 'Nolan wins free kick, Newcastle half (17 mins)', it was like playing *Championship Manager* in the mid-90s. But you know what? The whole thing felt weirdly liberating. After 24 years of having my every Saturday between August and May dominated by football, I had a legitimate excuse to take a step back.

The decision was completely out of my hands. I had my weekends back and discovered that it's easier to handle a loss when you're not paying too much attention. Not that we lost too much in the 2009/10 season.

Chris Hughton wasn't officially named manager of Newcastle until 27 October 2009, by which point he had been voted Manager of the Month once, had won eight out of the season's first 13 games (losing just three) and had the club sitting at the top of the table, a position they would relinquish for only one week during the remainder of the season. He was given no real funds to sign players – Danny Simpson and Zurab Khizanishvili came in on loan in August, and Peter Løvenkrands signed on a free ('from Ger-man-ee', as the song went) five months later. January saw Simpson's loan from Manchester United made permanent, while Wayne Routledge arrived from QPR and Mike Williamson from Portsmouth. The defence was further strengthened with the loan signings of Patrick van Aanholt from Chelsea, and Fitz Hall from QPR. Finally, with Ashley loosening the purse strings in a bid to guarantee promotion, Leon Best arrived from Coventry City.

After being officially named manager, Hughton's team lost only one more game that season. But that random 3-0 defeat at Derby in February was sandwiched between two colossal runs of form: nine wins out of 14 between October and February, and 13 wins from 17 between February and May. With the dependable Steve Harper in goal, the curly haired, sex god Fabricio Coloccini at the back, the experience of Nolan and Barton in the middle, and an emerging Andy Carroll up-front, the spine of the team was far too spicy for the Championship. Harper always talks about how they were horrible to play against, boasting that perfect combination of talent, experience, and utter shithousery.

Mike Ashley was busy doing some shithousing of his own to the backdrop of this resoundingly successful season. While Keegan's promotion chasers had been boosted by the additions of Robert Lee, Scott Sellars and Andy Cole, Hughton had to survive off scraps until halfway through the season. Ashley's shit-show PR machine was firing on all cylinders, too, a high point being in November 2009 when, with the club sitting at the top of the table and a feel-good factor finally starting to return, he announced that he would like to sell the naming rights to St James' Park. The news broke in a rare interview that also saw him admit he regretted buying the club in the first place. It's fair to say that it went down about as well with the Newcastle supporters as Prince Andrew's *Newsnight* interview did with the lads at Buckingham Palace. It was so typically tone deaf. From a position of burgeoning success and reduced anti-Ashley noise, the owner stuck his head above the parapet and once more wreaked havoc. So, in what was allegedly a move to entice sponsorship, St James' Park was temporarily renamed sportsdirect.com@StJamesParkStadium, even though nobody called it that … anywhere, not even the club in its matchday programme. Unsurprisingly the decision was met with huge fan protests at the following game (a 3-1 home win against Peterborough United) but more on all that later.

Like Grimsby in 1993, a party in Plymouth saw Hughton's class of 2010 win the league with two games to spare. Newcastle in yellow – just as they had been all those years ago in Lincolnshire – always looked likely to grab the one point required to secure top spot in the division. A first goal duly came on 20 minutes, with Andy Carroll sending a looping header into the corner of the net from a Danny Guthrie corner. It was the 18th goal of an interesting season for Carroll. On the one hand he had fully broken into the first team and thrived, but on the other he had also broken team-mate Steven Taylor's jaw (presumably *with* that other hand) after he had apparently sent texts to Carroll's former partner. That Taylor was standing in a wheelie bin at the time – or so the story goes – using it as a makeshift ice bath adds a certain level of comedy to the whole thing. One that I'm not against, to be honest. A second goal came just eight minutes later, from the one quality move of the game. Although Barton initially lost the ball in midfield, he quickly shrugged off his man to regain possession. He played a neat one-two with Guthrie, before sliding a defence-splitting pass through to Wayne Routledge, who rounded the goalie and sealed Newcastle's promotion back to the Premier League.

Newcastle absolutely walked the title in 2009/10. Hughton's side bagged 102 points, a club record, and more than Keegan did (or Rafa Benítez's team of 2016/17 would). They scored more goals and conceded fewer than any other side in the division, winning 30 games en route to the title. They were also unbeaten at home, the only time that has happened in my lifetime following the club. But it still didn't feel special, at least not to me. Perhaps this is simply about shifting sands, and moments in time. This just wasn't *my* promotion. Not the one that I followed home and away, and obsessed about as I was growing up in the north-east of England. I looked to the bench as the full-time whistle went at Plymouth, and that seemed muted, too. A few hugs, some handshakes, but nothing like the pandemonium at Grimsby all those years ago. Maybe I would have felt differently if I had followed it from home, going to the games again. The lads in the crowd certainly did. Tops were off and the Geordies were ready to party. I never quite understood Newcastle's away following taking their tops off. 'Shoes off if you love the Mags' was a step too far for me, so I'm pretty glad I missed the more extreme version. Warm weather, fair enough, but other than that I'm more of a 'wear gloves, if you love the Mags' sort of bloke. Not that this is an easy line to walk. A guy at the match once took me to task for wearing a scarf. 'What's that thing for?' he said incredulously, as the snow fell around us.

Newcastle wrapped up the season with a 2-2 draw at home to Ipswich – Jon Walters' 94th-minute equaliser for the Tractor Boys taking the gloss off the trophy parade somewhat – and then a 1-0 win away at QPR. You couldn't argue that it had been one hell of a turnaround at St James' Park, and Hughton and the players deserved nothing but respect and admiration for the way they picked up the pieces after relegation, got rid of the dead wood, and went on to win the title. But there was no rallying cry at the end of it all. No rabble-rousing from Hughton, claiming that Ancelotti and Chelsea needed to watch out, we were after their title. Of course this wasn't Hughton's style, and football's landscape was unrecognisable from that of 17 years previously. The finances in the game meant that it had become increasingly difficult for such magical moments to occur. If you go up, you just bloody try and stay up. You can think about being a bit better after that.

One person who was making statements, however, was Mike Ashley. And from the heart of his Sports Direct empire – what I presume to be a hollowed-out hill somewhere in Buckinghamshire – he made sure that the goodwill built by a successful promotion campaign would not continue for any longer than absolutely necessary. Newcastle became the only club in Premier League history to go into a new season without a bonus structure being agreed upon. An air of mistrust from the players, fans, and a generally shitty atmosphere grew once more around the club. We hadn't even played one game back in the Premier League, but at Mike Ashley's Newcastle United it was business as usual.

9
All Guns Blazing

19 August 1995
Newcastle United 3 Coventry City 0
Lee, Beardsley (pen), Ferdinand

The first day of a football season is unequivocally the best day of the year. Christmas and birthdays might *sound* good, but they're fraught with familial danger. First day of a holiday? Exciting in theory, but that's just a wheelie suitcase full of hassle. Pancake Day? Fair enough, that is decent, but the reality is that nothing can truly match the unbridled joy of a whole new year of football stretching out in front of you. Just think about it. Which other day has the ability to wipe clean the transgressions of the previous 12 months? You might say New Year's Day, but I'm not so sure. That's basically all hangovers and dark regret, or at least mine are.

The first day of the footy season, on the other hand, is redemption in the sun. Here, all the mistakes and heartache you endured last season simply disappear into the ether. The big misses and lost opportunities, that time you fell asleep in the toilets at Molineux and missed the second half, even the indignity of relegation. When you walk into a stadium for the first game of the new season none of that matters.

You've probably spent some time in a beer garden, the pitch is a brilliant green and you think, 'You know what? I fancy us to win the whole bloody thing this year.' I have never had that feeling more than on 19 August 1995.

Such fresh optimism was a far cry from the atmosphere surrounding the club just seven months earlier, when Kevin Keegan fronted up to an irate group of supporters on the steps of St James' Park after selling star striker Andy Cole to Manchester United. 'Cole Sold For £7m!' screamed the sandwich boards of Newcastle's local paper, the *Evening Chronicle*. At least I think that's what they said, I was pretty close to tears at the time.

When Cole missed his first big chance for Newcastle, I was sitting in a temporary stand on a miserable Wednesday night at Maine Road, Manchester. The ball had dropped to him in the box at around the ten-minute mark, but rather than the 'gets the ball, scores a goal' scenario we had built a whole song around, his instinctive shot flashed high over the bar instead. As the Mitre Ultimax whistled towards the back of the North Stand I was so shocked that I tipped Bovril into the jacket of the man sitting in front of me (I didn't tell him). Missed chances by Cole for Newcastle were incredibly rare. Don't get me wrong, the guy must have popped a few efforts wide of the mark in the 20-odd months since becoming the fulcrum of our attack, but for the life of me I couldn't remember them. After signing for a club record fee of £1.75m from Bristol City in March 1993, he had been utterly imperious in front of goal.

A lithe, gazelle-like mover, Cole wore cycling shorts under his actual shorts – something I tried for a while but was so skinny that it just looked like I was wearing two pairs of shorts – and he had the enviable knack of being in the right place at the right time. He had an air of surly cool about him, too, and while he would feature in the typical football magazine canon of *Shoot!*, *Match*, and *90 Minutes*, you also would see him in things like hip-hop bible *The Source*. I feel confident labelling that a first for a Newcastle player. Not only did it take Cole just 70 games to score 55 goals for the club, but the 1993/94 season had seen him hit 41 alone, breaking the 70-year goalscoring record of legendary Newcastle centre-forward Hughie Gallagher in the process. After the miss at Manchester City – a game that would end up 1-1 courtesy of Mike Jeffrey's first and last goal for the club – our talismanic striker never scored another Newcastle goal again. Largely because Keegan sold him just six weeks later. It did not go down well.

To Newcastle fans of a certain vintage, the Cole bombshell felt like momentarily stepping back in time. Selling your top man to a bigger rival was such a late-80s Newcastle move; a shift back to horrible old habits. But despite the air of pessimism that had suddenly returned to the club, there was one crucial difference to this particular big-money departure. This was not the Newcastle of old.

It's hard to say how many people were calmed by Keegan's beige trouser-and-roll-neck combination on the St James' Park steps that day, but I firmly believe his outfit helped pacify supporters on a deeply subconscious level. I don't think the look was in any way deliberate, not like when members of parliament pick a tie colour that polls well with floating voters. But as he wearily faced off with fans about the transfer, arms outstretched like a fed-up Jesus, I couldn't help but think, 'Hang on a minute, Kevin looks a bit like Roger Moore in *Live and Let Die* here. Surely that's a good sign?'

According to Terry McDermott in his autobiography *Terry Mac: Living For the Moment*, both he and Keegan had decided that the time was right to sell Cole. In their eyes there had been a lack of spring in the step of Newcastle's number nine for some time. Even though he was averaging a goal every other game in the 1994/95 season, and had never agitated for a move away from St James' Park, the management team felt a little of the light had left his eyes. 'Manchester United came in with an offer in January worth a British record £7m, which we accepted,' said McDermott. But while it was a move that caused a meltdown among the fanbase, Newcastle weren't selling the family silver this time, they were planning for an attack on the title.

By 1995, I had struggled through some further A-levels at Durham New College after leaving the sixth form at St Leonard's RC Comprehensive, but in truth I felt lost. It seemed like everybody else had got their shit together so much earlier than me, and UCAS forms – the application route to university – had been sent out with the speed of Ruel Fox scampering after a ball over the top. I vaguely remember filling one out a few months before we left school, whenever the very last available moment was. I may have applied to do Forestry in Portsmouth in blind panic. But I'm not sure I wanted to go to university at all. I just didn't know what *else* to do. And so, as is my way, I did nothing, while occasionally mumbling words of concern. 'Don't worry about it,' people said. 'You'll get in through clearing. It'll all be fine in clearing,' like it was some sort of magical university wand. 'Great,' I thought. 'Now not only do I have no real life plan, but I've also got to find out what the hell clearing is, too.' During these times, only Newcastle United gave me any real sense of purpose, and I built my life around their fixture list. To their credit, they were doing a passable impression of a football club going places.

Ahead of the 1995/96 season, Newcastle made four signings who went straight into the first team for the opener at home to Coventry City. Goalkeeper Shaka Hislop joined from Reading for £1.57m, and I immediately warmed to his penchant for wearing a massive, untucked jersey, a chain over his shirt, and a pre-match preparation that included blasting the ball into his own net. Next up was England full-back Warren Barton, who briefly became the most expensive defender in English football after his £4m move from Wimbledon. Then the big one, QPR and England striker Les Ferdinand. The story goes that, originally, Keegan wanted to pair Cole and Ferdinand up front. But while the mind boggles as to the carnage those two might have caused together, the reality was that he eventually joined for £6m as Cole's successor. If the signings had stopped there we would have been more than happy, but the club were in no mood to rest on their laurels, and the dashing French winger David Ginola also arrived, signed from French giants Paris Saint-Germain – under the noses of Barcelona – for the criminally low fee of £2.5m. If you would like a solid indicator of how much life at Newcastle had changed in a short space of time, Ginola's signing was apparently delayed for 24 hours as he was on a modelling assignment with the supermodel Claudia Schiffer. That almost never happened with Billy Askew.

At time of writing I have seen 40 seasons' opening fixtures while supporting Newcastle. Some good, some bad, all memorable in their own way. But Coventry in 1995 is the one that always sticks out in my mind as the picture-perfect opener. St James' Park was bathed in bright sunlight, and the club's now-iconic Grandad collar Adidas shirt was everywhere. The team had just enjoyed a sparkling pre-season that read: played six, won five, drawn one, goals scored 15 (including six for Ferdinand), goals conceded three. Confidence could not have been higher as we welcomed opponents who, with all due respect to Ron Atkinson's side, were simply there to make up the numbers, echoing the role played by Bristol City three years earlier on Keegan's managerial debut.

Life in England around 1995 felt exciting and there for the taking, too. It was soundtracked (at least for me) by the Charlatans, Black Grape, and Oasis. If I wasn't at the match or thinking about football, I was reading about Tony Wilson, Ian Curtis, or Shaun Ryder. A female friend once said, upon inspecting my bookshelf, that they were all either about football or music. I took that as a compliment when she was, in fact, noting my rather limited selection. What can I say? I'm with the Stone Roses' bass player, Mani, on this one, 'After football and music, what else is there?'

There is greatness in these moments, even though they're often terrifying. I was secretly wracked with nerves as to where my future lay in 1995, but life came with raw excitement, too. Sure, you have no idea what the hell you're doing, but anything is possible. Astronaut, hitman, professional breakdancer, it's all up for grabs. There's an almighty power in that. The key is being able to grasp that energy and do something with it.

The feeling of optimism at Newcastle was further boosted by the completion of St James' Park's redevelopment, mandated by the post-Hillsborough disaster Taylor Report. For the first time in its 103-year history the ground became all-seated, with a roof that sheltered everybody from the elements (at least in theory). St James' Park was now all shiny industrial pipes and big grey angles. As it loomed over Strawberry Place it felt like we had a stadium to rival any team in the world.

There were downsides, of course, because it meant an end to standing on a terrace with your mates, jumping about and generally being daft. I had waited until the very last moment to make my move to a more respectable, seated life, holding firm in the Milburn Paddocks until the Gallowgate

End development was finally complete. I teetered on the brink a few times, of course. I was offered a season ticket in the Leazes End midway through the 1993/94 season, and was allowed to try it for one game before committing. It felt all wrong. For a start, my mate Mikey and I were stuck in one of those sections housing only three or four seats in a row, like we'd been naughty and had to sit separately from the group until we saw the error of our ways. Secondly, Ray Wilkins. QPR's player-manager completely spooked me that day. I mean, it's not often you see a former England and Milan legend sporting a shaving foam beard is it? I stared as he signed some autographs nearby, without making any reference to it at all, as a bit of the foam glooped off his chin and on to his sleeve. What the hell was that about? Butch Wilkins had completely got into my head, and I couldn't think about anything else for the rest of the game. The bad omens were confirmed when a QPR side featuring Darren Peacock and Les Ferdinand (who scored) picked up a surprise 2-1 win. I immediately decided to go back to the Paddocks until the following season.

As I clicked through the turnstile and walked up to my seat in the new Gallowgate End, roughly around the area once known as the Scoreboard, I considered the heaving mass of Geordie aggro it once was. All the years I had spent daydreaming about standing on this terrace, and how amazing it felt to become part of that crowd. We had shared so many good times together. There was the rubbish pitch invasion after the Hull game in 1991 of course, and East Stand Kenny Everett's sheet of A4 paper that same day with the words 'Going Down' on it. This banner, if you can call it that (you can't), was aimed at Sunderland who were busy being relegated from the First Division at the time. Every five minutes or so he removed it from his jacket pocket, carefully unfolded it and displayed it to a cheering Gallowgate Corner. There was the time Gazza turned up to a game at home against Derby County stood in the Corner, and was given good-natured abuse for 45 minutes, and also the moment we all realised that Ant McPartlin, at the time known as PJ from *Byker Grove,* was standing behind us. He had to face a few, shouted-from-distance, questions as to whether or not he was getting it on with Spuggy, his famed ginger co-star. I never saw him at a match again. But there was little time for sentiment, the game had kicked off and Newcastle were playing like the 1970s Brazil side.

If you start a game with attack-minded midfielders such as Lee Clark and Robert Lee, wingers of the darty and dribbly kind (Keith Gillespie and David Ginola respectively), the guile of Peter Beardsley and the power of Les Ferdinand up front, then you're not aiming to grind out a 1-0 win. From the moment that Lee scored a leaping, looping header after just seven minutes, the only question was how many goals Newcastle would score. That it remained 1-0 until the last ten minutes was probably the biggest shock of the day. Although Beardsley blasted home a penalty, winning the spot-kick himself on 82 minutes, the big moment of the day came just 60 seconds later – the goal everybody, with the exception of Coventry, wanted. With St James' Park bouncing in the late afternoon sun, Lee arced a ball down the right channel towards the Gallowgate End, and Ferdinand shot into the picture. He took one touch to push it past the on-rushing goalkeeper, John Filan, and another to angle the ball just inside the right-hand post. The stadium went nuts. Keegan and McDermott leaped for joy, I got my new neighbour into a friendly headlock, and our star centre-forward was off the mark in game one. He went on to score 18 more before we had even got to Christmas.

In his autobiography, *My Life in Football*, Keegan describes how the board once chastised him for publicly talking about his desire for Newcastle United to go and dominate English football. The feeling from the upper echelons at the club was that this sort of hype would bring too much pressure. But for Keegan it was a no-brainer. Why shouldn't a club like Newcastle aim for the top, and why shouldn't they put that ambition on record? Keegan had embraced pressure his entire career, and he knew that out of pressure comes diamonds.

10

Everything Must Go

2 February 2011
Fulham 1 Newcastle United 0

For a short time in 2010, Andy Carroll led the line for Newcastle United with such ferocity that I could only assume it was part of some convoluted ransom demand, and that he had been told he would only see his family again if he obliterated every centre-half in the Premier League.

> 'Jesus, man, why are you doing this?'
> 'Never mind that, just give Rio Ferdinand a torrid time this afternoon and await our next call.'
> *phone clicks off

It felt good watching a Geordie centre-forward play for his hometown club with such forceful passion. Sure, it was early days, but Newcastle had something going on. There was a fear factor about us and, dare I say, even a winning mentality, too. Hah! What a fool I was. Allowing cautious optimism into your life is the worst thing you can do as a football fan. The clogged veins of Newcastle supporters everywhere had suddenly been injected with the merest drop of hope, and in the blink of an eye we went from wondering if we would stay up to philosophically explaining (after a few pints), how we had an outside chance of Europe. Regardless of realism, a feel-good factor had slowly returned to Tyneside once again, so it should have come as no surprise when Mike Ashley promptly sold our ponytailed beacon of light at the first big-money opportunity. It felt like someone had died that day. Cards on the table: I had to leave work early.

Carroll was once almost cut from Newcastle's academy. A left-footed player, he had been asked to fill in at left-back due to injuries, and some of the coaches there felt like he wouldn't quite make the grade. Thankfully John Carver, in charge of the academy at the time, had seen him play up front, and a two-year scholarship was forthcoming. Having signed his first professional contract with the club in July 2006, Carroll made his first-team debut just one month later, a late substitute for Nolberto Solano as Newcastle picked up a priceless 1-0 away win against Palermo in the UEFA Cup. Occasional substitute appearances followed, he grabbed a goal in a 2-0 pre-season win over Juventus – earning praise from Gianluigi Buffon – and then had an 11-game loan spell at Preston North End. But it wasn't until 2009 – as big-name strikers deserted our sinking ship following relegation to the Championship – that Carroll really got his chance to shine. Under the calming influence of Chris Hughton, a Geordie strike force of Carroll and Shola Ameobi began the 2009/10 season. By the end of it, Newcastle had won promotion back to the Premier League, and Carroll's 19 goals topped the club's scoring charts.

Despite posting significant numbers in the Championship, Carroll was never a prolific goalscorer. Big and strong, he could bring players into the game, and he was surprisingly decent with his feet, too, so he was about more than just putting the ball in the back of the net. His role in 2024 behind the striker at French side Amiens bore further testament to that ability. He had plundered goals at England youth level, but his professional career shows him to be a one goal in every three or four games sort of striker.

Injuries eventually took their toll on Carroll, and he never seemed to get a good run of appearances under his belt after leaving St James' Park. As a footballer, he may have peaked in those first 18 games of the 2010/11 season, from the all-left-foot hat-trick in the 6-0 demolition of Aston Villa, to the towering header that ensured a first win away at Arsenal since 2001, taking Newcastle to fifth spot in the table. His England debut came just ten days later, as our Samson-esque striker looked set to write his name into Newcastle's number nine folklore. But of course much to everybody's regret (including his own), it didn't work out that way. Carroll scored five more times in eight games for Newcastle, one of them a long-range banger in a 3-1 home win against Liverpool. Six weeks later, as the transfer window slammed shut, and with Newcastle sitting eighth in the table, Mike Ashley sold Carroll to Kenny Dalglish's side for a British record £35m.

I was a kid when Newcastle had sold Chris Waddle, Peter Beardsley and Paul Gascoigne in the space of just three years. Three exciting homegrown players shipped off to balance the books and win trophies elsewhere. The sale of Andy Cole seven years later was a blow too, but for the first time ever that hadn't been enforced on the manager. In fact the Newcastle board thought that Keegan was crazy to part company with their star striker. But this was tactical. It allowed Newcastle to move up a gear and buy Les Ferdinand. Although Andy Carroll wasn't in the same bracket as those big-name players, the situation felt depressingly familiar and a gut-wrenching revert to a pre-Keegan type.

The 34-year-old Finnish-Albanian striker Shefki Kuqi was a player without a club when Newcastle signed him on a short-term deal in February 2011. Often wrongly cited as the Carroll replacement (the club allegedly tried to bring in Diego Forlán for that purpose, only for collective arses to drop when they saw his financial requests). Kuqi arrived on Tyneside in one of the most bizarre signings of the club's modern era. And bear in mind that this era included Fumaça – the most un-Brazilian, Brazilian footballer ever. By the time he arrived on Tyneside, Kuqi had already spent a decade in the UK, playing for Stockport County, Sheffield Wednesday, Ipswich Town (he did pretty well there actually, 26 goals in 68), Blackburn Rovers, Crystal Palace, Fulham, Swansea City, Derby County, and then Newcastle. I think the biggest shock for me wasn't that he had signed for the club – it didn't serve you well to be easily spooked during Ashley's ownership – it was that he was five months younger than me. I mean, seriously, the guy looked late 40s minimum. It wouldn't have surprised me if we discovered that he also lived with a family of bears, maybe in a caravan somewhere, all of them just growling at stuff together. Alas, Kuqi's time on Tyneside was all too brief. Six games, no goals and on to his next adventure, like a not very good Jon Stark, the self-styled 'soccer mercenary' from the *Roy of the Rovers* comic.

Carroll's sale wasn't the first time that Ashley had pulled the rug from beneath the feet of Newcastle supporters that season alone. Chris Hughton was given the manager's job in 2009 and, free from the shackles of his usual caretaker suffix, brought relative calm to St James' Park, taking a disparate group of characters and building a close-knit first-team squad. He achieved promotion at the first time of asking; and his start to life in the Premier League had been quietly satisfactory, too, overseeing five wins out of 16 – including the 5-1 demolition of local rivals Sunderland – and a comfortable mid-table position. He had the confidence of both fans and players by November 2010, which was just around the time that Ashley sacked him, replacing him with the former West Ham manager Alan Pardew. At the time, a Sky Sports poll claimed that Pardew had just 5.5 per cent of a supporter vote. Most people on Tyneside were surprised that it was even that high.

I felt sorry for Pardew during the Carroll sale. The guy had only been at the club for six weeks. He'd overseen seven games (three wins, two draws, two defeats) and the club was sitting in a healthy eighth position. Presumably emboldened by early success, the former Crystal Palace midfielder came out fighting during the deadline day rumours about Carroll.

'We need to have a big-club mentality and hold on to our best players,' said Pardew, clearly unaware of Ashley's glorious blueprint for the future of the club. 'Andy's career path is here. He has already proved that playing for Newcastle United will not hinder his international career, so why does he need to go? He loves it here and loves the fans – and long may it continue.'

Oh Alan.

In a matter of hours Pardew was forced to about-face, and rumours have persisted ever since regarding whether Carroll really had asked for a pay rise just five months after negotiating a new contract (something the striker denies), or whether that was simply how the club played the narrative. But away from the doublespeak, Pardew lost his number one striker in the blink of an eye. Something that presumably wasn't in the brochure when he signed on to become manager.

Two days after Carroll had gone, a rather lifeless Newcastle lost 1-0 to Fulham at Craven Cottage. It was a big, half-arsed sigh of a game. On 67 minutes, Damien

Duff dispossessed José Enrique down the Newcastle left to rush in and grab the winner. Isn't that typical? Just when you think you're at rock bottom, a former player – one who never quite cut it at your own club – decides that you can still come down a notch or two, and delivers a good old shit sandwich. To be honest, the result barely registered with me that day. I was still bereft about Carroll.

Some people claim that there's pride in seeing a player your club has developed leave and succeed elsewhere. But there's not, it's just shit. Even more so when it's a local player. These are the ones you hope will know what it means to wear the shirt, and have an ingrained desire to run themselves into the ground for the club and its supporters because, deep down, they're still one of them. These are the players you hope will want to stay at the club for ever.

Hindsight is a beautiful thing, of course, and we all now know that Carroll's move to Anfield didn't work out. There were injuries and a strange reluctance from Liverpool to adopt a style that would get the best out of their record signing. We know, too, that Carroll didn't want to leave, and he has since said that he was praying to fail his medical, just so he could come home. Even taking into account a few decent years at West Ham, he was quite never the same player after leaving the north-east. Who knows, maybe that would have always happened? Perhaps his early career form at Newcastle was the anomaly? We shall never know.

Looking at the sale of Carroll in terms of business, £35m for a homegrown talent with half a decent season in the top flight under his belt represents astonishing value. That money, if spent wisely, could add depth and quality to a squad – and aided by the hugely French-based scouting of Graham Carr it did just that, leading to the permanent signings of Hatem Ben Arfa, Yohan Cabaye, and a roaringly good 2011/12. Brighton operate in a similar way today, with a great scouting network that recognises young and under-the-radar talent, develops them at the club, embeds them into the first team for one or two stellar seasons and then sells them on for a healthy profit. But what does that say about you as an entity?

Your club occupying this middle ground of the football world is a little bit heartbreaking. You might sign or develop a player with the potential to be world class, but you'll never see him reach those heights in the shirt of your club. He'll have long since been tapped up by a team that would rather be in a Super League, playing Real Madrid four times a season and banking obscene amounts of cash.

On the day that Newcastle sold Andy Carroll, I turned down a polite offer from a colleague to go out for some after-work drinks in Dubai. As soon as the words 'Sorry mate, I'm just too upset about Andy Carroll' came out of my mouth I felt absolutely ridiculous. After all this was a normal human being I was talking to, one whose days were not dominated by the eccentric whims of a football club. But I didn't care. Carroll had gone and I felt like a spurned lover. All I wanted to do was go home, pour a glass of wine, and watch a YouTube video of his greatest goals.

In the 1980s, with a stale and unambitious board, Newcastle United was known as a feeder club, and a great north-east production line would develop young players only to sell them on to bigger, more successful teams in England. It was a fundamental reason why the team eventually stagnated, and slowly ebbed away into second-tier obscurity as the region fell into decline alongside it. Now, under Mike Ashley, this football netherworld seemed once again our destination.

11

A Beautiful Game

27 August 1995
Sheffield Wednesday 0 Newcastle United 2
Ginola, Beardsley

David Ginola could make anything look good; and that's now, in 2025. In 1995 it was like he'd been sculpted by the Flemish artist François Duquesnoy to sit in the Louvre. You could barely look at him, he was so handsome. I firmly believe that if, on his first day at the club's Maiden Castle training base, Kevin Keegan had explained to Ginola that Newcastle's home shirt was actually a bin bag he would have still looked great in it. Anybody watching him that day, as he nonchalantly skipped over flying tackles, would probably have thought, 'Hmm, that bin bag; not bad is it? Probably goes well with some cords.' Thankfully, the Frenchman would not be reduced to such madness. He was born to wear the most iconic Newcastle strip of all time.

In 1995, the replica shirt business was going through a regeneration across the country, and Newcastle were at the forefront of its renewal. Prior to that, in the decades when hooliganism gripped the English game and your main matchday aim was to come home without a dart in your eye, very few people wore their team's shirt to a game. In the 1970s, the nation's rough and ready terraces saw a combination of flares, big collars and a scarf tied around each wrist. Then, in the 80s, the nascent Casual scene heralded a continental shift towards Adidas, Lacoste, Sergio Tacchini, Fred Perry and more – largely the spoils of Liverpool's cross-Channel European adventures from the early part of the decade. Those labels would be joined by CP Company, Aquascutum and Stone Island in an essential matchday uniform. Wearing your club colours was almost embarrassing by comparison. It took until 1990 and the World Cup in Italy before that mentality started to change – when England and Paul Gascoigne taught us that it was OK to wear a shirt to the match and your heart on your sleeve. But it was the launch of the Premier League two years later that saw a genuine gear change when it came to your gear.

In 1992, Sky Sports' very first advert for the breakaway FA Premier League sought to capture all the glamour and commercial opportunities found across the Atlantic in American sport. Those early days look quaint now, but the advert is an exercise in brand-building. It starts off in black and white, featuring the likes of John Wark, David Hirst, and Tim Sherwood chatting awkwardly as they head off to play football with a team made up of one player from each side in the top division. They pull on Sky Sports football shirts, along with a healthy selection of tasty Asics and Lotto boots, and suddenly the advert sparks into life with vibrant colour. It also gets a bit odd. Anders Limpar splashes some water on his face like he's in a Brut advert, while Gordon Strachan gets a massage. John Salako is in the shower, and a topless Tony Daley is lifting some weights. It's like a late-night TV advert for a risqué chatline. But it was kind of brilliant, too, and Premier League club shirts were featured heavily, making a case for their primary role in the fan experience from thereon in. This didn't resonate with the old guard of course – it would take more than Vinnie Jones getting a shiatsu for Liverpool's Annie Road End crew to ditch their Pringle knitwear – but it did have the desired effect on younger fans like me.

A replica shirt was essential to my matchday experience at the time, and that of all of my pals, too. Even when Newcastle switched sponsors from Greenalls back to Newcastle Breweries a few seasons earlier, and my mam had to stitch on a god-awful patch the club sent out featuring the famous blue star – complete with a weird black bit that blocked out the old sponsor at the same time – I remained unfazed. In a time before football shirts were updated each and every season, I wore that shambolic kit every week for at least two years with genuine pride.

In the pre-Premier League era, merchandise wasn't deemed to be the cash cow that it is now. Slick football boutiques and fashion brand collabs might be the norm in 2025, but the first Newcastle United shop I ever went to was a shed at the top end of the club car park. I absolutely loved it, of course, and as the years went by I forced various relatives to take me there so I could just stand and stare at whatever was on display, hoping that they would realise that if they bought me something, we could leave. In 1989, a club shop in the city's Green Market took on a distinctly Samba feel, in celebration of our new centre-forward, Mirandinha. The first Brazilian to play in English football, Francisco Ernandi Lima da Silva – as his mam called him when he was in trouble – was brought in to replace Peter Beardsley. No easy feat. However he was a full international, wore Hi-Tec boots with big flapping tongues, and would often shoot from around the halfway line. Upon his signing, in a moment of cultural confusion, the city instantly sold out of sombreros. Stocks must have been fairly limited to start with, but still.

To me the club shop was more than just a place to waste your hard-earned cash. Back when I was utterly reliant on my dad to take me to the match (I only saw about a third of the season's home games) the club shop was my only regular connection to Newcastle United. It was there, among the bobble hats, pennants and footballs that my obsession truly blossomed. Genetic codes entwined … cut me open and I bled, if not black and white, then certainly a signed picture of club captain Glenn Roeder.

In those days, despite my love of anything featuring a Newcastle badge – shirt, hat, stapler, seriously, it didn't matter – I was playing catch-up when it came to the latest kit. I don't want to name names, but it was all my dad's fault. For a previous birthday he had bought me a no-brand white football shirt with black pinstripes. The material was at once both rough *and* smooth, and he tried to pass it off as a Newcastle top. 'It's their third kit,' he said to me, refusing to relinquish eye contact as the excitement of the big day visibly drained from my face. You've got to hand it to him. As far as I can tell he pretty much invented the concept of third kits on the spot that day.

My dad and I only spent three seasons going to the match together regularly, but those early games come back to me in memories of fatherly love rather than football. I remember my first-ever game, and his making sure we had my Newcastle scarf flying from the car window. I remember him lifting me over people's heads so I could get to the front of the West Stand Paddocks against Spurs, after I had forced us to go there and then started to cry because I was too small to see anything. I remember how he would grip me tightly when we made our way back through the crowds to the car after each game. I remember him giving me his gloves when my hands were so cold that they had gone numb.

As he was a refugee, it was unsurprising that Dad had no time for the merchandise demands of a nine-year-old. He was a very talented footballer himself, once, and even on the books of Newcastle United for a while. Having signed for the club on amateur forms in 1962 he played a few games at centre-forward for the reserves, even keeping the legendary Bryan 'Pop' Robson out of the starting line-up. But he was nervous and couldn't shake the feeling that he hadn't quite shown them his best. After an away game at Huddersfield Town – in which he'd scored with a diving header but also injured his knee after colliding with the post – he approached legendary manager Joe Harvey to apologise.

'I'm so sorry, Mr Harvey,' he said, as Newcastle's bus inched its way home on a wet Wednesday night in West Yorkshire. 'I know that I can do better.'

'No, son, don't worry,' replied Harvey. 'There's definitely something about you that we like.'

My dad was rightly proud of that, but he quit Newcastle shortly afterwards. It cost him a fortune to travel by bus and rehab his injury with the club, and he was making more money working in a factory during the day and playing for Spennymoor United on a weekend, so that was that. As someone who had come to the country with just the clothes on his back, financial security was always his priority. That instinct never left him.

So, despite being an excellent player, Dad didn't understand the concept of spending money on football. If he was bad at buying a shirt then he was even worse when it came to boots. 'Expensive boots won't make you a better footballer, Andrew,' he quite rightly said, before regaling me with the story of how he had once played in women's shoes – after his own had been hidden as a parental punishment – yet was still the best player on the pitch by a mile. As a result, I was forced to wear some unusually bendy, yellow-flashed Dunlop boots for ages, briefly earning the nickname 'Banana Feet'.

When it came to Newcastle shirts, I absolutely loved our Asics kits of 1993 to 1995, despite the fact you would generally catch the material with your fingernail or anything remotely sharp within five minutes. They're now, quite rightly, considered grail shirts for retro kit hunters, but the eventual move to Adidas took us to another level. We were suddenly cool. Run DMC, the Beastie Boys, Predators, Copa Mundial, Tango footballs – especially the Subbuteo ones – the iconic West German kit of Italia 90, and now Newcastle United.

What I liked most about that shirt was its versatility. It looked good wherever I wore it. Playing football, watching football, drinking eight pints of Snakebite in Hanrahan's while talking about football, it was simply impossible to look out of place in the thing. It was seriously hot property, too. Adidas's first order of 180,000 shirts had flown off the shelves, but even if you managed to get one it was advisable to keep your eyes on it. After one hasty post-match liaison at Newcastle's Station Hotel, my friend Pete woke up the following morning to find that, while his wallet and valuables remained on the table, his Newcastle top was gone. The shirt was sparking some sort of sexy crime wave.

In 1995, with the all-new Premier League clicking into gear and football attendances around the country on the rise, Adidas decided to change how they made football kits. Instead of bashing out a crappy polyester top with a stick-on badge that nobody wore, the concept and delivery behind each shirt would be more akin to that of a fashion house, with smart fabric choices and a thoughtful infusion of local culture. Newcastle were one of the first beneficiaries of this strategy. The Grandad collar and buttons, for example, were a nod to the type of shirt worn by working-class men during the city's industrial heyday, while the burgundy and blue horizontal stripes of the away kit referenced the colours of Newcastle West End, who had merged with Newcastle East End to form Newcastle United 103 years earlier.

No stranger to the wonders of capitalism, Newcastle chairman Sir John Hall welcomed the Premier League's desire for showmanship with open arms. Keen to capitalise on the city's excitement at the club's new signings, he even transformed the kit launch into a fashion event; one with some interesting talent choices. Peter Beardsley was my first hero at Newcastle. He was an absolutely astonishing footballer, but even he must have questioned why he featured so prominently in that show. If you have Les Ferdinand and David Ginola on your books, your first port of call for a modelling assignment should not be the 'canny wie lad with a toothless grin', as he was described in the 1989 song of the same name. That Harry Rodin song was once played by John Peel on Radio 1, incidentally. But for the life of me I'm not sure why. With club officials – including Kevin Keegan – watching on, Newcastle treated this kit launch like a major event, and if you thought Peter Beardsley was an unusual catwalk choice, then Pavel Srníček wandering on stage looking like he was about to be tried at the Hague for war crimes was absolutely staggering.

I had finally stumbled to a place at university by this point, and at Sunderland of all cities. I'll level with you, I didn't know what to do with myself, so I signed up for a course in Computing and went where a few of my mates were also going. You will be unsurprised to discover that things did not go well. After starting the term with diligence and effort, my endeavour ran dry after about three months. I was distracted by this new thing called the internet, and a football management game on it. The rest of the year was spent making the most of cheap student promotions and drink deals (one quid for a Turbo Shandy, as I recall), and wearing the new Newcastle top as I played five-a-side in the city. Being stationed in the home of our greatest foes, as Newcastle rampaged towards a possible league title, felt intoxicating (admittedly that could also have been the Turbo Shandies). It felt like I was embedded with the enemy, tasked with bringing them down from within (but, again, like I say, the Turbo Shandies).

While both the home and away kits became instant classics that year, what elevated them above their thoughtful design was the Newcastle Brown Ale logo sitting on the front. That resonates even more in 2025, when local sponsors have all but disappeared from the top flight of English football, replaced largely by overseas betting companies. Newcastle Breweries were the club's very first shirt sponsor in 1980 and apart from a six-year hiatus between 1985 and 1991, when the Warrington brewery Greenalls took over, they featured on the front of every Newcastle shirt until 2000. This bond ran far beyond geographical familiarity. Newcastle Breweries had been instrumental in the club signing Keegan as a player in 1982 – they actually paid part of his wages – and, with a factory just across the road from St James' Park, their influence was olfactory as well as ocular. It sent out a strong message of local identity, too, and was another reason for pride whenever you saw that strip. It's also worth mentioning that it just looked great on the front of a football shirt. The five points of the blue star represented the five founding breweries in Newcastle, and its retro design and burst of colour against the black and white made for an irresistible mix. It was an honour, rather than a necessary evil, to have this sponsor's logo.

When you buy a football shirt from your club shop in 2025, there's often an option to purchase the 'Pro shirt', replete with better cut and improved ventilation, making for a top that pretty much fits like a second skin. In 1995, however, it was one-size-fits, meaning that the shirt looked totally different on each player. Rob Lee's untucked jersey gave real extra-from-*The Office* vibes, for example, while Beardsley's occasionally fastened-up collar was fully schoolboy. Keith Gillespie could have been even quicker if his shirt hadn't billowed out behind him like some sort of parachute. Still, in their own way they all looked like legends in that kit. And none more so than David Ginola.

Although Kevin Keegan's side had earned their nickname as Entertainers long before the 1995/96 season, it was this game, the third of the season at Hillsborough and with the Sky cameras rolling, that saw the rest of the country sit up and take notice of our title chances. Newcastle had followed a 3-0 opening-day win at home to Coventry with an impressive 3-1 away victory at Bolton in midweek. Now, clad in their burgundy and blue away kit, they dazzled on a Sky Sports *Super Sunday*, with a masterclass by Newcastle's new Gallic hero.

Ginola didn't score many goals for Newcastle, it's easy to forget. Just six in 58 games (stat-obsessed NUFC Twitter would have had him written off after a couple of bad performances). But the first of those six was an absolute belter, and a goal that signalled his arrival in England. After receiving the ball from Beardsley on the left after 53 minutes, the Frenchman took just seven touches, pushing the ball from instep to the outside of his boot and back again as he made his way infield in search of an opening. Suddenly, and without much backlift, he sent a rasping drive into the far left-hand corner of Kevin Pressman's goal, and erupted in the way he often did after scoring – like he really was annoyed about something.

While goals are all well and good – especially when fired from a Nike Tiempo boot like a projectile missile – shortly afterwards I fell in love with Ginola even more (a love that became official just three days later, when he absolutely destroyed Middlesbrough full-back Neil Cox in our next home game). After his goal, the former Paris Saint-Germain man was understandably feeling pretty good about himself, strutting around the pitch with his chest puffed out and his head held high. He received possession midway inside the Wednesday half, all balance, poise, and great body shape. As he scanned the pitch before making his next move, he suddenly spotted a blur of blue and white in his peripheral vision. It was Dan Petrescu, and he wasn't very happy. The life of a football player must be amazing, but imagine if an opposition player could just take the piss out of you for 90 minutes, making you look utterly rubbish. Well that was the situation Petrescu found himself in against Ginola that afternoon, and he had decided that enough was enough. Unfortunately, it was about to get worse. Spotting the Sheffield Wednesday man's wild lunge coming a mile off, Ginola nonchalantly flicked the ball up and over the defender in a split second, like some sort of bullfighter, allowing the Romanian international to zip past, off the pitch, and into another football dimension altogether. It was glorious.

Not to be outdone by Newcastle's new superstar, a moment of genius made on Tyneside sealed the win 20 minutes later, with Peter Beardsley cutting in from the byline and instinctively firing a shot beyond Pressman from the most ridiculous angle you ever saw. The ball looped across the box and cannoned in off the far post. If it had been anybody else you might have labelled it a mis-hit cross, but this was Peter Beardsley. It was just what he did.

After three games and three wins, Newcastle sat majestically at the top of the Premier League table. At least it felt majestic to me. It was early days, and nobody was thinking about the title yet (we were *all* thinking about the title), but if the soaring levels of local pride were anything to go by then Keegan's team had already done its job. The games couldn't come quickly enough at St James' Park. Best thing about it all? The fun was only getting started.

12

The Stadium Shakedown

3 December 2011
Newcastle United 0 Chelsea 3

It was the @ symbol that finished me off. Just one measly little character, but it tipped me over the edge. Well, three little characters if you count Mike Ashley and Derek Llambias. The brains behindsportsdirect.com@StJamesParkStadium. A crass, poorly thought-out, and awfully long-winded attempt to drive revenue into the club. Why is it like an email address? Why are there no spaces? Why does it feel like something Elon Musk would name a child? The debacle was testimony to both men's talents – how to turn 119 years of football history into an everything-must-go sale in the blink of an eye. They might as well have just called the place '50 per cent Off Slazenger Shorts' and had done with it.

Ashley delivered the news in his usual reverse Willy Wonka-style, crushing dreams just as the team was sitting on top of the Championship, and looking good for an immediate return to the Premier League. Allegedly the original plan had been to rename the stadium altogether. After that was understandably met with grave vengeance and furious anger – along with the tabling of a motion in parliament that called on Ashley to reconsider – Llambias shot back. Hold up guys, there has been a mistake. We were always going to keep St James' Park in the title, yeah, of course we were. Can't believe you thought that we wouldn't, hence the @ symbol. The club searched for a suitable sponsor for both shirt and stadium name, but in the interim kept the new title. Just as a showcase, you understand, leaving Ashley's Sports Direct with thousands of pounds' worth of free advertising until such time that the naming rights were purchased. Nothing to see here.

This strategy was nothing new for Ashley. Since his arrival in 2007 the stadium had been slowly covered by Sports Direct logos popping up on every available surface. Things are a little murky when it comes to the numbers, but while the owner claimed that he only inserted Sports Direct into advertising spaces yet to be purchased, fans' suspicion was that he only paid a fraction of the full market value, effectively hobbling the club's commercial matchday opportunities for more than a decade. Just part of the reason why NUFC is now having to play catch-up when it comes to navigating the current Profit and Sustainability rules (PSR). It's funny, the Premier League now has Fair Market Value guidelines to ensure that an owner can't disguise their investment, but that's intended in relation to a deal that *makes* the club millions, not one where the owner is possibly getting something on the cheap.

That Ashley first wanted to use sportsdirect.com and not even Sports Direct felt like it devalued the whole thing even further. In what could be the finest-ever example of poundshop self-promotion, the football stadium that had been the backdrop to my life was now reduced to a discount sports store website plug. I'm amazed that he didn't just have the new name spraypainted on the wall.

Commercialising the naming rights of a stadium is a powerful way to help your club succeed in modern-day sport. In 2009 it was about competing with oligarch-level wealth, but now it's more a case of coping with your PSR responsibilities. Either way, a smart commercial approach to every aspect of a football club is increasingly what separates the haves from the have-nots.

In the NFL around 80 per cent of teams play at a branded stadium, compared with roughly 30 per cent of football clubs in the English top flight. My first memory of this came at Middlesbrough in 1995, when they opened their newly built home as the Cellnet Riverside Stadium – part of a £3m deal that saw the telecommunications provider feature on the front of their shirts, too. That said, some time later their ground was also named the Captain James Cook Stadium for a day, so I guess the Smoggies aren't too concerned about what they call the place. Fuss-free branded stadiums usually have one common denominator: they're a newbuild. Although Arsenal and Manchester City now happily play out of the Emirates and Etihad stadiums, can you imagine if a sponsor had tried to rename Highbury and Maine Road as the Forbidden Planet Arena and the Claire's Accessories Stadium? There would have been an uprising.

The new stadium moniker at Newcastle was never formally used as far as I can remember. I don't recall seeing a sign, possibly because it was so long that it wouldn't fit, but largely because the whole city – and wider football world – decided to ignore it.

One of the biggest mistakes Mike Ashley made was taking St James' Park to be a mere football stadium. He assumed it was a place where, every few weeks, a match happened and that was that. He was technically correct, but that's not what it is. St James' Park is a home to the team, but it's home to the fans, too – far more so. Players come and go, but the supporters are in it for the long haul. St James' Park was the backdrop to my life between the ages of nine and 31. Not just in terms of football, but during my formative years. As music has the power to forge identity, build opinion, and make you who you are, so too does football. All the good times, all the struggles, all the bollocks life throws at you, was against the backdrop of Newcastle United. I came to St James' Park and forgot about it all for 90 minutes, and by the time the game finished I usually had a fresh perspective on things, too. There's an awesome power in that.

Back in 2008, I came home from Dubai for Christmas and managed to catch a couple of games at St James' Park. Stoke first, and then Arsenal in a seat not too far from my old season ticket spot in the Gallowgate. Having that specific view of the pitch brought everything rushing back to me. It was like hearing an old song, or getting a waft of a familiar scent. I had tears in my eyes. I mean, not furiously blubbing, but clearly emotional. We lost that day but the moment, half an hour or so before kick-off, was special. It was an acknowledgment of everything that had come before. Other than my family, this place and these people had been the one constant in my life. Devaluing it for the sake of commercial opportunity was trampling on everybody's connection to this famous old stadium.

There have only been two occasions in my life when I have cried in relation to the Magpies, at least if you're talking proper tears rolling down the cheeks, not just welling up to clips of the Champions League win over Paris Saint-Germain on Twitter. The first time was in 1998, when Alan Shearer's goal against Sheffield United took us to our first FA Cup Final in my lifetime. I hadn't been able to get a ticket so I watched the semi-final in a Durham pub with a friend who thought I was being utterly ridiculous. The other time was, erm, watching the movie *Goal.* I realise that this is a bit shit. But in my defence I had been travelling around Australia for six months and watched it on a plane. Seeing St James' Park, in that moment, simply overwhelmed me. I blame the altitude.

During the 1995/96 season, my first glimpse of the new Gallowgate End stand overawed me. My club, at the very heart of the city, suddenly had one of the best stadiums in world football, and that made me beyond proud. That might be a weak boast, but when you support a team that never really wins any silverware you have to find victories elsewhere or risk going mad from the sheer bleakness. Maybe it's the occasional big-name signing, or an iconic managerial appointment. Perhaps it's simply having the best strip in the league, or a stadium that is the envy of Europe's top clubs. It just needs to be something that you can shout about enough to sustain you and your passion, while the usual suspects hoover up all the trophies. St James' Park was undoubtedly one of those sources of joy.

Newcastle were again on an upward curve when Ashley decided to piss everybody off again and rename St James' Park for a second time – in the 2011/12 anomaly season under Alan Pardew, when a side featuring Hatem Ben Arfa, Yohan Cabaye, and Demba Ba flew out of the blocks and went unbeaten for their first 11 games. On 9 November, Derek Llambias laughably explained how our ancestral home's name was putting off potential suitors, and so they would now change it to the far snappier Sports Direct Arena until somebody bought the rights. Ten days later, against Manchester City, Newcastle lost for the first time that season. Two weeks later, they were beaten 3-0 by Chelsea, their first home defeat of the season. You could say that these were simply bad results against two of the league's best sides. But I say, pah! That's exactly what they want you to think. These were no mere defeats, they were thunderclaps from the beyond. The football gods showed their disapproval of Mike Ashley once again, and who could blame them?

In fairness, the Chelsea game was a bit of a stitch-up. After ending a poor first half 1-0 down to a Didier Drogba goal – Tim Krul had also saved a Frank Lampard penalty, and David Luiz should have seen red for a foul on Ba – Newcastle absolutely dominated the second 45 minutes. Ba had a header off the post, Drogba thwacked a header off his own bar, and Shola Ameobi raked a shot off the woodwork, too, as the Magpies chased an equaliser. Then came the sucker punch, two of them actually – Salomon Kalou on 89 minutes and Daniel Sturridge two minutes into injury time – as Pardew's team paid the price for being profligate in front of goal against one of the big boys.

In 2012, the payday loan company Wonga controversially sponsored the club in a £24m four-year deal, stadium naming rights and all. Their choice of name? St James' Park. While nobody really wanted a loan company known for its astronomical interest rates on the front of their shirt, you had to admit that this was a PR masterclass.

For Ashley it was all simply business, and therein lies the problem. A football team isn't just a commercial enterprise. How can it be? It holds the key to happiness for literally thousands of people around the world. It's a weekend escape, a ready-made group of friends, a first thought in the morning and a last one at night, a priceless relationship with your parents or siblings. A football club lives and breathes, and deals squarely in hope. And if you neglect its beating heart you should be ready for the cardiac arrest that follows.

13

Sir John Hall's Geordie Dream

3 December 1995
Newcastle United 6 Wimbledon 1
Ferdinand (3), Howey, Clark, Albert

When I was young I knew the type of club chairman that I wanted at Newcastle United. He would drive a Rolls-Royce and wear a fur coat. He would be a cigar smoker and prone to the occasional inflammatory statement. Finally, in his spare time, he would hang out with a celebrity or two. Oliver Reed, perhaps, or Vicki Michelle from *'Allo 'Allo!*. Turns out I was just visualising Malcolm Allison managing Manchester City in 1972, but you get the picture. I was after a bit of a character, a bloke with bucketloads of cash and a readymade soundbite up his gold-cufflinked sleeves. One thing was certain. Whether it was Michael Knighton believing he was going to buy Manchester United for £20m in 1989 – amazingly doing keepy-uppies on the pitch like a new signing – or George Reynolds trying to buy Faustino Asprilla for Third Division side Darlington in 2002, it was certainly the era for a wheeler dealer.

When I began supporting Newcastle, the club was miles away from having the type of millionaire chairman who would come to dominate English football towards the end of the century – the likes of David Moores at Liverpool, Martin Edwards at Manchester United, or even Ken Bates at Chelsea. Bates bought Chelsea for a quid back in 1981 and helped steer them back into the top flight three years later – the same year that Arthur Cox's Kevin Keegan-driven Newcastle were also promoted. He won several major trophies in the 20 years that followed, before eventually selling up to Roman Abramovich in 2003 for £140m. It was the first instance of oligarch involvement in English football and would, once again, change the financial requirements of successful ownership, this time from millionaire to billionaire.

Bates was an ideas man, his peak moment being a plan to deal with hooliganism inside Stamford Bridge by erecting an electrified perimeter fence. It was basically one step away from having snipers on the roof, and he actually had the thing built, too, the mad old bugger. Thankfully, the Greater London Council thought the idea to be a touch dangerous, and Ken's hoped-for voltage never materialised. The fence was eventually dismantled.

When it came to Newcastle's boardroom power struggles of the late 1980s and early 90s, however, I'll level with you: I didn't have a clue what was going on. I was 13, and far too busy playing *Yie Ar Kung-Fu* on the Spectrum or figuring out how to talk to girls. The political in-fighting at my football club felt a touch out of my remit. I turned up at the match and shouted 'Sack the Board', of course, but I sang about almost anything if the Gallowgate End had a chant for it. Case in point, the regular song focussed on police killer Harry Roberts. 'Harry Roberts is a friend, he shoots coppers' went the line every time a policeman entered the terraces to deal with some bother. Pretty wild when you think about it. I mean, what next, something detailing our support for the Great Train Robbery?

I do remember recognising Gordon McKeag's face, as the club's under-fire former chairman was public enemy number one. I clocked his tie, blazer and mad wavy side parting and decided on the spot that he wasn't for me. It was an awfully blinkered opinion but, in my defence, it was backed up by numerous other half-cocked speculations on the terraces. All equally negative, all leaving me in no doubt that this could not be the man to take us forward. Not with that hair.

Gordon McKeag was a man of his time, and his boardroom battle with Sir John Hall pitted an autocratic dynasty against an emerging business elite. Up until then, a seat on the board was a prestigious community role, a ticket passed from father to son that meant the club had effectively been controlled by the same four clans for decades: the McKeag, Seymour, Rutherford and Westwood families. But as the club gradually slipped into decline – from a powerhouse FA Cup-winning side in the 1950s to the verge of bankruptcy 40 years later – multiple shareholders decided that enough was enough. Although he had only been chairman between 1988 and 1990, McKeag had been a part of the board that sold the trio of Chris Waddle, Peter Beardsley and Paul Gascoigne to balance the books between 1985 and 1988 – quite ironic when you consider that he would later describe Sir John Hall and the Magpie Group's attempted takeover as 'selling the family silver'. But while the sales of Newcastle's generational local talent temporarily placated the bank manager, it did little for the ire of the supporters, or the club's fortunes on the pitch for that matter. Newcastle were relegated from the top flight in 1989, one year after the sale of Gascoigne. Now it was time for change.

Full disclosure, I knew even less about Sir John Hall than I did McKeag in 1991. But when I discovered that he was the bloke who had built the Metro Centre in Gateshead – then the biggest shopping mall in Europe – I got on board pretty quickly. Anybody who thought it was a good idea to stick a big fuck-off rollercoaster in a shopping centre was all right by me. As it happened, the Metro Centre and Newcastle United had become the twin pillars of my weekend activity. If Newcastle were away from home, my pals and I hopped on a bus to Gateshead instead of St James' Park, often carrying a small transistor radio so we could keep in touch with the game. Shopping certainly wasn't on the agenda, so it was a toss-up between Metro Land, an indoor funfair with rides, games and an arcade that boasted not one but two *After Burner* simulator machines; or by trying to get served at Harvey's Wine Bar and, as my mate Pete so eloquently puts it, 'doing some fingering if you're lucky'.

Eventually we would make a dash for Dixons electrical store around 4.40pm, joining an anxious-looking group of men all staring at its collection of TVs in the window, as the day's football scores revealed themselves via *Grandstand*'s vidiprinter. Oh, the things this unspectacular stretch of mall must have seen over the years, hosting the joy of victory and stench of defeat on its almost too-beige tiles. I wonder how many people stormed straight into the store and bought a portable telly or hi-fi system based purely on the endorphin rush of a last-minute winner. Literally thousands I'm guessing. They were probably cheered out of the place post-purchase, too, kissing staff on the cheek and firing finger guns as they went. I am steadfast in my belief that the 90s were simpler, yet more impulsive times.

The story of Sir John Hall's reluctant battle to buy Newcastle United is a long and protracted one that played out between 1988 and 1992. It's been told on many occasions and, let's face it, nobody really wants me to go into the finer details here – least of all you. But the salient points are these: After watching Newcastle slowly crumble as a football force thanks to poor management, a lack of investment, and a dearth of real ambition, shareholder Malcolm Dix became something of a thorn in the side of McKeag and the rest of the board, agitating for change via the newly formed Magpie Group. But revolution does not come cheap, my friends, and after a short while Dix realised he needed some financial muscle if he was going to oust the board and change the club's future.

Enter Sir John Hall, the Ashington-born, Newcastle-supporting son of a miner who, with his Cameron Hall company, was more than happy building the Metro Centre thank-you-very-much. Owning a football club seemed like far too much trouble for Hall, and was certainly not part of his grand plan. So, it's hard to say why – and how – he was eventually talked into joining the fight. People have a tendency to dismiss his motives as purely financial. But while Hall certainly wasn't a football philanthropist in the mould of Blackburn's Jack Walker, getting into it for a quick buck still sits at odds with the times. This was all prior to the Premier League's post-Sky Sports commercial boom, so nobody was making huge sums of cash owning a football club. And even if they were, only the most optimistic soul could have envisioned making any profit out of a thoroughly downtrodden Newcastle United.

Initially Hall wanted the fans to own the club, while also adding some new faces to the board. The Magpie Group drew up a brochure detailing how they would help inject finances into the club as well as improve the stadium, and suggested that shares be made available for the fans to buy. Hall then travelled around the region, trying to whip up interest, but the drive failed – much to the amusement of the existing board members. The battle was far from over, however, and became pretty complicated too, playing out like some sort of spy novel, with bugs, doublespeak, and misinformation. Deep down Hall felt that the football club needed a leader, a person to help smash the historical four-family grip. As a result, he was eventually convinced by his son Douglas and other members of the Magpie Group to go after the missing shareholders. They used private detectives and even genealogists to help track the people who had bought some of the 2,000 ten-shilling shares originally issued by the club in 1892. Hall eventually purchased 79.2 per cent of the club for an estimated £3m.

From the moment of takeover Hall smartly surrounded himself by a small nucleus of trusted board members: Douglas, long-time business ally Freddie Shepherd, and Freddie Fletcher – who had helped guide Glasgow Rangers out of their own years of funk in his role as commercial director – made up its inner circle. Although the club was saddled with debt from the off and the promised transfer funds were, famously, slow in filtering down to Kevin Keegan, it only took the 1992/93 promotion season for the boardroom to fully embrace the project. Two years later, and with Newcastle at the sharp end of the Premier League, they had developed a taste for grand gestures, wanting every signing to be bigger and better than the last. From favourite sons to foreign superstars, nobody was off limits as a potential transfer. The biggest surprise was that these lofty ambitions were increasingly coming from the boardroom rather than the manager's office.

Every club has a list of great players that they apparently almost signed, usually just before that player was able to establish himself at a major club. Zinedine Zidane to Blackburn Rovers is generally considered the peak of such what-the-fuck-ism in this regard (Jack Walker didn't fancy him as they already had Tim Sherwood, fair play).

Newcastle had a list, too, but instead of up-and-coming talent their targets were firmly established stars, meaning that it was a fantastical time for transfer rumours – which are always far more fun than actual signings anyway. We had some belting gossip on that front, from the potential glory of homecomings for Paul Gascoigne and Chrissy Waddle to the sheer exoticism of Jean-Pierre Papin, George Weah, Dennis Bergkamp, and Rivaldo. Scanning the football rumours round-up page on Teletext was enough to leave you breathless, meaning you would often have to jump on to the Bamboozle quiz page just to calm down for a bit. Suddenly Shepherd and Douglas Hall were driven to purchase marquee signings for the club, with the zenith of such have-a-go heroism coming in Rome, with an impromptu crack at one of the finest footballers on the planet.

According to Keegan, Shepherd decided sometime around 1993 that he would like to try and sign Roberto Baggio from Juventus. There had been no contact with the player, his agent or the club, Shepherd just fancied it. So, he grabbed Douglas Hall and assistant manager Terry McDermott (Keegan refused to go) and flew out to Rome on a whim, with the three of them rocking up to the Stadio Delle Alpi like Del Boy, Rodney, and Uncle Albert. Hall allegedly knocked on the door, introduced himself, and then enquired who he should speak to about signing Baggio. It was mental. The way Keegan spins it, Shepherd felt they could do a deal for the Divine Ponytail and be back home in time for tea. That optimism must have quickly evaporated when they were left sitting in the Juventus reception, waiting for a president who would never arrive. The whole thing is batshit, especially that two experienced businessmen thought they could pull it off in the first place. It's something you would come up with after eight pints down the pub.

The famed *Evening Chronicle* journalist John Gibson always described the board of that era – in the nicest way possible – as a 'bunch of chancers', and their efforts to sign Baggio from one of the biggest clubs in the world were ultimately amateurish and embarrassing. But I couldn't help but fucking love them for it. The local news that week featured Shepherd trotting to his car and retrieving a Newcastle shirt with Baggio's name on the back, a permanent smirk playing out on his face. It was the type of unhinged ego that could make you great. That or you explode in a fiery ball of your own self-importance. Either way, it was entertainment. I felt amazed that my club was being mentioned in the same breath as these teams and players, even if it was largely just by way of hype. It was a sign of the rapid progress we had made. In 1992 the £250,000 signing of Brian Kilcline had almost put the club out of business. Three or four years later we were trying to pick up the best player in the world on a last-minute trip to Italy. Talk about *la dolce vita*. It felt like a dream that I would eventually wake up from to realise that we had actually just re-signed Kevin Dillon on a free.

Hall Snr. left such transfer star-gazing largely to Shepherd and Douglas, but he was a master of spin himself. After building the Metro Centre and then saving Newcastle United he had redrawn himself as a vanguard of the north-east. The man spearheading regional regeneration, first through retail and then through sport. Now it was the Geordie Nation versus the world, with Hall famously stating he wanted a team of 11 Geordies at St James' Park. To get them he would set up an academy in the mould of Ajax's famed Sportpark De Toekomst to ensure that the club never lost great local talent again. That one never came to fruition, unfortunately, but his big sporting club plan did, at least for a while. Hall wanted Newcastle to eventually become an overarching umbrella of sporting greatness like Barcelona. As a result he invested in ice hockey, basketball and rugby all under the Newcastle name, even going as far as signing Va'aiga Tuigamala for Newcastle Falcons in a world record £1m deal. It was a nice idea and, again, I got a warm fuzzy feeling being compared with a club like Barcelona. But unfortunately Hall had forgotten one thing. Few people in the region were bothered about these other sports, and neither was the London Stock Exchange. When Newcastle decided to float in April 1997, only the football club was welcomed. Everything else eventually fell by the wayside.

While the Newcastle Sporting Club dream was ultimately a bust, the £16m spent on Les Ferdinand, David Ginola, Warren Barton and Shaka Hislop in the summer of 1995 was going great guns by the time the Magpies reached matchweek ten at home to Wimbledon. The team had won eight of their first nine fixtures, scoring 20 goals in the process and conceding only seven. The one reverse had come via a 65th-minute Jim Magilton winner for Southampton at The Dell, a ground where we had presumably once done something terrible, as we had only ever won three league games there in our entire history.

Ferdinand, in particular, was looking every inch the superstar striker. Not just because he had already notched ten goals in his first nine appearances (six in his last four), or because he was apparently dating TV's Dani Behr, but because his all-round game was so impressive. The archetypal number nine, at the time, was a fox in the box, a rebound merchant in the mould of Gary Lineker or Andy Cole. Nothing wrong with that – just watch the video of Newcastle's 1993/94 season and enjoy the staggering amount of tap-ins Cole gets by simply following up every shot. Ferdinand could do untold damage in the box, too, as the Wimbledon game would illustrate, but what I liked about him most was that he could do it all on his own as well. Two games earlier at Everton, around the 11th-minute mark, he had spun his man just inside the opposition half, and proceeded to rampage towards goal. The Toffees' defence backed off, not sure whether to stick or twist. In the end they gave him enough time to simply blast a shot into the bottom-left corner from just outside the box, leaving goalkeeper Neville Southall looking thoroughly unimpressed. It was no fluke. A week later on his homecoming at former club QPR, and with the scores delicately balanced at 1-1, Ferdinand was involved in a race with centre-half Danny Maddix, following a long hoof out of defence by Warren Barton. Ferdinand made it look like his former team-mate was playing in Cuban heels, giving the Jamaica international a yard head start and still beating him to the ball, blasting it home from the edge of the area. We had signed the complete striker, who could seemingly destroy defences at will. Just like the ridiculous levels of confidence that had spread after our 11th straight win in the 1992/93 promotion season, it now felt like we would simply bulldoze every team that came before us (with the exception of Southampton away because, well, the curse and that).

Even now, as a fully grown adult, I have a checklist for what makes a match perfect. It should be a Saturday 3pm kick-off, but crucially during winter so that you end the game with the floodlights on. It should be a full house and a high-stakes game, meaning that the entire city is up for it. We should win by three clear goals, ideally one of which being a calamitous own goal, and another an absolute thunderbastard. An opposition player should be sent off and, hopefully, an outfield player will end up in goal. Finally, a fan should briefly run on to the pitch, caught only after a slapstick attempt by numerous stewards to catch them. It's a lot to ask, I know. By the time Wimbledon came to St James' Park in early December the club was not only starting to fully realise its potential on the pitch, but was also about to come perilously close to achieving that perfect-match bingo full house.

Back in the 1990s there was a bit of needle in any Newcastle v Wimbledon game. I mean, it was Wimbledon – Joe Kinnear was their gaffer at the time – and their whole shtick *was* needle, but there was an extra sprinkling of spice to this occasion. Maybe it stemmed from the infamous 1988 FA Cup tie where Vinnie Jones got to grips with Gazza, or perhaps it was just John Fashanu and his 'awooga' catchphrase from *Gladiators*. That had nothing to do with football, it just annoyed the shit out of me. Either way, the Dons were Premier League pantomime villains by 1995. Thankfully, on this occasion, it was Newcastle who were about to put on the performance.

In truth, the damage was done in just nine first-half minutes, courtesy of some good old-fashioned wing play. First Keith Gillespie crossed for centre-half Steve Howey to send a looping header into the Leazes End goal on 31 minutes. Four minutes later, on the other wing David Ginola was busy holding off two Wimbledon defenders before whipping over a ball to Ferdinand – his majestic leap meaning that he was already in the air, waiting – who headed in powerfully at the near post for his seventh goal in as many games. Four minutes later and the action quickly reverted back to Gillespie on the right, with the Irishman's run and cross met by a diving Ferdinand header, and the ball popping up and over the onrushing goalie and into the net. Half-time, 3-0, game over. But the fun was only just getting started.

After two minutes of the restart we were firmly in Holy Grail territory, with the Wimbledon goalkeeper Paul Heald

– already on a yellow card for time-wasting – launching into a Forrest Gump-esque tackle on the galloping Ferdinand, and quickly receiving his marching orders from referee Graham Poll. I realise that there is no evidence of the beloved Tom Hanks character's defensive abilities, however I feel strongly that he would have made a tackle like this – all wild-eyed and full-blooded. A goalie going off is always a golden moment for a fan, especially if an outfield player has to take their place. It's just weird. From the minute they stick on the oversized jersey to the inevitable struggle pulling on the gloves and that first, incredibly awkward, save (usually with the feet), it simply adds to the drama tenfold. When that player is Vinnie Jones then things jump up quite a few notches. I can still hear the cries of 'dodgy keeper' now. To his credit, Jones made a decent fist of things in net. Despite playing like Sylvester Stallone in *Escape to Victory* (generally feet-first and catching the ball all funny), he opened his account with a fine double save, first palming away a long-range Ginola shot before booting the follow-up effort from Gillespie against the post and away. Suddenly it was a Vinnie Jones love-in on Tyneside and, for a good spell, the Gallowgate End couldn't work out whether to cheer for him and his unlikely saves, or demand a glut of goals. In the end we did both.

With almost the entire second half still to play when Jones went in goal, it wasn't difficult to comprehend my glee. Newcastle certainly weren't finished, but now it was worldies only. First Lee Clark arrowed a left-footed shot into the top corner from 20 yards that no goalkeeper in the league would have saved, let alone a future movie hardman. Marcus Gayle actually pulled a goal back for Wimbledon at some point, but it barely registered with the crowd. Ferdinand grabbed his hat-trick with a shot from close range (that Jones almost saved), and then Philippe

Albert scored what, on reflection, might be an even better goal than his yet-to-come chip over the head of Peter Schmeichel. Picking up the ball on the left-hand side of the Wimbledon half, the Belgian stormed forward, played a one-two with Scott Sellars, and instinctively curled a shot into the top corner with the outside of his left boot like he was prime Roberto Carlos. We ended the game in a weird parallel universe, where the Newcastle crowd serenaded both their victorious team *and* Vinnie Jones, picking up a ninth win in ten games in what was rapidly becoming a season of pure fantasy football.

Sir John Hall was the first chairman I was fully aware of as a football fan. Gordon McKeag was more a template of a chairman, a cut-out that I didn't understand. Hall felt real. He looked a bit like an eagle, and would pronounce the word Premier quite unusually, replacing the letter e with the letter y to result in the word 'Prymyr'. I'm guessing that this was simply a byproduct of his Ashington accent, but I became obsessed by his every interview just in case he said it. So, when Hall would big-up Newcastle's chances of eventually winning the Prymyr League, I couldn't really concentrate on the actual plausibility of the statement any more. Things had gone beyond.

As I became older, I watched the success of a man whose politics were in such stark opposition to the area in which he operated – a region utterly decimated by the industrial privatisation spearheaded by Margaret Thatcher's government. When Hall took the money he had made from the Metro Centre in 1986 and, one year later, bought Wynyard Hall – a huge slice of country estate owned by Marquis of Londonderry – he became something of a beacon for Thatcher's 'do-it-yourself nation' (hence the 1991 knighthood). The Marquis family had controlled numerous pits in the area, and the purchase was presented as the son of a miner buying out the pit owner – and of Britain being a place where anything was possible. It is fair to say that the millions of unemployed in the UK at the time – a rate sitting at 10.4 per cent, just 1.5 per cent shy of its 1984 peak – did not share the sentiment. Whether an owner's politics should be open to debate is another question altogether of course, one that's complicated even further by the controversies surrounding the current ownership.

According to a final set of figures laid out by the club in 2008, Hall and Shepherd, the other major shareholder, earned almost £146m from their time at Newcastle, and that's frowned upon by a growing number of supporters. I have a slightly different view. I admit that the money made from the club's Stock Exchange flotation in 1997 feels slightly incongruous, especially as it has been since claimed that the initial share price was far too high. The shares were purchased largely by fans who had cobbled together some cash in order to own part of their club, just like Hall had wanted them to all those years ago. You can lump me in with that group. In only his second known instance of spontaneity, my dad decided that we should become part-owners of the club, too, picking up a small amount of shares to dip our toes into the water. I say we – he was the one who bought them, very kindly adding my name to the proceedings. I'll level with you. It was not as exciting as I had hoped for. I got no free tickets, no access to the players' lounge, and they never once consulted me over transfer dealings. Not so much as a questionnaire (e.g. do you want to sign Des Hamilton: yes or no?). But it still felt pretty cool owning part of the club, no matter how tiny and insignificant. At least it was for me. Every few months my dad would just look at me with a shake of his head and say, 'Eeeeh, we made a mistake buying those shares, didn't we, Andrew? They stitched us right up.'

Yet I still have nothing but love for Sir John Hall. To my mind he helped save Newcastle United from disaster, whether it was by putting in an initial £500,000 to kickstart the Magpie Group's push for control in the early 90s, the millions required to hoover up the shares needed to take control, or the £685,000 he spent in a 40-minute phone call to prevent the club from going under after the bank had pulled their overdraft facility in 1992. Hall and others certainly made more than their money back, but the alternative was potentially the end of the club as we know it. I know which scenario I prefer.

In the space of just three years the landscape for the Magpies had changed utterly. From the verge of oblivion, the club now sat on top of the pile and boasted a side that played with flair, passion, and an absolute ruthlessness. Newcastle were starting to become a global brand, and Hall was a major part of that transformation. Suddenly, it felt like nothing could stop us.

14

Mike Ashley's Dodgy Pint

30 August 2008
Arsenal 3 Newcastle United 0

Would you like to hear something terrifying?
Up until recently there was a whole generation of football fans who had only ever known life at Newcastle United under Mike Ashley. That feels almost impossibly cruel to me. Like inadvertently being on some extreme 80s game show, where a barrel load of Cockneys (the collective noun) take your undying support, love and passion, then gleefully grind it all into dust. When you think it can't get any worse they simply laugh, maniacally, and bring out a bigger and better grinder. We're basically talking about a Geordie *Squid Game* here, with Ashley as the massive Red Light, Green Light girl. To these poor innocents, the era of Kevin Keegan's Entertainers is like some sort of fuzzy dream. A football utopia where superstars signed on the regular, the goals were aplenty, and Newcastle Brown Ale rushed by like a big, boozy stream.

Two things come to mind when I consider this (three if you count wondering how we can make that stream a reality). Firstly, in the interest of cold, hard facts, while the halcyon days of mid-90s Newcastle United were truly wonderful, they yielded exactly the same amount of trophies as Mike Ashley's Newcastle United: none. In *Fever Pitch*, Nick Hornby maligns the fact that Arsenal could only muster two major trophies in his first ten years supporting the club. What I would give for such a purple patch (try 40 years, three Second Division titles, and an Intertoto Cup winners' certificate, mate). Secondly, and I realise that this sounds bizarre 18 years after the fact, but when Ashley purchased Newcastle in 2007, he did so as the club's Great New Hope.

The face of football was changing in 2007, just as it had done in the 1990s. Four years earlier, Roman Abramovich had paid £140m for Chelsea and promptly took them on a £213.5m spending spree, delivering the Premier League title in just two seasons. A further two seasons down the line and Abramovich, ably assisted by José Mourinho, had added another championship, a second League Cup and an FA Cup to the Stamford Bridge trophy cabinet. Not only was this a stunningly successful power grab – Manchester United had won a staggering eight of the first 11 Premier League titles – but the Russian was feted like a hero. It was a sign of football's burgeoning global power and influence. We might have been several years away from the term 'sportswashing' entering the football fan's lexicon, but you could argue that the seeds were first sown in west London. The immediate ramifications for everyone else were slightly simpler. If we wanted to challenge for major honours, we needed oil baron-levels of financial clout – signalling the extinction of local businessmen owning their hometown, top-flight football club. While Sir John Hall took his team to the brink of glory in 1996, even by his own admission he could not compete with the new money on the Premier League table. In truth, despite his successes, he had never wanted to own Newcastle. At 74 he was looking to retire, not overly extend his finances for another crack at the title.

For every exhausted leader there is always a younger man desperate to take his place. Like Benny Blanco from the Bronx in *Carlito's Way*, or that guy who does pretty much the same thing in *Layer Cake* (and who even looks a bit like him, now that I think about it). Around this time, somewhere in the wilds of Buckinghamshire, the businessman Mike Ashley had just come into some serious cash, and he was looking to invest. In just 25 years Ashley had taken a single sports shop – purchased thanks to a £10,000 starter loan from his parents – and turned it into Sport Direct, a thriving retail group that included the sports chain Lillywhites and famous old brands such as Donnay and Dunlop Slazenger. In February 2007 it became Sports Direct PLC and was floated on the London Stock Exchange, after which Ashley sold a 43 per cent stake to investors for £929m. He retained the other 57 per cent which was, at the time, valued at a cool £1bn. That same year he was named the 488th wealthiest man in the world on the *Forbes* Rich List, with a net worth of £2bn. He had a hankering to do something big.

On 23 May 2007, Ashley purchased Sir John Hall's 41.6 per cent stake of Newcastle United for £55,342,223. By 26 June he had acquired 90 per cent of the club and, on 18 July, had the shares of Newcastle United PLC delisted from the London Stock Exchange. In total he paid £134m to become the sole owner of the club. But although this sudden change of ownership model might have ordinarily set alarm bells ringing, I was too busy doing some big-picture thinking to be overly concerned with a looming dictatorship.

At the time, Mike Ashley was billed as being a reclusive billionaire. Not quite in the Howard Hughes, Kleenexboxes-on-the-feet, mould, but still a man with serious wealth and a penchant for making quick decisions. His purchase of Newcastle was done so rapidly, it has been said, that there wasn't even time for the usual due diligence processes – something that would cost him £45m after his team initially failed to notice an unpaid loan obtained by Freddie Shepherd. Perhaps we could expect a reckless attitude in the transfer market, too? Maybe he would sanction a move for Neymar in return for the use of St James' Park as a concert venue in the off-season. Essential stadium and pitch maintenance could occur during June and July, but late May would be reserved for Mike-Stock, a week-long festival with Ashley the only guest. There, a litany of 90s bands would play hours of music each day, a bit like The Beatles in their Hamburg years. All of his favourites would be invited: Five, Atomic Kitten, and the Vengaboys, playing on loop until Mike fancied a bit of quiet time. At which point East 17 would rush onstage to perform an acapella version of 'Stay Another Day' until he fell soundly asleep. Such is the life of an unpredictable billionaire, I reasoned.

On a slightly different note, I looked at it like this: spend £500m over five years and see where that gets us. If the investment delivers success on the pitch then the finances flooding into football must surely find their way on to your bottom line. If not, sell up or run the club in a different way with our blessing, safe in the knowledge that your other 57 per cent of Sports Direct is safe and sound. At the time I found this idea to be perfectly reasonable. It's a typical football fan's opinion of course. One that develops in the pub and is regularly posted on Twitter in outrage. It has little regard for the actual finances involved in running a football club, but we fans rarely operate in such ruthless reality. We are the dreamers. I also appreciate that expecting someone to plough huge amounts of their hard-earned personal fortune into making Newcastle United a successful club is, on many levels, a fairly unreasonable request. While on one hand a person who buys a team does so with an obligation to finance it on to greater endeavours, on the other there's a huge amount of financial difference between simply running a club and making one successful in the modern game. Owners are businessmen first and foremost, and even the most hardened supporter-turned-owner would want to make at least a bit of money. Not that spending huge sums of cash in football automatically equates to success. In the last ten years Tottenham Hotspur have spent close to £1bn on transfers, and yet have zero trophies to show for their fantastical outlay. Admittedly that is quite funny.

Ashley's tenure at Newcastle started positively. The new chairman, Chris Mort, made all the right noises about sensible financing, reducing debt, and having a better focus on signing the right players. They threw their support behind new manager Sam Allardyce, himself only in office for 15 days, and went through an impressive pre-season, beating the likes of Celtic, Sampdoria and Juventus. Even the much-maligned Albert Luque was scoring goals. But Allardyce was never a popular appointment with the majority of Newcastle fans, and I felt it was only a matter of time before Ashley dropped the axe. That decision came just eight months into Big Sam's reign and, after 20 games and with the team sitting in 11th place, he was (probably unfairly) relieved of his duties. Two weeks later Kevin Keegan was anointed for his third incarnation at St James' Park. At this point Ashley was making a mockery of his 'reclusive' reputation. In fact the bloke seemed to be in Newcastle every other week, taking in the match, drinking in the city's Bigg Market and buying rounds of drinks whenever he did. Unsurprisingly, the fans were quite taken by this early enthusiasm/free Smirnoff Ice. But apart from a freak fifth-placed finish in 2011/12, this was where the good times ended for Ashley on Tyneside.

Eight months after hiring Keegan, Ashley stood among the Newcastle fans at Arsenal's Emirates Stadium. On 46 minutes, with his side already 2-0 down to a Robin van Persie brace, he proceeded to down a pint of lager in double-quick time (he once described himself in court as a 'power drinker'). Now let's be absolutely clear about this; there are bad pints and there are *bad* pints. While one might result in a dodgy stomach and your head in a toilet bowl, the other could change your life. Ashley's at the Emirates felt like the latter. The rest of the game passed like most Newcastle games away to Arsenal usually do. The home side purred, finding a fluidity that had deserted them in the first few matches of the season. In the second half they killed the whole thing off with a neatly angled shot by the Brazilian midfielder Denílson. The away team's attacking intent amounted to a Nicky Butt header that smacked off the bar in the second half. It ended 3-0, but it could have easily been five or six. Four days later Keegan quit as manager for the second time, and the Tyneside public declared war on Ashley.

There were times during the 14 years of his ownership that seriously made me consider whether the whole thing was an elaborate piss-take, and that Ashley would eventually unmask himself, like a *Scooby Doo* villain. Everything would come tumbling out then, oh yes. He was actually from Pennywell in Sunderland, and had sworn vengeance over the Mags after Peter Beardsley's New Year's Day derby hat-trick in 1985. From that day on, young Mike worked furiously day and night, shunning friends and family, to become rich enough to buy his most hated football club.

Once in charge he completed his life's masterpiece, slowly and painfully bringing the club down from the inside. If that had been in any way true then I would have actually had some respect for his efforts. As it was, the circus that followed felt like a cruel joke without the pay-off. A heartless, seemingly never-ending, and painfully unfunny joke that devastates you to your very core. The football equivalent of an episode of *Mrs Brown's Boys*.

Supporting Newcastle under Ashley sometimes felt like being on the run from the mob, living on your nerves and watching your back. I quickly realised that we were most vulnerable when good things happened. We might celebrate the occasional big win or decent run of form. But as soon as we allowed ourselves to feel even just that little piece of joy we were finished, because that usually meant Ashley and his team were beavering away behind the scenes to cause some sort of mayhem.

I'd walk into a new season like Tommy from *Goodfellas* going into that basement (transfer deadline day), thinking that I was about to become a Made Guy (sign Hamza Choudhury on loan from Leicester), only to realise I had made a terrible mistake and, instead, would be shot in the back of the head (fail to sign Hamza Choudhury on loan from Leicester). I'm pretty sure I've nailed that metaphor.

The lack of communication from the club was even more baffling. In the era of the Entertainers, Newcastle United and the community thrived off each other's energy, and the news from the local press was the lifeblood of us all. In a pre-internet age I couldn't wait to buy the *Evening Chronicle* each day, and would eagerly scan its back pages in the hope of discovering some fresh transfer news, or to read a title battle cry from the club. Under Keegan's instructions, training sessions at Durham's Maiden Castle were made public, with thousands in attendance every day (there was a hot dog van and everything). The spirit felt joyous, and the resulting fan fervour ensured that the club not only became a far more lucrative beast – through merchandise, season ticket sales, and the increased TV coverage of a team that had captured the nation's (and Sky Sports') imagination – but crucially it enabled the fans to feel part of what was happening at the club. Keegan wanted Newcastle's success to be for the supporters, and that came across in the all-consuming passion with which it was reported in the local press. Through the good times and the bad, I felt that the local writers wanted success for the team they covered almost as much as I did.

Ashley, meanwhile, fell to a siege mentality whenever things turned sour. In 2013, after the *Evening Chronicle* led with a front page splash about an anti-Ashley march, the enraged owner slapped an immediate ban on journalists from the *Chronicle* and its Trinity Mirror Group's sister papers the *Journal*, and *Sunday Sun*. While there was nothing revolutionary in the act itself – there was barely a British football journalist who hadn't been banned by Sir Alex Ferguson at one point or another – it's believed that Ashley was one of the first people to offer a workaround to the problem. If the banned papers wanted access, they could always pay for it. And to think people say the guy didn't innovate! It's said that the owner banned more than ten journalists in his time at the club, and while that comes across as childish and petty, the subtext is far darker. Instead of working alongside the local media, as was historically the case, the club would instead direct all eyes to its in-house reporters and club-owned social channels. That way they could control the message, a move straight out of any budding dictator's handbook, but Ashley had forgotten one of its other key tenets: win hearts and minds. It occasionally occurred to him in the rare moments that his interest suddenly flickered to 'on', and he acted out of character hiring Keegan, or Shearer, or suddenly breaking the club's transfer record. But it always lacked the substance and follow-through required to make any real, positive change.

When Ashley purchased Newcastle in 2007, he said, 'I bought this club to become part of its passion and it has worked. I feel at home here already. I love the place, the club and especially the fans, who wouldn't?' But it was exactly this passion that he would go on to almost kill. In a region so fiercely proud of its history, tradition, and football team, Ashley's Newcastle systematically stripped away almost everything that the fanbase held dear. He was bafflingly obsessed with only signing players under 25, and then selling on any talent at the hint of a decent transfer fee. There was the heartbreaking treatment of Argentinian winger Jonás Gutiérrez, who was dropped after developing testicular cancer and denied the extra games required for a contract extension. It was the stadium – the 'Cathedral on the Hill' as Sir Bobby Robson called it – left rusting, unloved, and with spots of mould lurking in dark corners. It was the training ground that wasn't 'fit for purpose', and the commercial opportunities that had gradually been cannibalised by a sea of red and blue logos. It was Shearer's Bar on the Gallowgate End, renamed Number 9 in what seemed a fit of pettiness. When it came to the end, Ashley's contempt for the club shone through like one of his zero-hours Sports Direct contracts, rendering the dreams of the people utterly worthless.

If you're reading this book and do not support Newcastle United, firstly, fair play. I realise that you've taken a leap on this one, hopefully it's worked out for you. Secondly, I want to point out that no Newcastle fan – at least not one of genuinely sound mind – feels that this club has a divine right to be successful. The myth that all Magpies supporters believe they should be in the Champions League because of a few good seasons under Keegan, Kenny Dalglish and Sir Bobby Robson is utterly deranged, but is a story that has been perpetuated by certain pundits who seem to have an axe to grind with the club and its fans. If I have learned anything from my time supporting Newcastle at all, it's that we are a far more pragmatic bunch than we're often given credit for. Sadly, history has taught us to expect the worst. But we always hope for the best. At least we did, until Mike Ashley arrived and took the hope as well.

15

The Reality Check

27 December 1995
Manchester United 2 Newcastle United 0

I'm pretty sure that the football beam-back became a thing in the mid-90s. You remember the beam-back? If your team had a big game coming up away from home, where tickets were scarce and thousands of fans wanted to go, the club would hastily erect a Jumbotron screen in the middle of the pitch and charge you a tenner to watch. Although being at St James' Park always seems magical to me, this whole experience felt a little strange.

The rules for a beam-back are essentially the same as for any other game, and I think that's where the problem starts. You put on your replica shirt, grab your scarf, follow the same pre-match pub routine, and head to the ground. But the players aren't there. They're miles away and, in their place, lies a massive grainy vision of their endeavours. Behaviourally there's a lot to unpack, too. As the game progresses you offer a traditional, 'go onnnnn' when your team attacks, and a 'wheyyy' if a ball is ballooned over the bar by the opposition. These are both perfectly acceptable responses. They're reflex actions, the football equivalent of having your kneecap tapped with a hammer. But should actual matchday singing be part of the occasion, as well? If Newcastle are in the ascendancy, should we sing 'Blaydon Races' – as was the norm when taking the opposition apart in the mid-90s – even if the team is out of earshot? Does a packed house down the pub blast out a few rounds of 'United!' towards the screen during the match? I've been out of the country since 2007, so maybe it happens at those Boxpark games during international tournaments – a quick bit of Elmer Bernstein's 'Great Escape' theme and then it's back to chucking pints of lager at each other. I've got no idea. But I do know that I never walked downstairs to find my dad watching the match and singing the 'Magpie Ranger' song. More's the pity.

Singing builds the atmosphere and camaraderie, and makes it feel special, like you're almost there. I get it. But the whole experience is unusual. Familiar, but strangely disconcerting. That's how I felt when Newcastle went to Manchester United in December 1995, for a game that Sky Sports was already gleefully promoting as a title showdown: like I was wearing some exciting, yet tiresomely familiar pants.

Unable to source tickets, I was reduced to watching the game on a big screen at St James' Park. I was sitting in the Leazes End, wearing my shirt, scarf, and feeling a bit odd at the tail end of a few 'Toon! Toon!' chants, but I was also concerned about our god-awful record at Old Trafford. Mind-blowingly, we were half-expected to win. That prediction felt like a set-up. Even if David Ginola hit a 94th-minute goal to put us in the lead with seconds on the clock, I felt sure that Alex Ferguson would have flown past the speed of light – like Christopher Reeve in *Superman* – reversed time, and still somehow got the win, taking the physics of Fergie Time to a whole new level.

The fact is that there are some football grounds where you just don't win. Like it's against god, or nature, or something. Whatever the reason is, the minute you go there you're fucked. You can play there every season for decades and still not manage to come home with a win. It doesn't matter how much your line-up changes over the years, who your manager is, or what sort of form you're in. You turn up, you lose, you go home. It's tradition. Newcastle have quite a few of these destinations. A win at Stamford Bridge, for example, is about as rare as a win at Anfield. Four wins in my lifetime at Chelsea compared to three at Liverpool. Quite astonishing, really.

I count myself incredibly lucky to have been at Anfield on the day that we picked up our only Premier League win there to date. When I was growing up I felt that Liverpool had to play at Wembley several times a season. Other teams would play there, too, sometimes, Manchester United or Everton, but it felt like Liverpool were contractually obliged to be in all cup finals. The teams of Bob Paisley and then Kenny Dalglish were simply imperious. So, watching us beat them on their own ground in 1994 was a boyhood dream come true. And we didn't just beat them, we battered them 2-0, with goals from Andy Cole and Robert Lee. Under Graeme Souness the hosts were a team in transition, but I couldn't have cared less. I remember getting into the ground extra early so I could stare at the Kop for a while, watching it fill up. This was the last day of service for this iconic terrace. The place where Liverpool fans had sung Beatles songs in the 1960s, and what seemed like the backdrop to almost every big game on TV. It was the final game before the Kop would be made all-seater in order to comply with the Taylor Report and a sad day for football fans everywhere. If that wasn't poignant enough, it was also the day after the fifth anniversary of the Hillsborough disaster, so Newcastle fans laid wreaths around Anfield, and even inside the ground on the pitch before kick-off. After the match and although they had been soundly beaten, I remember being hugged by the Liverpool supporters in gratitude for our gesture. It was one of those rare moments that went far beyond sport.

If Stamford Bridge and Anfield were dodgy venues for Newcastle, Old Trafford was on a different level. The last time a Newcastle team won there was four years before I was born, in 1972, a 2-0 victory with goals from Stewart Barrowclough and John Tudor against a Manchester United side featuring George Best, Bobby Charlton and Denis Law. I can only assume that we wronged some sort of shaman on the way home, because, fucking hell, we hadn't been able to buy a win there ever since. And that's presuming someone had even tried to. No last-minute winner off somebody's arse. No wholly undeserved three points thanks to a grossly incorrect refereeing decision. Not a dickie bird. So you'll understand that although Newcastle went there two days after Christmas 1995, ten points clear at the top of the table and having lost only two of their previous 20 games (with three draws), I still couldn't see us winning.

When it comes to football, I am not an optimistic man. The smallest thing will set me off in my doom mongering, too. A team that hasn't won for ages ('well they're bound to beat us'). A player who hasn't scored for months ('100 per cent guaranteed to notch'). My dad betting on us to win and then deliberately telling me about it because he knew that it would wind me up ('well you've absolutely fucked it, there'). I used to sit next to a bloke at the match who, prior to every Newcastle corner, would shout, 'Here we go, big Al at the far post, get in!' and I cannot tell you how much that bothered me. I mean, look, it was Alan Shearer so I'm certain that he got more than his fair share of goals from corners. But if you try and call it before it happens then surely you're decimating the odds of it *actually* happening? It was infuriating – on a football *and* mathematical level.

So, with my glass set permanently at half-empty, I looked elsewhere for help. While footballers are renowned for their weird good luck rituals – Gary Neville would sit on the toilet for 15 minutes with his kit on, while Johan Cruyff would slap the Ajax goalie Gert Bals's stomach – at least they had a level of control over the outcome. How we expect the good luck rituals of fans to make a difference is anybody's guess. Not that it matters, I still have loads of them. I'm not sure how these things get started. Maybe we get a win one day, then I'm desperate to repeat it, but realise that I have zero impact on proceedings. As the feeling of helplessness seeps into my entire being, I switch into survival mode and begin to make arbitrary connections. Maybe if I wear exactly the same things, the same result will happen? Well that's not weird at all.

By the mid-90s, my lucky matchday uniform had been honed to near perfection, to the point where it felt truly ready to deliver the title. As with all good teams, the key was a strong spine: the oldest part of the kit (or shall I say most experienced) was my underwear, some Calvin Klein boxers that weren't so much worn as utterly decimated. They didn't even have an underneath part to them any more, making them, basically, a very short dress that should have gone in the bin years ago. But as long as the waistband remained, and the results kept rolling in, the pants stayed in the team. After that it was some black Stüssy jeans, a Newcastle top, and a brown Gio-Goi jacket with a yellow stripe down the arm. From a distance I resembled a traffic warden.

It didn't end there, either. I also had a lucky walking route from the centre of town up to St James' Park. To my mind victory absolutely hung on my taking this route, without deviation, ahead of every home game. So, it didn't matter where I was, or what pub I was drinking in. When I was heading to the ground I would have to go back to Grey's Monument and begin the official journey. Along New Bridge Street, left up Northumberland Street, left into Eldon Square and all the way through to the exit on Percy Street. Cross over, head up Leazes Park Road, take a left on Strawberry Place, and then into St James' Park via turnstile number 59. Once at my seat I had to re-tie my shoelaces and stuff whatever was inside my pockets into the left one, because the team on the left of a fixture is the home side. Only then was I ready.

As the season had been going so well I had, understandably, put an increased emphasis on my lucky outfit. That was OK when I was at the match. But what about when we were away, and I couldn't afford a ticket? No problem, just crack on as per usual. So, from the confines of my childhood bedroom, and with the blinds remaining closed (not sure how that became part of it), I would get up each Saturday, generally with a stonking hangover from a Friday night out in Durham, and pull on my full matchday outfit. I would stand unsteadily (because standing felt like being at the match), listen to the game on the radio and sweat, shake, and generally feel pretty terrible. The whole charade was a source of amusement to my family, and it remains so to this day. What I will say is this: In those few seasons, Newcastle had their best top-flight away record since I began supporting them, and that went back to normal the minute I stopped doing it. Coincidence? (I mean, yes, obviously, we just had a good team, but still. The clothes etc.)

Occasionally I would look at these bizarre rituals and evaluate my actions through a sobering prism of reality. I mean seriously, just how does the guy in the old, ripped underwear, with one trouser pocket filled to bursting, have any sort of influence over the results of Newcastle United Football Club? In the cold light of day it's hard to make an argument in my defence. I know what you're thinking. What happens if I rationalise it further and question just how much my actions have ever helped my team at all? A team without a major trophy since 1969? Well, I haven't found the right formula yet, obviously.

Sometimes I wish that I was one of those other people. You know the type: optimists. The lads and lasses who are always certain that Newcastle will win. Absolute perverts the lot of them if you ask me. Occasionally I wonder what it must be like for these people in their day-to-day lives. Some sort of stress-free fucking utopia I'm guessing but, alas, I shall never be one of them. So, when Newcastle turned up at Old Trafford that day I wasn't expecting much. That feeling was heavily reinforced when our former number nine, Andy Cole, did what he did best.

It always irked me when Manchester United fans would sing the Andy Cole song after he had signed for them, the one that we had so skilfully created. Not only were they rubbing salt in the wound, but the sheer lack of originality was staggering. Surely they could have worked on something new? Why not do something to the tune of 'Gold' by Spandau Ballet, for example ('Andy Cole … GOAL!')? There are loads of options, obviously. That's just a suggestion. Either way, six minutes into our 'title decider' 90 per cent of the ground was singing it, as Cole took a defence-splitting pass from Roy Keane and rifled home a first-time, side-footed shot from the corner of the box. It was a very good finish, and his body shape was textbook. Firm leg, head over the ball, wallop. As he celebrated I cursed him from my seat in the Leazes End 148 miles away, wondering just how close you needed to be for a curse to actually work.

Ten minutes after the goal, another disaster, as the home defender Phil Neville did a job on his former team-mate Keith Gillespie, injuring the Northern Irish winger who had been so integral to Newcastle's fantastic early season form. Les Ferdinand missed a great chance shortly afterwards, blasting a shot straight at Peter Schmeichel when one-on-one with the Danish goalkeeper, and that was the highlight of our attacking intent. Seven minutes into the second half, a raking 30-yard pass by David Beckham found Roy Keane in oceans of room on the Newcastle left. He took a touch and sent a low volley past Pavel Srníček to make it two. Game over, and then some. Cole should really have had a hat-trick.

Maybe this comes down to big-game experience? Maybe it's about nerves, or complacency. But there are some teams that can raise their game when it truly matters. Manchester United had drawn three and lost two of their previous five games, but they knew that allowing Newcastle to pull 13 points clear of them in December could have been a fatal blow to their hopes of the title. So, buoyed by the stakes, they utterly dominated against a Newcastle team that had dropped just six points from the previous 42 available, and suddenly the lead was down to just seven. Still big, but manageable for the chasing pack.

Although I left St James' Park with a familiar, defeat-at-Old-Trafford feeling, I wasn't distraught. We were flying, this was just a blip. I think the players felt the same, too, with Les Ferdinand later claiming that they were often a little blasé after their occasional defeats, and only started to panic when it was too late. What was certain, however, is that Kevin Keegan wasn't panicking. In fact he was about to do something that would blow everybody's mind.

16

The Fever Dream

2 May 2012
Chelsea 0 Newcastle United 2
Cissé (2)

There were times when I doubted that the 2011/12 season at Newcastle ever really happened. We scored great goals, beat sides that we almost never beat, and were genuinely exciting to watch. It felt so out of character. I can only liken it to a TV show that makes a freak episode, like Bouncer's dream in *Neighbours*, or the *Seinfeld* one where they go to India for a wedding and the whole thing runs backwards. It was weird, intoxicating, and confusingly brilliant.

Football teams occasionally experience a freak big season like this. One that comes out of nowhere and skews all the metrics. It starts with some good, confidence-building early season form. Five or six games in and you pass the 'we've usually lost by now' stage. After that, the rub of the green helps you pick up points from teams you often lose to. Not big-hitters, but bogey sides like Brighton or Ipswich. Maybe after that you do take a big scalp, possibly even two. Now confidence is suddenly sky high and you're operating on pure momentum until you hit the finish line. Leicester City's Premier League title win of 2015/16 is the best example of such a feat in recent English football. The Foxes finished 14th the previous season, spent around £30m on ten players in the summer and then somehow won the championship. It was like the entire squad had been replaced by football-playing replicants. Every week you would expect the wheels to come off, but Claudio Ranieri's men just went on and on. As a fan you dream of the miracles that sport can occasionally deliver; you try and imagine what they would feel like if they ever happened to you. But you never really believe that they will. There can be no Leicester fan alive who expected to win the Premier League. But then they did and, rather than Manchester City or Arsenal picking up their umpteenth title, you have this fantastic underdog story instead, one that will be passed down through generations of misty-eyed Leicester supporters who were lucky enough to experience it. How great is that?!

Although Newcastle were some way off title-winning heroics in 2011/12, it was the one top-flight season under Ashley that we had a team with something about them, a bit of attitude and attacking snark that would have interested the likes of Kevin Keegan and Sir Bobby Robson. We have to give some credit to Alan Pardew for this. Not that the fanbase always did. Even after this stellar year (he was eventually named LMA Manager of the Year and Premier League Manager of the Season), the guy never shook off his Ashley stooge tag. But I always quite liked him. For me he was never in the same mould of meek compliance as Steve McClaren or Steve Bruce. Pardew at least had some fire in his belly – just ask the Hull City midfielder David Meyler who Pardew head-butted in a touchline fracas down at the KC Stadium in 2014. He also called the then-Manchester City manager Manuel Pellegrini a 'fucking old cunt' as they won 2-0 at St James' Park, which is undeniably funny. Despite the fact that Pardew's time on Tyneside ended badly – with fan protests, a sackpardew.com website, and some truly awful form – I've always respected how he showed real pride in holding the Newcastle manager's job, and continues to talk up the fans and club even now as a pundit. What cannot be in any doubt, however, was that after the initial shock of having to sell his star striker Andy Carroll just two weeks into the job, Pardew helped assemble a side with real talent for the season that followed, aided largely by the work of 'super scout' Graham Carr, and his French network of unearthed gems and off-radar talent.

This was a season also notable for granting Fabricio Coloccini a pass to shag all of our wives, thanks to some stout defending and cultured play on the ball. I wonder if he ever cashed in on one of those terrace anthem offers? Just turned up on someone's doorstep unannounced, explaining that he was into it and leaving the husband downstairs while he made hay with his missus. Maybe he would bring a home perm kit with him to soften the blow? At least that way the cuckolded partner could have 'curly hair too', as the song also dictates. I'm not sure what would happen if you had a sudden change of heart and *didn't* want Coloccini to shag your wife. I suppose a chant from the Gallowgate End isn't legally binding. So, even if he got litigious I imagine the local court system would have found in your favour. Up to you, really, innit.

A selfless, complicated love of Newcastle's captain aside, the team's defence wasn't exactly known for being a particularly tight unit. In fact, despite many successes that season we also took some absolute pastings away from home, and from bizarrely unexpected sources, too. There were drubbings at Norwich, Fulham and Wigan that read 4-2, 4-2 and 4-0 respectively; results that would have been a real problem had we not been so sparkling going forward most of the time. In that respect, four players in particular caught the eye.

In Hatem Ben Arfa Newcastle had a player of prodigious talent who, on his day, could be described as a tricky winger x fucking hell, did you see that? With a delicate touch, an instant drop of the shoulder and a frighteningly sharp burst of pace, the Frenchman's talents deserved a bigger stage ... the Bernabéu or Camp Nou, perhaps? But for whatever reason Ben Arfa was never fully able to retain the discipline and focus required to maintain the Ballon d'Or-winning form he so often had in him. Across the pitch from the enigmatic winger there was Yohan Cabaye, at £4m a bargain-buy midfielder from Lille who could control the game, pass the ball short and long, and was the best free-kick taker we had seen since Laurent Robert. He also had a bit of a nasty streak in him too, the perfect combination of artistry and arsehole. Up front, Demba Ba was a free transfer revelation from newly relegated West Ham United, and for a bloke with a supposedly dodgy knee I can't remember him missing a game. He could score any type of goal, too, from two-yard tap-ins to 20-yard tit-blitzers, towering headers to free kicks and flying volleys.

To my mind, Ba was one of the most complete centre-forwards the club has had in its modern era, and he was only eclipsed that year by the goalscoring madness of his Senegalese strike partner Papiss Cissé. A £9m January signing from German side SC Freiburg (a rare fit of generosity from Mike Ashley), Cissé's 12 goals in 13 games often came via unorthodox finishes and from bizarre angles, like bullets in *The Matrix*. But they came at the cost of his strike partner's form. Although Ba would score on Cissé's debut against Aston Villa, and end the season as Newcastle's top scorer with 16, he didn't score again for the rest of the season after that game.

I was certainly much more fun to be around in 2011/12. Even now, at the age of 49, I find it astonishing how the form of Newcastle relentlessly dictates my mood. Win and I feel lighter. I'm more receptive and gregarious, and I open myself up to life's rich possibilities that little bit more. Lose and I'm a dick. At least in the immediate aftermath. That's one improvement from when I was a kid, actually. Back then it took me days to get over any loss. Now it's just a few hours, but I still sulk with glazed eyes, dipping in and out of conversations as I consider how we managed to snatch defeat from the jaws of victory this week.

Life just seems that much better when my football team starts posting regular wins, too. Rather than carrying the heavy toll of defeat on my shoulders as I lurch into Monday, a win means that I bounce into work with a mood that sets positive action in motion across the board. In Dubai I was now four years into my adventure, and was finally starting to feel more settled. I had recently taken a job with a new men's magazine called *Edgar*, and while it wasn't quite the *Esquire* or *GQ* that I craved, it allowed me to act upon my own ideas as well as interview fun and famous people. In an interview about watches with the *300* star Gerard Butler I asked him, for some unknown reason, if he would punch a baby panda in the face as long as nobody ever found out about it (he surprisingly would), and I quizzed the Rock and Roll Hall of Fame inductee (and Newcastle United fan) Bryan Ferry way more about a forthcoming Toon match against Fulham than I did his seminal work with Roxy Music. I can't exactly remember what I said to Pamela Anderson in a 2am interview by a nightclub bathroom – I was too busy thinking what my teenage self would have thought about it all – but I'm sure that it was also good.

On the pitch it was a season punctuated by big moments, too, from Ryan Taylor popping one over the wall for a 1-0 win at Sunderland in game two, to the collective relief of Ba's first goals for the club, finally arriving four games into the season in the form of a hat-trick at home to Blackburn Rovers. Four games (and two more goals) later he grabbed another hat-trick, this time away to Stoke in the type of game that Newcastle generally lose. Away from home during midweek, the usual run of things is to start reasonably well, miss a good chance and then end up losing by two. But this season we simply blew them away for a comfortable 3-1 win. There was an invigorating 3-0 home win over Manchester United, featuring a fine, hooked volley from Ba – reminiscent of Duncan Ferguson's goal against the Red Devils at the same Leazes End goal eight years earlier – and a bending, dipping, 30-yard Cabaye free kick that went in off the crossbar. After that there was Papiss Cissé's debut goal for the club, an arrowed, 18-yard half-volley into the top corner of the Gallowgate net in a 2-1 win over Aston Villa, and a 2-0 home win over Liverpool. The latter was particularly enjoyable for the fact that returning striker Andy Carroll barely got a kick, and returning full-back José Enrique ended up in goal, after Pepe Reina was sent off with ten minutes to go. But it is the Chelsea game that everybody remembers.

Stamford Bridge always throws up mixed emotions for me. It's the site of my first-ever unsupervised away match, so quite rightly holds a certain place in my heart, but it's also somewhere that we rarely win. It's the ground where, after a late Les Ferdinand goal snatched a 1-1 draw in the 1996 FA Cup, I had a run-in after the match with a large Chelsea fan who bowled up to me in the crowd and bellowed, 'You Geordies are maggots!' It was kind of funny, but it was also fucking terrifying. He was wearing a massive overcoat, so I wasn't 100 per cent sure whether he was going to chin me or get his cock out – or which would have been worse, for that matter. Thankfully it was neither, and he staggered off into the night, like a pissed, fairly aggressive Barry from *EastEnders*.

During Euro 96, the illusionist/spoon bender Uri Geller claimed he had helped England beat Scotland in their crucial Group A game by moving the ball with his mind. Geller was hovering over Wembley in a helicopter at the time, England were 1-0 up thanks to an Alan Shearer goal, and Scotland won a penalty. As the Leeds United man Gary McAllister strode up to strike the ball, it suddenly rolled forward just an inch or so and England goalkeeper David Seaman saved the resulting spot-kick. Geller took the credit – well who else could? He had a soft spot for the Toon, as well, and later helped them end their 28-game London hoodoo in 2001 as he ran around Highbury 11 times during the match to somehow help Sir Bobby Robson's side to a 3-1 win, a victory that took them to the top of the Premier League. So far, so abso-fucking-lutely normal.

Unsurprisingly, I could only think that Geller was at it again as Newcastle slowly began to sparkle at the Bridge in their third-to-last game of the 2011/12 season. Coming off six wins in the last seven games, Pardew's men attacked with fluency and intent, and when André Villas-Boas's side came back at them they looked comfortable and solid at the back. The game was finely balanced, but then we held an ace up our sleeve (no, not Geller). Our number nine was scoring goals like they were going out of fashion.

It's often said that Papiss Cissé's two strikes, in what would become Newcastle's first league win at Stamford Bridge for 26 years, are the finest brace in the club's recent history. I wouldn't argue with that, largely because I can't remember any others off the top of my head. But, controversially, I preferred his first-half goal to his 94th-minute second. I mean, don't get me wrong, who doesn't love a dipping-bending-outside-of-the-right-boot-physics-defying freak of a goal? Certainly not me. Even Didier Drogba was into it, laughing about its sheer ridiculousness with Alan Pardew just moments afterwards, and the Chelsea striker was still on the pitch at the time. But there's also part of me that thinks he just got lucky. I know that professional footballers have the ability to do things with a ball that us mere mortals cannot comprehend, but I have since read that the Senegalese was utterly exhausted at this point – understandably so – and when the ball came back to him from Shola Ameobi he simply decided to crash it towards goal, as he didn't have the energy to try and keep hold of it and run the clock down. So, it was either sublime skill, blind luck, or the work of Uri Geller, and I'm not taking any other explanations at this point.

Away from sorcery, Cissé's first goal that night was pure class, and a move that devastated Chelsea in seconds. First the striker calmly accepted a pass from Italian left-back Davide Santon on the edge of a crowded box. He instinctively flicked it up with his right foot and, finally, crashed a left-footed volley past Petr Čech in what looked like the very same action. It was perfect in every aspect, and will always be the better 'footballing' goal as far as I'm concerned.

For a minute or two after that win down in west London, with Newcastle sitting in fifth position and with two games left of the season, it looked like we might actually sneak into a Champions League position. With the riches that come from Europe's elite club tournament then, who knows, maybe this story could have turned out differently, with Ashley sucked into a desire to build the best team in the country. I doubt it, but maybe. As it was, our sliding doors moment went the other way. We promptly lost the last two games of the season, missing out on fourth place to Tottenham by just four points, and ended up in fifth spot – our third-highest Premier League placing ever – and with qualification to the Europa League.

The season had given us all a glimmer of hope. Maybe it was going to be OK after all, and it would be like *Moneyball*. We would unearth lower-league gems, or foreign talent that hasn't bloomed yet, and we would do it all while gradually progressing and improving. There would be a trophy, or maybe even two, and people would make movies and write books about how we did it. Either that or I would wake up one day to discover that, actually, the whole season had been a dream, like Bobby Ewing's death in *Dallas* in 1986, and in fact we had finished 16th, after a late-season rally pulled us away from relegation in the nick of time.

But for the moment, Newcastle were back among the country's elite, sitting at the right end of the table and worthy of giving anybody a good game. Mike Ashley once more found himself at a crossroads with the club and its supporters. Surely now was the time to build and develop? Surely now we kick on? Unfortunately, the owner didn't quite see it that way.

17

Tinooooooo

10 February 1996
Middlesbrough 1 Newcastle United 2
Watson, Ferdinand

In the six months that passed since Newcastle's opening match of the season against Coventry City, and game number 25 at Middlesbrough, much had happened. Motorola had released the world's first flip phone (it cost around a grand, but then you can't put a price on a sense of self-importance). In boxing, Frank Bruno had won and then subsequently lost the WBC world heavyweight championship, and Oasis and Blur had gone head-to-head for the number one spot in the UK. Oh, and the Magpies were 12 points clear at the top of the Premier League. Which was the most surprising bit of the lot.

The club's fine four-match winning run since January was paralleled by a transfer saga rumbling along behind the scenes, stemming from the 2-0 reverse at Manchester United just six weeks earlier. It was an exotic, hare-brained saga that would twist everyone's melons.

Newcastle had followed that December defeat with solid wins over Arsenal, Coventry, Bolton and Sheffield Wednesday – while Fergie's men dropped five points during the same period – yet still conversations at the club persisted about solidity and stoutness. Attack-minded football was swashbuckling fun, sure. But don't forget defensive duty and being a touch more difficult to beat, Kevin. Kevin? KEVIN!? Keegan responded to the muffled accusations of defensive creakiness in the only way that he knew how – by signing the Colombian striker Faustino Asprilla. Because if attack is the best form of defence, then a wildly unpredictable attack (that is possibly armed) is surely even better? It was a signing very much in tune with the football times.

In the fourth season of Premier League football, clubs were increasingly becoming defined by their transfer activity. Gone were the days of scouting a hardworking prospect from the second tier, getting him up on the train and then having him pose with the gaffer on the pitch, the pair of them holding either end of a club scarf. That particular trope always reminded me of the pasta scene in *Lady and the Tramp*, actually. But the player and manager rarely kissed at the end of it. Or ate the scarf, for that matter. The whole concept of the new signing photoshoot almost went too far in 1994, after Bryan Robson was appointed player-manager at Middlesbrough. Somehow Robbo was convinced to pose in the most literal interpretation of a situation ever. Shorts, socks and boots at the bottom, jacket, shirt and tie at the top – he was a player-manager, *geddit?* Thankfully, football marked it down as mid-90s exuberance and the whole thing was never mentioned again.

The first great influx of foreign talent arrived in the Premier League for the 1994/95 season, players such as Ghanaian number nine – and thunderbastard originator – Tony Yeboah at Leeds, Dutch winger Bryan Roy at Nottingham Forest, American striker Cobi Jones at Coventry, and the unpredictable Nigerian forward Daniel

Amokachi at Everton. After a fine first season back in the top flight – finishing third and qualifying for the UEFA Cup – Newcastle had been shopping, too, with Keegan neatly combining his USA 94 co-commentary duty with a bit of much-needed player scouting, returning home with the busy Swiss full-back Marc Hottiger and the Dane-chipping Belgian central defender Philippe Albert. But it was Tottenham Hotspur who changed the game when it came to big signings from abroad. Having picked up Gheorghe Popescu and Ilie Dumitrescu from PSV and Steaua București respectively – the pair having performed admirably as Romania reached the World Cup quarter-finals – Tottenham gaffer Ossie Ardiles then took things into the stratosphere by signing the German legend Jürgen Klinsmann from Monaco for £3m. He would become the Premier League's first genuine foreign superstar.

At the time, Klinsmann was something of a divisive signing for Spurs, and the German carried with him the reputation for being a diver. He was a roller and a twister. A shyster from across the Channel, and English football, with its firm belief in sportsmanship and all, would simply not stand for this type of behaviour. One self-deprecating, headlong dive in celebration of his debut winner against Sheffield Wednesday later, of course, and all was forgiven. But there was more than one way to make a first impression in a new country. Eighteen months later, Tino Asprilla wandered into Newcastle during a blizzard. He wore a fur coat and carried a look of suspicion normally reserved for a Mafia boss eating at a new restaurant. The fans instantly loved him.

A wild signing for a wild time. Asprilla was the type of bloke who shot guns in the air to celebrate the new year (he was on probation for that), and allegedly kept the company of porn stars and drug cartels. In 1998, after being sent off for fighting with Paraguayan goalkeeper José Chilavert, a hitman apparently called Asprilla seeking permission to kill the Vélez Sarsfield number one for his on-field transgression. The permission was not forthcoming, but it was a measure of the worlds in which Asprilla moved in when he wasn't playing football. Not that he was a model of convention when he crossed the white line on a Saturday, of course.

On the pitch the Colombian wore black boots with a bright red Diadora logo. He would pick up the ball and stumble into his stride, shirt untucked, socks half down. To the uninitiated it could look like he didn't have a clue what he was doing, but the former Parma striker developed his game in Italy when Serie A was the most technical and merciless league in the world. This was a time when the likes of Paolo Maldini, Roberto Baggio, Marco van Basten, Ruud Gullit, and Alessandro Del Piero lit up its iconic stadiums. Anybody who underestimated the languid playing style of Asprilla would, more often than not, end up paying the price (that's not the hitman again, I just mean he could carve your team up in seconds given the opportunity). Asprilla seemed to operate on pure instinct half the time, reacting to the merest hint of a move towards the ball when it was under his control with a dodge or swerve, a flick or a turn. Watching him often felt like studying the boxer Prince Naseem Hamed, who would judge his bobs and weaves by staring at his opponent's feet to work out where an attack would arrive from. Asprilla's game was utterly enthralling. You just never knew what he was going to do next. In fairness, I'm not sure that he did either.

Asprilla arrived in Newcastle with the team once more on the up, and it's always said that the big plan was to bed him in gradually. He could be the match-winner that we kept up our sleeves should we need a bit of magic, along the road to becoming champions. Then after having had time to settle, he would be fully ready for the Champions League season that followed. But in many ways Keegan and Asprilla were similar. Both men operated on impulse. The Colombian had flown into Newcastle on the morning of the game at Middlesbrough, and was set for a largely symbolic place on the bench that day. He was never actually meant to play, and had already enjoyed a glass or two of wine with his lunch. But then things started to look a little dicey on the pitch. Newcastle were a John Beresford own goal down, and decidedly short on ideas. Keegan decided to go nuclear and told Asprilla to get warmed up.

I have only played football once after drinking. It was at training for the University of Sunderland team, following an impromptu afternoon drinking session with my then-girlfriend (and now wife), Alexandria. The performance was something of a mixed bag. On the plus side I had *a lot* of confidence. On the minus I discovered the next day that I had, apparently, spent around an hour booting the ball 20 yards over the bar whenever it came anywhere near me. I mean, I can't remember it, I was pissed.

Until Asprilla's arrival, Newcastle were having one of those games. You know the type. Passes a yard misplaced, control a little sloppy, runs ill-timed and shooting, well, shooting like me after the above-mentioned drinking session. Then the whole thing went bananas. The Colombian jogged on in his long, lazy stride, wearing black gloves and making a sign of the cross as he did. In that moment you could sense the atmosphere change inside the Riverside Stadium. Asprilla was a superstar and, even if they might not admit it, the Middlesbrough fans were almost as excited to see him take to the pitch as Newcastle's were. At least until he picked up the ball seven minutes later on the far left-hand side, twisted Steve Vickers inside out like a pair of jeans in the wash, and sent over an inch-perfect ball to the head of Steve Watson for an equaliser.

The actual finish – a real smart header – is almost incidental. The whole thing is about Asprilla. At first he looks like he's jogging to answer the door. Zero urgency. Although Vickers stands him up, he's utterly powerless to stop the debutant from cutting inside and on to his right. By the time his vision does fall into focus, Asprilla has done him again, Cruyff-turning back on to his left and chipping the ball into the box. If I had been the Middlesbrough number four I would have walked off the pitch and gone to live in the woods for a year just to get my head right.

Newcastle went on to win the game 2-1, the Colombian discombobulating everyone to such extent that when Les Ferdinand scuffed a shot from the edge of the Middlesbrough box, it somehow managed to bobble its way underneath Gary Walsh and roll apologetically into the back of the net. Asprilla almost added a third himself, glancing a header just wide at the death. But it remained 2-1, and a hugely important win on the road. But my standout memory remains another piece of Asprilla wizardry.

When a season finishes it's funny the minutiae you remember, often for life. Naturally the goals and games are there, the wins and losses, if you're lucky perhaps even a trophy, but often it's a millisecond in time that burrows deep into your frontal lobe. A trick, a pass. Some effortless control or an outrageous step-over. For me there were two standout moments that season. In the reverse fixture at St James' Park earlier in the season there was David Ginola on Neil Cox. The Frenchman was on his own touchline at the Gallowgate End. Fenced in by the Middlesbrough full-back, he refused to panic. He dragged the ball with his studs on top, right, left, then right again, leaving Cox utterly bamboozled, like a dog trying to figure out which cup a treat is hidden under. If it had been a cartoon, Cox's skin would have fallen off in shock.

Back at the Riverside, Asprilla's trickery for Newcastle's equaliser turned out to be just a palate cleanser – an amuse-bouche, for those of you who like their football chat laid out in fine-dining terms. With Newcastle 2-1 up, and the clock ticking down, the ball found its way to the Colombian on the halfway line. He instinctively flicked it to the left of the onrushing defender with a stroke of his right boot, and then pushed past him with his left in one fluid movement. But going past him once was not enough for Asprilla. So, with the Middlesbrough man still trying to work out where the Colombian was, Asprilla rolled the ball backwards and through the defender's legs for the most outrageous reverse nutmeg I have ever seen. You'll notice that I decided not to name the Middlesbrough player in this passage. Partly because I can't work out exactly who it was, the footage is pretty grainy, and partly because this man will likely have a family. Dredging this up could very well destroy everything he has gone on to build since that fateful day.

For all of the amazing things that Asprilla could do on the football pitch, it was equally true that he also did some amazing things off it. His soirees while at Newcastle were infamous, and he would often invite taxi-loads of people back to his home from nightclubs such as Julie's or Legends to party until the early hours. And then, when he wanted to get rid of them he would call his neighbour David Ginola to come down and turf them all out. Quite ironic, as it was by mentioning the Frenchman in the first place that he had convinced half of the women to be in attendance. But the truth is that Keegan probably handled Asprilla better than any other manager ever did, giving him enough freedom to live his life and still do his thing for the team. This was undoubtedly one of KK's big strengths – man-management.

It's no surprise when, after Keegan left Newcastle halfway through the following season and was replaced by the furrowed brow of former Liverpool and Blackburn manager Kenny Dalglish, the whole thing imploded. Although Asprilla would bag his iconic Champions League hat-trick against Barcelona in September, they would prove to be his last goals for the club. His final appearance just four months later, a turgid display in the FA Cup third round at Goodison Park before being hooked for Ian Rush (who would bundle home the winner), told you everything you needed to know about the direction of the club.

I think that what makes the football life of Asprilla so enjoyable is that – apart from possessing an outrageous, natural ability – he was the total antithesis of a football player in 2025. That's not a dig at current players; Asprilla thought that football should be fun, and that's exactly how he played. Admittedly, that wasn't always easy to watch. Sometimes I'd prefer he squared the ball to a team-mate for a tap-in rather than attempt to take on a fifth man. Or maybe, after scoring against Metz in the UEFA Cup it would have been better if he had not taken off his shirt, stuck it on a corner flag and hoisted it into the air in celebration – getting a yellow card that would keep him out of the following round. But that wouldn't have been Tino. Give me his unpredictability any day over the guys who are media-trained to within an inch of their lives, posting identikit social media epitaphs after each and every game.

Despite becoming a grandfather quite recently, the 55-year-old has seemingly not changed one little bit, and has no intention of doing so. 'My life is much the same,' he once explained about retirement. 'I go to parties, dance, drink, eat, and meet women. Many women. I will never change. Joy is my destiny – and it's a good destiny to have.'

After the win at the Riverside, there was plenty of joy on Tyneside. Although Keegan's men had begun to tire as the season pushed into its final straight, they were now grinding out victories by one-goal margins – like all good title-winning sides do. Now, they had added another mercurial match-winner to their ranks, and it was going to take one hell of a team to stop them. Down the road in Manchester, Alex Ferguson had some thoughts about that.

18

Oh Noooooo

14 April 2013
Newcastle United 0 Sunderland 3

You know you're having a bad season when somebody punches a horse in the face. That's not a saying, as far as I'm aware, but it probably should be. It certainly feels like a very Newcastle-under-Mike-Ashley thing to talk about. A moment of utter lunacy from a supporter in a season where the team reverted depressingly to type, making the fifth-placed finish of the previous year look like a figment of everybody's imagination.

What I remember most from this season (even more than a bloke trying to punch a horse) is the utter face-scraping, mind-bending frustration of it all. I guess this is what football is all about. A game of the finest margins, where agony and ecstasy sit in precarious and constant balance. That's part of the reason why we love it so much. The width of the post, the stretch of a leg, a moment of hesitation. Consider England's 1990 World Cup semi-final with West Germany, for a moment, and Chris Waddle's extra-time shot that cannoned off the inside of the post. A few inches to the left and it would have been a goal. England would have likely progressed to the final, and very possibly beaten an average Argentina side to win the World Cup. Instead it was tears in Turin and an eventual fourth-placed finish. Maybe the universe simply disapproved of Waddle shaving off his mullet for the game?

Mike Ashley was certainly skilled in the dark arts of frustration. You just couldn't read the guy. One minute he wanted to sell the club, the next he refused to leave until we won a trophy. In a sport where a spine of consistency is integral to success, supporting Newcastle between 2007 and 2021 felt like a massive game of snakes and ladders. No sooner were you making progress than a Sports Direct-sponsored snake – probably wearing a Donnay jacket – popped up to drop you back down to where you had started … or even worse.

For Ashley and his team, Newcastle's surprisingly good form of 2011/12 must have felt like vindication. After all, this was proof that his financial model for the club could work. The fact was that the previous season had been fun. Some big wins, lots of goals, real attacking flair, and a return to European competition at the end of it all after an absence of six years. If Ashley was unwilling to plough big amounts of his own cash into the club, then a strategy that saw incremental improvements felt like a reasonable compromise. The only problem was that this model relies on stellar recruitment at all times, and in reality that's just not possible, especially as the rest of the football world was starting to cotton on to Graham Carr's work in France, and looking to unearth diamonds of their own there too.

In terms of the balance sheet, there are certainly examples of the process. Players such as Yohan Cabaye (bought for £4.3m and sold to Paris Saint-Germain for £19m) or, better yet, Moussa Sissoko (bought for £1.5m and sold to Spurs for a bewildering £30m), showed that huge margins could be made if you got things right. But for every Demba Ba, Papiss Cissé, Hatem Ben Arfa and Gini Wijnaldum there was an Emmanuel Rivière, Rémy Cabella, and Florian Thauvin. In fact there was Siem de Jong, Henri Saivet, and Achraf Lazaar, too. That list is not to belittle those players. I'm a firm believer that, sometimes, a move isn't right for a multitude of reasons. If your recruitment rests on spotting a future star, and signing them when they're young and far cheaper, you should factor in that some of these men will simply not settle on Tyneside, or in English football for that matter.

At this point, the only certainty was that we were stuck with this business model for the foreseeable future. Anybody who thought that the previous season's results might fuel the owner's thirst for a successful football team was to be sorely mistaken. Yes, the potential riches of Champions League qualification might have technically been two or three decent signings away, but this type of risk didn't seem in Ashley's business lexicon when it came to his football investment. Why spend all that money when a multitude of factors could still mean that you end up in mid-table? Far better to minimise financial outlay and hope for another season of over-achievement, feeling safe in the knowledge that the club was surely too good to be relegated. So, while the fans wanted a commanding, ball-playing centre-half, a world-class right-back and a speedy left-winger, their only real first-team signing that summer was the full-back/midfielder Vurnon Anita from Ajax for £6.7m. There was certainly nothing wrong with the man from Curaçao. Anita was a tidy player who never let anybody down. He just wasn't what was needed to take Newcastle on to the next level. Although the season started well enough, with only two defeats in the first ten games, a ghoulish mid-November to mid-January saw them lose a staggering ten out of 13, with the Ashley swingometer moving from OK, to shit, to shitter in the blink of an eye. As a result, the Magpies remained entrenched in mid-table mediocrity for the entire season, doing just enough to keep downwind of the swirling threat of relegation.

There were some distractions in the cup this season. Not in the League Cup or FA Cup, of course, oh god no. 'He's ruined us for the cups,' I often said of Ashley, but our poor form actually stretched back to Hall and Shepherd as well, those two apathetic finals aside. We haven't really been a cup side since the 1950s. But what I would say is this: how about you at least look a bit interested in winning them? If only for appearance's sake. Definitely don't say that the cups aren't a priority. That's a terrible message to send out. Claiming disinterest in the only two trophies you could potentially fluke all the way to glory seems almost intentionally divisive to me. But although Newcastle made traditional third-round exits from both domestic cup competitions in 2012/13, they did fare slightly better in the Europa League, eventually losing 3-1 in the quarter-finals to Benfica (who would go on to lose the final 2-1 to Chelsea).

The OGs among you will also recall that this season saw the first and last French Day at St James' Park. I'll probably tell my children about French Day, in lieu of any trophies to talk about. What we forget is that this was another distraction in and of itself. While Rafa Benítez was busy being thoroughly disliked as interim manager at Chelsea – despite winning the Europa League – he also pinched Demba Ba from our line-up and plunged us into some barren months in front of goal. As Chelsea had activated Ba's £7m release clause, there was nothing that the club could do about it. However Newcastle's precarious position in the league – they were sitting in 15th place as Ba headed off to west London – meant that Ashley was forced into action in the transfer market. First came Mathieu Debuchy from Lille in early January. He was followed just a few weeks later by the highly rated centre-half Mapou Yanga-Mbiwa and attacking midfielder Moussa Sissoko from Montpellier and Toulouse respectively, while the striker Yoan Gouffran arrived from Bordeaux. Finally, the young full-back Massadio Haïdara joined from Nancy. The five new signings linked up with Yohan Cabaye, Hatem Ben Arfa, and Sylvain Marveaux in the first-team squad, as the fruits of the club's French scouting network went into overdrive. The new boys had an immediate effect, too, as Newcastle secured an exciting win away to Aston Villa, and then at home to Chelsea in quick succession, with Sissoko scoring twice and catching the eye as a marauding midfielder.

Three games into this Gallic influx – the other result being a 2-1 defeat at Spurs in which Gouffran scored – and we were all apparently so taken by our new signings that the club's marketing team decided to acknowledge this love-in with French Day, to coincide with the home game against Southampton. It's amazing that this really happened. It's like something you would do at school when you were a kid. The gist appeared to be this: we might be struggling in the league and have sold our best striker, but don't worry about that, we've just bought a load of French lads, so get a tricolour on your face and *shaddap* about it. At least that's what I took from it. Maybe I'm being a little harsh, and the French contingent took it as a lovely gesture. It probably was really, wasn't it? Something to help them settle in. Cabaye and Sissoko scored that day, too, as we beat the Saints 4-2. So maybe it was a marketing masterstroke. It just felt … weird.

As it turned out, even being super-French couldn't help Newcastle with their season, as they bounced depressingly from victory to defeat with alarming regularity. We took some absolute pastings too, shipping seven goals at Arsenal, four at Manchester City, and six at home to Liverpool. Cissé's unerring form in front of goal deserted him for large parts of the season, while injuries to Ben Arfa and Cabaye hamstrung the fluency and consistency the team had enjoyed in the previous year. The misery peaked on 14 April, which is where our story returns to a man punching a horse.

There was a time, when I was very young, that I thought Newcastle and Sunderland were the only two football teams that existed, and that they would play each other every week like in some rubbish, two-team Super League. I'm not sure whether that spoke of the absolute passion of north-east fans, or just of my own limited intelligence. But I did know that, as a supporter, you were either one or the other, and there was nothing in-between. I don't remember anybody at my school in Sacriston supporting Liverpool just because they won all the time. You picked your favourite local team and then loved it more than life itself until, well, death. You would hate any team in direct opposition with your own (start with your local rivals and work outwards from there) and even refuse any association with the colours of such teams. It was a bit like the Bloods and Crips in LA, only far more ridiculous. There was once a man in Newcastle who stopped eating bacon because, when uncooked, it resembled the red and white of Sunderland. If you were serious about your team it was advisable to maintain a similarly foolish outlook, even when people thought much less of you because of it.

Because football was so ingrained in everything we did growing up, a derby game felt like the whole world was at stake. 'The form book goes out of the window' is the hackneyed phrase, because the pressure is so great that it usually boils down to who wants it most on the day. But I think that these games disassociate from the wider context of football, too. Whatever the result, your mind instantly leaps to your Sunderland-supporting mates. Win and you cannot wait to see them, so you can laugh at them. Lose and you go into hiding with the doggedness of Saddam Hussein after the invasion of Iraq.

With the above firmly in mind, you can perhaps appreciate how I felt in 2013 as Sunderland pulled three absolute worldie finishes out of the bag for their first win on Tyneside in 13 years. First Stéphane Sessègnon pounced on a loose pass from Jonás Gutiérrez to beat Tim Krul from 20 yards. Papiss Cissé then had one wrongly disallowed for offside, before Sunderland struck with two late goals as we desperately chased an equaliser. First Adam Johnson curled a left-footed shot past Rob Elliot on 74 minutes, before David Vaughan hit a ball better than he had before or since, to ping an 82nd-minute shot into Elliot's top bin. The 1990 Second Division play-off semi-final aside, I had never actually seen Sunderland beat us by more than a one-goal margin, and it was disorienting. Even looking at it now makes me think that somebody has made a mistake, and it was actually us who won 3-0. This defeat was the first of their 'famous' run of six victories in a row over us, but it's only now that I feel almost certain Sunderland were doing something rather devilish when it came to the new manager bounce phenomenon.

You know the drill: a struggling side gets a new gaffer and, for a while at least, they turn into world-beaters. There are stats to back this upturn in points, too, with the new manager often having a five-game spurt where his team far over-performs their current plight. It's generally used as the last throw of the dice in order to stay up, but it felt like Sunderland were hiring and firing managers just to win the derby with Newcastle. Consider these facts: Paolo Di

Canio, installed as Sunderland manager on 31 March 2013, defeated Newcastle 3-0 in his second game in charge. Gus Poyet, installed as Sunderland manager on 8 October 2013, defeated Newcastle 2-1 in his second game in charge. Dick Advocaat, installed as Sunderland manager on 17 March 2015, defeated Newcastle 1-0 in his second game in charge. Finally, Sam Allardyce: installed as Sunderland manager on 9 October 2015, defeated Newcastle 3-0 in his second game in charge. From 2013 to 2015 Sunderland were averaging two managers per season – three in 2013 if you count Kevin Ball as caretaker. I'm fairly sure there should have been an investigation into this one. I'm not sure of what type, or by who. Can we do anything retrospectively? Let me know if anything comes to mind.

Everybody handles defeat differently. My friend Saul, for example, is one of those optimists we mentioned a few chapters ago. He'll come in with a fact that shows, really, this result means nothing, and that everything is still going to be great. Personally, after a derby loss I will be an absolute pain in the arse for days. Moody, irritable, and utterly indignant if anyone dares utter the phrase, 'Hey, it's just a game.' Some fans, as we have seen, will fight each other. An idiotic waste of time and energy in my opinion. And just once, a single fan will try to punch a horse.

When you're frustrated, the emotion-processing part of your brain releases cortisol and adrenaline, as your body goes into fight or flight mode. But your body doesn't want you to be stressed, so it also releases dopamine to create feelings of satisfaction, and serotonin to help you try and avoid aggression. We must presume that Barry Rogerson – the man who actually squared up to a horse in the style of a Victorian-era pugilist following that gut-wrenching defeat to Sunderland – acted just before his own chemical reaction could slow his roll.

After initially claiming he was acting in self-defence (the horse started it?), Rogerson eventually pleaded guilty to violent disorder and was sentenced to one year in prison, but only served six weeks. In an extra twist of crazy, the moment was later immortalised by the Geordie artist Sam Wood, with his painting of the incident picking up a staggering bid of £1,100 when it went on display.

As for Newcastle, it was another season of wasted opportunities; part of an exhausting ritual now playing out at the club every single season. There seemed to be no planning for the future. No project in place, not in the traditional sense at least. You might argue that a club operating on what it generates is the very model of sustainability, and that's something all clubs should aim for. But in reality the whole thing tore me up inside. Players would pass through like ghosts, with no real love or connection with the city or the club, and very little desire to become part of the region's history. There would be performative kissing of the badge after a goal, and social media declarations following a win, but it all felt so disposable and empty. Like we were part of the journey but never considered the destination. No matter how much you tried to hope for better days, it was hard to escape the fact that Newcastle United now felt like a football club without a soul.

19

Peter Schmeichel's Massive Hands

4 March 1996
Newcastle United 0 Manchester United 1

One of the big problems I have with modern football stadiums – other than their needy obsession with being as useful and as aesthetically pleasing as possible – is that you can no longer play the floodlight game as you travel around the country. You might be in a car or on a train, minding your own business, when you suddenly catch sight of some iron monstrosity rising out of a provincial town like an alien tripod from *War of the Worlds*. First sighting confirmed, and football buzz activated, the race is then on to identify the team, and ground that the floodlights belong to. Tactics vary here. Some people use football knowledge tied in with a basic sense of geography to offer an educated guess. Others just press their face up against the window and stare at it for as long as possible, hoping for inspiration to strike. It's a high-stakes competition where reputations can be made and lost. Discovering that the floodlights actually belong to a rugby ground is never anything less than devastating.

When I was young and would drive across the Redheugh Bridge from Gateshead into Newcastle with my dad, we always fought to see who could find the stadium on the skyline first. He was at a disadvantage here, what with having to also watch the road. But then I was about seven, so what the hell did I know? Either way, its place among the neo-classical, gothic, and renaissance architecture of the city was almost always revealed by those four looming floodlight towers. I still play the game today, actually, by myself whenever I travel into Newcastle. And while the floodlights are long gone, St James' Park thankfully remains one of the few grounds still visible as you arrive in town. As someone who now lives away from the north-east, I cannot tell you how much happiness the sight of that giant Milburn Stand offers me every single time I see it. It tells me that I'm home.

Home comforts were certainly in rich supply for Newcastle in the 1995/96 season, and as the football year rolled into March, the record at St James' Park stood at a beautifully perfect played 13, won 13. Some time later, those not in possession of the facts would take great joy in explaining how Kevin Keegan's gung-ho attitude towards defence had ultimately been his side's undoing. But the truth is that the opposition had scored in just six of those 13 games, and not one team had managed more than a single goal. That sounds pretty miserly to me. Those stats should have made Tyneside supremely confident as Manchester United arrived for a big game under the lights, but in reality we were all just shit-scared. Don't get me wrong, we wanted to believe that this was the year we would finally end our 40-year wait for a major domestic trophy, but Newcastle fans have been starved of success for far too long to genuinely believe something like that. As a result, the boisterousness that had kept us sane during years of underachievement merged with a catastrophising that had simply become second nature. The city simmered with possibility, cautious optimism, but mainly fear.

Kevin Keegan returns to Newcastle United as manager for the first time, changing my world overnight.

David Kelly celebrates scoring the most important goal in modern Newcastle United history, as fans invade the pitch to mark potential survival in the First Division.

Joy as Newcastle United win the First Division title at Grimsby. Fuelled by eight cans of Skol, I later end up lost in a nearby garden.

Sir John Hall's investment saves the club from oblivion, and helps turn St James' Park into one of the best stadiums in Europe. RIP the terrifying Gallowgate End toilets.

David Ginola scores his first goal for the club, bewitching Sheffield Wednesday defenders and Newcastle United fans alike in the process.

Tino Asprilla against Middlesbrough – a debut that could only have been improved if he'd worn his fur coat for the last 10 minutes.

Kevin Keegan slumps over the Anfield hoardings as Stan Collymore strikes late to dent our title hopes. Meanwhile in a Durham pub, a gambolling Sunderland fan goads me.

Spurs boss Gerry Francis consoles Les Ferdinand, as the Entertainers' great adventure ends in second place.

Mike Ashley, decked out in a Newcastle shirt, never truly understood what it meant to be the custodian of this great club.

Kevin Keegan returns to Newcastle United for a third time, in a final stab at glory that felt doomed from the outset.

Newcastle fans vent their fury at Mike Ashley's treatment of Kevin Keegan, as their team loses miserably at home to Hull City following his departure.

Joe Kinnear speaks to the press – f-bomb presumably imminent – as he shocks the football world to become interim manager at Newcastle United in 2008.

Papiss Cissé celebrates his iconic goal against Chelsea, but was the 2011/12 season stellar, or a scientific experiment that never really happened?

Alan Shearer directs his frustration at a bottle of water, as Mike Ashley's Newcastle United suffer relegation for the first time during his ownership.

Rafa Benítez brought hope and pride back to St James' Park under Mike Ashley, at least for a short while.

Steve Bruce in a pose that feels indicative of his time at the club – resigned to defeat – as he watches Newcastle serve up a dire performance at Bramall Lane.

Miguel Almirón scores the club's first Champions League goal in 20 years, en route to a famous 4-1 victory over Paris Saint-Germain at St James' Park.

At St James' Park with Spugsy (right). No matter how many years pass between visits, this will always be home.

Three seasons had now passed since the launch of the Premier League, and Sky Sports was fully into its razzmatazz-parping stride as the title race moved into the final straight. The footage from that day is quite extraordinary. The opening credits are like a clip from the 1987 dystopian death-chase movie *The Running Man*, starring Arnold Schwarzenegger. It starts simply enough, with a player in a changing room putting talc into his Asics boots (bit weird), but then suddenly a massive Premier League trophy bursts out of a generic stadium to a backdrop of fiery skies. The music moves towards air-grabbing electro on steroids, as loads of flags appear and, for some reason, an apache gunship flies into view. But just when you expect the screen to cut to three former *Running Man* contestants, and the voiceover to announce, 'Here they are, Whitman, Price and Haddad, basking under the Maui sun, their debt to society paid in full,' it instead just hypes up *Monday Night Football*. Finally, it gets excited by the fact that the whole thing is sponsored by Ford Escort. We had been getting this type of Americanised build-up for weeks, now. An incessant wall of hyperbole surrounding the most exciting season of top-flight football in history. The big one, the ultimate title showdown, the Premier League decider. In truth, it was hard not to get a little swept away by it all.

The problem was that my whole matchday routine had been affected by the pressure. Although I had started going to watch Newcastle play, first with my dad, and then with my group of pals, it had become something of a solitary experience by the 1995/96 season. By this point my nerves were frayed, and I felt so invested in the outcome that it was even hard to relax with a load of mates at the pub ahead of the game, or talk to people during the match, either for that matter. Certainly nothing more than a throw-away comment or two. Pre-match was spent worrying about formation and fitness, doing everything I could to turn any available statistic into a dark omen of defeat. During the game, meanwhile, I was simply glued to what was happening on the field, unable to take my eyes away from the action. It was only after the match that I realised how exhausting it is to offer that type of concentration for 90 minutes. It's the ultimate act of being present. I could never understand people who left before half-time to be first in the queue for a pint, or committed the cardinal sin of leaving before full time to get a jump on the traffic. Being at St James' Park was all I thought about through the week, so the idea of leaving early for any reason made no sense to me. Sometimes I would find myself contorted into an awkward position, frozen in time as I stared unblinkingly at the action unfolding before me. It was often physically painful, at least once my brain registered the uncomfortable posture, but then my football OCD would explain, in no uncertain terms, that if I moved then the team would surely concede as punishment. Sit painlessly *and* win the game? Who the hell did I think I was?

There was certainly nothing comfortable about the atmosphere inside St James' Park on 4 March 1996. It felt like we were going to war, and everywhere you looked people fidgeted with nervous possibility. What if this was the night? All the years of mediocrity, all the pain, all the suffering. Win tonight and perhaps everything changes?

You could tell how big the game was by the fact that most fans had left the pub early to be there, and the vast majority were already in their seats by the time I got there, blasting desperate howls of 'HOWAYYYYYY!' out into the cold night air. As the levels of hysteria intensified, it felt like a ritual sacrifice could be next. Admittedly a bold move by the marketing team, but perhaps something to banish the bad spirits once and for all, a bit like they did at Trabzonspor in Turkey. Instead of a goat, however, it could have been our former centre-forward George Reilly, to signify the years of toil and hardship as we passed into the next, hopefully more successful life.

A Sky Sports clip showing the players coming out of the tunnel that night has stayed with me for ever. In fact the sight of it brings everything rushing back like a big old slap around the chops. As a camera focuses over the stadium, lights blaze out from its edges like a furnace, and a bloodcurdling roar reverberates from the stands. At a glance it looks like the Colosseum in Rome. If the Colosseum was on fire, packed with 33,000 frenzied Geordies, and ready for a night that would shape its destiny.

As both sets of players walked out, the home side held a four-point lead at the top of the table and still had a game in hand over Fergie's men. But nobody in the stands was thinking about that, they were baying for blood! And the players responded with ferocity. To this day I don't think I have ever seen such a one-sided first half in my life. The stats will tell you that we had 61 per cent of all possession that night, but that doesn't offer half the story of our domination. So I'm going to do it here, now, below, in a style not too dissimilar to *Championship Manager*.

2 minutes: CHANCE
Asprilla flicks on a ball for Ferdinand to race after into the box. He pushes it forward with his thigh, but hesitates pulling the trigger for a split second, allowing Schmeichel to smother the ball with his huge frame as the striker gets his shot away.

4 minutes: DANE STOPS PLAY
Ferdinand meets a long ball forward on the halfway line,

he cushions it to Beardsley who finds Asprilla on the right. The Colombian runs with the ball before releasing a teasing through ball back to Ferdinand. Although shadowed by Ronny Johnsen, this time the striker gets his shot away with decent contact. But Schmeichel – who appears to be getting bigger with each attack – moves a giant palm to the right, parrying the ball into the air before catching it at the second attempt.

8 minutes: DANGER
Asprilla's socks are half down. He looks like he's been playing for eight hours straight, but continues to plague the Manchester United backline. This time he passes from near the right corner flag to Peter Beardsley, whose left-footed shot from just outside the area skids at Schmeichel dangerously enough for him to make a dive, but it never looks like going in.

9 minutes: CLOSE
A neat passing move involving Asprilla, Warren Barton, Robert Lee, Beardsley and Ferdinand sees the latter bundle his way towards goal. Ferdinand's touch is slightly heavy and the ball runs away from him, but his half-shot squirms past Schmeichel, rolling inches past the post. About 20 metres behind the goal, in the Gallowgate End, I'm dangerously close to a type of Beatlemania frenzy.

20 minutes: OFF THE BAR
Philippe Albert's curling free kick arches up and over the wall, but can't come down quick enough. It hits the right-hand side of Schmeichel's crossbar, with the Dane's flapping hand nowhere near it. The ball bounces up into the air, and when it lands it's completely sliced by Gary Neville into the path of Ferdinand. The striker, lurking in

the six-yard box and so deadly all season, spins, turns and smashes the best chance of the game high over the bar and into the Gallowgate End.

32 minutes: IT'S GOING TO HAPPEN
Ginola flicks a ball inside before laying it off to Asprilla. The Colombian then rolls the ball to an on-rushing Peter Beardsley, who takes a touch and hits a half-decent shot from the edge of the box. It's too close to Schmeichel, however, and he gathers it while staying on his feet.

40 minutes: IT'S HAPPENING
Ginola, increasingly an influence, wins a high ball on his chest with Denis Irwin for company. The Frenchman spins and pushes the ball past his marker. Suddenly Lee Sharpe appears, recklessly diving in only for Ginola to skip past him, too. Someone in the crowd screams. They don't shout, they *scream*, as Ginola juggles the ball on his thigh at speed down the left wing. He gets to the byline before cutting past Irwin, again, and flashing a ball across goal. Ferdinand throws himself at it, his toe is inches away from contact, and it flies past Schmeichel's left-hand post. The chance is met by an 'Oooof!' from the crowd so loud that later reports claim it was heard in China.

41 minutes: ONLY A MATTER OF TIME
Ferdinand and Asprilla combine smartly on the edge of the box for the latter to thwack a shot at Schmeichel, with the big goalkeeper falling, exhaustedly, to his right to save and the half eventually comes to a close. At this point the entire English-speaking world is baffled at how Newcastle are not simply out of sight. On a good day Ferdinand could have had a hat-trick. On a better day he could have had four. All to play for in the second half.

52 minutes: BOLLOCKS
Cantona scores for Manchester United.

When you concede a goal at home it's always a strange sensation. Your heart sinks and thousands of people instinctively put hands on heads. There's a split second of silence, and then you hear the away fans erupt in the near distance. At that moment, you hate them with a passion. You look at your players to see how they respond. You want a sign that this isn't over. But as Eric Cantona wheeled away in celebration, the players on the pitch looked as shell-shocked as the fans in the stands.

After the former Leeds striker's goal there were chances. Half-chances, really, but opportunities nonetheless. Ferdinand with a header on 73 minutes, while Lee wriggled free in the box for a split second with three minutes remaining, but was unable to get any heat on the shot. The whistle went and there was suddenly nothing. Just a deafening, deathly silence, followed by a muted round of applause from all four sides of the ground. Keegan's men had absolutely given their all, and you had to love them for that. But once again Newcastle had come up short when it truly mattered.

You'll be unsurprised to read that I don't often watch this game back. Even after a 29-year cooling-off period, Cantona's winner still has the power to take the air from my lungs. There's a view of it from behind the goal that I *have* watched hundreds of times, however. You can see the Frenchman's shot cannon off the churned-up pitch, and the ball fly past the lunging dive of John Beresford, beyond the despairing fingertips of Pavel Srníček and into the net. No matter how many times I watch it I cannot fathom how it beats the goalie. How Srníček isn't able to extend his arms an inch or two further and parry it away to safety. Maybe it was the speed of the shot, maybe just the bounce? Sometimes I think he'll get it, that the big Czech will suddenly push a hand out and change history, but he never does, proving once and for all that time travel is impossible.

As a final side note on the Sky Sports production (seriously, I'm obsessed with it), there is four or five minutes of post-match coverage on YouTube that is quite mad. 'Job done for the night,' says host Richard Keys, thanking the Philips airship for capturing images like it was an emergency full-back who had come on at the last minute. Meanwhile his partner in crime, a youthful-looking Andy Gray, is busy dealing with a massive wall of media and an absolutely tiny telly. He pops in a video of some crucial match footage before using cutting-edge tech to circle players with a pen on the screen, operating the whole thing with the aplomb of a man absolutely nailing a moon landing.

Never before or since has a defeat stuck so vividly to my memory. Even now I can summon up the sights and sounds of it all. The ear-splitting, heart-thumping, fist-clenching awful beauty of it all. That the result didn't go our way is, even now, absolutely earth-shattering to me. Thirty seasons of football later and I can still hardly believe it.

In the years since that fateful night, Keegan and various players have claimed that this was not the game which killed our title hopes. They instead push that on to the match at Liverpool and sometimes Blackburn. Statistically they're correct, of course. After Cantona's strike ended our 100 per cent home record, we remained well in charge of the title race. In fact it took Manchester United 11 more games before they leapfrogged us into first place. But you wonder about the psychological effects of it all. Manchester United had now beaten us both home and away. At St James' Park, in particular, they took our best and absorbed it by a combination of quality, experience, and sheer good fortune, stealing the three points with a second-half sucker punch. In these moments champions are made. Despite the years that have passed, and the numerous personnel changes at the club, it's a final hurdle to success that Newcastle have yet to master.

Despite the pain, I can't help but look back on this match with a sense of honour. I had always disagreed with Keegan's opinion of Newcastle fans – that we don't mind watching a team lose, as long as it plays good football, is entertaining, and always gives its all. But maybe I was wrong.

I was incredibly proud of how far we had come in a breathlessly short space of time. And the fact that we had done it playing football that was often irresistible to watch, made the journey feel all the more sweet. Some years later, and in keeping with that line of thought, Newcastle fans famously unfurled a banner that read 'We don't demand a team that wins, we demand a club that tries'. There can be no game which embodies that sentiment more than the one at St James' Park on 4 March, 1996. It was beautiful and exhilarating and exhausting and devastating. But although the battle was lost, the war wasn't quite over.

20

Rafa Benítez's Big Heart

15 May 2016
Newcastle United 5 Tottenham Hotspur 1
Wijnaldum (2), Mitrović, Aarons, Janmaat

If the 2011/12 season felt like some sort of wild-eyed fantasy for Newcastle fans, then the final game of 2016 was a full-on hallucination. A mind-bending 90 minutes, where 50,000 Geordies packed St James' Park in the bright spring sunshine, roaring on an already relegated home side to a 5-1 battering of Champions League-qualifying Spurs. It was an atmosphere worthy of a title win in what turned out to be a weirdly enjoyable relegation party. This had nothing to do with the abject season we'd all just endured. This was a charm offensive, plain and simple. The objective: keep Rafa Benítez.

In something of a surprise, Mike Ashley had supported an attempt at better days in the previous summer transfer window, sanctioning a £48.5m spending spree. Four players duly arrived on Tyneside and they all looked pretty handy. There was the dynamic Dutch midfielder Georginio Wijnaldum, fresh from an Eredivisie title win with PSV. The promising young Serbian striker Aleksandar Mitrović from Anderlecht and his team-mate Chancel Mbemba, a highly rated Congolese centre-half. Finally, Florian Thauvin, a nippy French winger from Marseille joined the club. It was a quartet who came with a solid reputation in Europe, and genuinely felt like positive signings. Players who could develop at St James' Park, but who were already sparky enough to make a difference on the pitch. While not a headline-grabber at the time, we also signed a young centre-forward by the name of Ivan Toney from Northampton in that transfer window. Nobody really knows what happened to him, though.

This fresh pulse of owner interest had followed Ashley's first-ever live TV interview as owner of Newcastle United just two months earlier; a J.D. Salinger-esque surprise appearance on Sky Sports ahead of the final game of the 2014/15 season – which we needed to win in order to stay up (something that had, depressingly, become the norm). Despite the fact he had placed the club on and off the market more times than a dodgy flat in a rough part of town, Ashley declared right there and then that he would only sell Newcastle when they had won a trophy. That was all we needed. At our current trophy-winning rate that meant the guy would be with us for ever. But to his credit he then put his money where his mouth was. So it was a shame that he also put his money where Steve McClaren was, hiring the former England manager and once again reducing the air over the Tyne to an exasperated sigh.

Steve McClaren is one of those strange cases of an incredibly knowledgeable football man who could never consistently translate his skills over into management. Not that he hadn't enjoyed success over the years. After ably assisting Sir Alex Ferguson at Manchester United, coaching them to the treble in 1999, and Premier League titles in 2000 and 2001, he was brought on board by England with a growing reputation as one of the most astute coaches in the modern game. As manager of Middlesbrough he then delivered the club's first-ever major trophy with a League Cup win in 2004, also taking them to the UEFA Cup Final in 2006. Such was his standing at the time that he was then made England manager – given the task of improving upon Sven-Göran Eriksson's three consecutive tournament quarter-finals – but it would be his first real failure, with his Three Lions unable to make the cut for Euro 2008. After being sacked, McClaren dusted himself down and took unfancied Dutch side FC Twente to their first-ever Eredivisie title in 2010. So, why did he feel about as welcome in Newcastle as a suspicious fart in a pair of white trousers? Well, put simply, by the time he arrived at St James' Park – following later unsuccessful spells with VfL Wolfsburg, Nottingham Forest, FC Twente (again), and Derby County – he felt like damaged goods. There was also that weird Dutch accent he'd put on while in the Netherlands, which certainly hadn't helped his credibility. All things considered it felt like a very Mike Ashley appointment. Something sanctioned by a non-football person, possibly on the say-so of a bloke in the pub who had also tried selling him a stolen kestrel.

McClaren was widely acknowledged as a great coach, but he just wasn't cut out for management at the highest level. As a result, Newcastle's allegedly hoped-for eighth spot became 18th as a too-good-to-go-down-squad was out-played, out-thought, and out-battled almost every week. They managed two wins in a row only once (there were only nine wins all season), and after matchday three they placed no higher than 17th.

When it looked increasingly likely that Newcastle would drop, once again, into the Championship, Ashley went nuclear. You've got to hand it to the guy. When the club was in the shit – which was fairly often during his tenure – he would almost always pull something jaw-dropping out of the bag that made you briefly forget why you hated him. Keegan, Shearer, that mad trolley dash for French players in 2013. If the takeover had failed in 2021 I would have fully expected him to sack Steve Bruce with ten games to go and immediately install a managerial duo of Evel Knievel and Daniel Craig. The type of men you *really* need in a crisis. As it was he turned to a man who, at the time, felt about as likely to join us as the above-mentioned names (and bear in mind that Evel Knievel is dead): Rafa Benítez.

There was an excellent banner made by Wor Flags, bearing Benítez's face and the word: HOPE. It sums up everything that the man from Madrid represented when he rocked up at Barrack Road in 2016, with the team sitting in 19th place and with just ten games to save us from relegation. Strangely, when you compare the stats of Benítez and the man who would follow him, Steve Bruce, their numbers are spookily similar in the two full seasons that they managed us in the Premier League. While there were finishes of tenth and 13th for Benítez, Bruce fared just slightly worse, finishing 12th and 13th. In terms of points they secured identical numbers, with 44 accrued one season and 45 the next, and they had a total transfer spend in the same ballpark (Benítez with around £88.4m, and Bruce with a cool £100m), but the two men were poles apart in what they brought to the club.

After nine years of misery under Ashley, an appointment like Benítez felt otherworldly. His last club was Real Madrid for Christ's sake! His agreeing to join Newcastle felt like vindication that we were still relevant as a football club, that we could still attract elite names (attractive financial packages notwithstanding). Here was a manager whose recent CV included Liverpool, Inter Milan, Chelsea,

Napoli, and Real Madrid. Not only that but he came with a reputation for silverware, too, with a Champions League, an FA Cup, a Supercoppa Italia, a Europa League, a Coppa Italia and more all secured across the last 12 years. I'm not sure whether Benítez would have been the right person to take us forward post-takeover, but at the time he represented a link to something better, to greatness even. To Champions League nights and trophy wins, to some of the best players in the world and the hare-brained possibility that somehow, maybe they could even now be persuaded to join Newcastle. It was all simply by association of course. Even the most optimistic Newcastle fan couldn't have seen that in our future. But when you're desperately trying to stay in the fight and be recognised as a club of substance, a manager like Rafa Benítez makes you feel proud. You're stirred by the fact he has recognised something in your club that is worthy of his time. Also, let's be honest, it was dead funny because you knew just how much it pissed off Sunderland fans.

More than an excellent record as an elite manager, Benítez brought some much-needed warmth back to the club, too, establishing an immediate rapport with the supporters in the same way he had at Liverpool 12 years earlier. Very quickly it felt like if our new manager wasn't sitting in the dugout, or working on the training pitch, he was doing something for the community. Visiting children in hospitals, or handing out awards at football schools. I know this is now a mandated PR part of the job, but with Benítez it felt genuine, and in a time of rising poverty levels and food bank usage, these small acts meant something. If a football club is the heart of a community, then Benítez performed some vital CPR on Newcastle United in those early months. People talk about us 'getting our club back' following the PIF takeover in 2021, but I don't see it that way. That gave us a better chance of success in the future. In Benítez we had a person who genuinely connected with the people of the city. He made us feel like we mattered and that we were important to both him and the club. Now *that's* getting your club back.

The football improved under Benítez, too. I mean, how could it not? But I'm not sure whether I truly believed that even he could get us out of our predicament. So, I focussed on the fact he was at our club. Hoping blindly for a miracle like an eight-year-old. While being in Dubai remained helpful when it came to essential dissociation from football in times of trouble, it probably didn't help that my friend Mark, the editorial director I was working with on the Emirates airline inflight magazine at the time, happened to be a Sunderland fan. Typical isn't it? You go all the way to the Middle East and end up sitting next to a Mackem. But while Mark was originally impressed by the idea of Rafa Benítez ('he'll never come to your place'), he quickly decided, once he did come to our place, that the Spaniard was finished, rubbish, a has-been. So, our lunchtime chats would revolve around that same argument, supplemented by the debate over whether the Fairs Cup – Newcastle's most recent piece of silverware, won in 1969 – should be considered a major trophy. To finish that argument once and for all, Mark, yes it should.

After securing his first point in a 1-1 draw against Sunderland, I felt sure that Benítez's Newcastle were going to build on that momentum and get something the following weekend at fellow relegation candidates Norwich City. These are the games you have to win if you're to stay up – the fabled six-pointer. As we battled back from 1-0 down to 1-1, 2-1 down to 2-2, it seemed fate that Aleksandar Mitrović's 86th-minute penalty was going to be followed by a late Newcastle winner. This always happens, right? The team chasing all day snatches it late. Even my football OCD was working towards victory, and I felt sure that I had found a new lucky spot from which to watch the match: standing up, feet next to the grouting of two chosen-at-random marble tiles in my apartment. The two tiles equalled an away win. This is it, boys, I thought unusually confidently. It's happening! So, you can appreciate that Martin Olsson's 93rd-minute winner for Norwich was a real kick in the knackers.

It might not have been clear as the team trudged off the pitch that day at Carrow Road, but Benítez's sharp tactical nous aided by the blistering form of January signing Andros Townsend would soon help them turn a corner. The team were galvanised and suddenly had an attacking verve, defensive cohesion, and general passion that had been missing for much of the campaign. Unfortunately it was too little too late. Even a six-match unbeaten run to close out the season wasn't enough to save the club from tumbling back down into the Championship. If Benítez had been brought in just one month earlier then who knows? As it was, we stared into the face of a second relegation in just seven years. The only real question was whether the Spaniard would stay in the job, and attempt to gain promotion at the first time of asking.

Long before the match with Spurs even started on the last day of the season, it felt like the crowd at St James' Park had been singing the 'Oh Rafa Rafa, Rafa Rafa Benítez' song to the tune of 'La Bamba' for hours on end. To the point of madness, actually. It was only occasionally switched up for that other terrace favourite, 'We want you to stay, we want you to staaaaaaay', just in case the man in the dugout felt in any doubt as to the crowd's feelings. The players responded, too. This wasn't a nothing game, far from it. While the pressure might have been off the home side,

Spurs had something special in their sights, and the chance to finish above Arsenal for the first time in 11 years. That would only happen with a win. But just as terrace vitriol had spread to the players against Hull here eight years earlier, the sunshine from the stands in 2016 transformed them into the best versions of themselves. Gini Wijnaldum was dynamic, scoring early after a surging run into the penalty area to meet a Mitrović lay-off. Mitro himself gave a classic cameo, a powerful diving header to make it 2-0 and then a red card for an awful tackle on Kyle Walker. Mitrović is like every borderline psychopath I have ever played football with on a Sunday. A horrific, bone-crunching tackle is followed by a look of utter bemusement as to its consequences. Like they seriously cannot fathom what the problem is. The Serbian joined a very special club that day. A goal and a sending off is something that only five players had ever previously done in the Premier League, and we were all secretly just a little proud of him. It never quite worked for Mitro at Newcastle, but the guy has scored bucketloads of goals everywhere else. I liked him. And was also a bit scared by him.

Being down to ten men and conceding an Erik Lamela goal to make it 2-1 couldn't even come close to derailing the day. A Wijnaldum penalty at the Gallowgate End was followed by a lashed volley from Rolando Aarons, and a measured Daryl Janmaat pass into the net secured a quite bizarre 5-1 win over one of the best sides in the country. We all went home happy, safe in the knowledge that both fans and players had surely done enough to keep Rafa Benítez at our club for a little while longer. The clincher came two days later.

The Byker Bridge is a 17-minute bus journey from St James' Park. But you could walk it in 27 minutes on a sunny day if you fancied it. It was here that someone called

Figs reached out to Benítez in one of the most heartfelt messages I have ever seen. Two days after the Spurs rout it appeared, a spray-painted sign 100ft up on the side of the bridge that read 'Please stay Rafa. You're all we have left. Love Figs'. It's OK if you're tearing up at this bit. Figs was not wrong. He *was* all that we had left. Eight days later, whether moved by sentiment or merely hoping to ward off what could be a possible suicide attempt, Benítez confirmed that he would not activate the optional break clause in his contract, and would remain at the club after all. 'The love I could feel from the fans was a big influence for me,' he said, while presumably sending people out to make sure that Figs was OK.

One man can make all the difference at a football club. Now that Benítez had committed his future to Newcastle, the fans followed suit with loyalty of their own, refreshed and recharged for the season that lay ahead. We had just been relegated yet life felt good. That was all testament to the high regard in which the Spaniard was held on Tyneside.

Occasionally relegation can be something of a relief. While there's always the risk of falling through the trapdoor of subsequent demotions, like Leeds, Sheffield Wednesday, Manchester City, and Sunderland who all dropped into the third tier for a spell. It can also be a way of hitting reset, and reversing the fortunes at your club. Best case scenario it's a way to help ditch the dead wood and to move forward. Do it right and a second-tier season can help blood young players, rebuild shattered confidence, usher in a culture change and help grow team spirit. Even though it might be impossible to believe as a football fan, when relegation feels like the end of the world, sometimes down is actually up.

21

That's Entertainment

3 April 1996
Liverpool 4 Newcastle United 3
Ferdinand, Ginola, Asprilla

There's something a little old-fashioned about Newcastle United's 'Entertainers' tag from the 1990s, don't you think? It's like they were a troupe of slapstick Vaudevillian performers who travelled the country. 'Here they are ladies and gentlemen, for your viewing pleasure, the Entertainers!' Polite round of applause, then John Beresford gets fired out of a cannon.

It's a name which has gone down in Premier League history – as much for us blowing a 12-point lead as for playing swashbuckling football. That's another bizarre word to describe an attractive, attacking football team, actually: swashbuckling. Feels far more Musketeer than Magpie. The Entertainers tag was coined in the early 90s by BSkyB head of football – and lifelong Newcastle United fan – Vic Wakeling, the man who had been tasked with revolutionising how football played out on your telly, after Rupert Murdoch's firm had trounced the competition and snaffled up the very first Premier League broadcasting rights. Wakeling brought a whole host of innovations to the football revolution. He amped up the entertainment levels, and introduced camera angles that got fans closer to the action than ever before. But it was his journalistic background spanning the *Blaydon Courier* to Fleet Street – with the *Football Pink* in the middle – that meant he knew the importance of storytelling. So, having branded his old team as the most exciting in the country, he then made sure that they were looked upon favourably when it came to air time, at least according to former Newcastle chairman Freddie Shepherd. Pretty soon, the Entertainers were the talk of the Premier League.

In a time before broadcasting rights and global fanbases knocked the fixture list out of all whack, football felt about living for the weekend. A Saturday 3pm kick-off meant that you were out of the house by around 10.30am. The working week was a means to an end. A way of getting enough money to afford your season ticket was the goal. Not that this was solely about football, it was about the afterparty, too. Watching Newcastle at St James' Park in 1995/96 might well have been a riot of goals and big wins, but the game was only part of the day. Once the full-time whistle had blown, we headed into town to celebrate. You would start at Macey's, with its ridiculous drink promotions, and it felt like being on holiday. Music blasted out the place, as people streamed in with their Newcastle tops on, singing about Les Ferdinand or David Ginola. You would look across at your mates buying trebles for a quid along with pints of Foster's Ice, and would think, yes. I am exactly where I need to be. The evening's chaos was only getting started, of course. After that, a pub crawl fuelled by Two Dogs, or Carling, and Keegan. Definitely by Keegan. The football songs were never more than a street or two away, and the day's big game was dissected joyfully with strangers at the bar. The night ended in the way that nights like this should always end:

with a dodgy-looking takeaway. So, before heading home, you would head towards Munchies, a late-night snacking institution just down the road from St James' Park. Football was so ingrained in the DNA there that the owner would brandish yellow and red cards when things got a little too boisterous. They worked, too.

This wasn't just a Newcastle thing. If you grew up in the UK during the mid-90s then life felt full of excitement and possibility. A Labour government was preparing to oust the Conservatives for the first time in 18 years (Newcastle were languishing in the Second Division under Bill McGarry last time Labour had been in power), while culturally it suddenly felt like our small island was at the centre of the universe, with sparks of energy firing off in all directions. Whether it was Damien Hirst winning the Turner Prize for cutting up a cow and putting it in formaldehyde, or Danny Boyle making one of the most iconic British movies of all time with *Trainspotting*, creative energy that had been slowly simmering for years exploded, slap bang in the middle of the century's final decade.

The cultural possibility swirling in the UK fused with the excitement of following Newcastle United. Often literally, and the 1995/96 season will always feel inextricably linked with live music to me. There was Shaun Ryder's Black Grape at the Riverside a few weeks before the season started, and both the Stone Roses and Oasis at Whitley Bay Ice Rink before the end of the year. Those last two gigs in particular made up the second part of great football and music Saturdays. You started the day at the match – and with a great Newcastle win – then ended it in the Wagon Wheel pub, ahead of seeing two of the finest bands of a generation. It felt like you were flying.

After years of austerity, violence, and dwindling attendances, football in England seemed different, too. For better or worse it had become mainstream. In many ways this was the middle-classification of the game that had been coming since Italia 90, and which would eventually change football beyond all recognition. But that dystopian future lay some years off. At the time it was exciting to find your favourite sport – and team – featured everywhere. Whether through slightly more grown-up football magazines such as *90 Minutes* or *Goal* (Les Ferdinand in a Newcastle shirt was the latter's very first cover), or on TV, where you couldn't move for an irreverent sports or football programme. From the 1991 magazine show *Standing Room Only* to the early lad culture of *Soccer AM*, and the rowdy quiz show chaos of *They Think It's All Over*, football was now cool, and two programmes encapsulated that more than any other.

The main downside of football being manhandled by satellite television was that if you didn't subscribe to the broadcaster – which my dad didn't – you rarely saw any live games, save for an occasional FA Cup tie on the BBC. 'If you want to watch Sky, Andrew, go and sit on the roof,' he would say, laughing along to his own gag every time I badgered him about it. But in 1992, Channel 4 decided to fill this vacuum by acquiring the rights to Serie A in Italy, and launch a programme called *Football Italia*. At the time, the Italian league was the most glamorous in the world, and was littered with the biggest names in the game. We're talking Franco Baresi, Paolo Maldini, Ruud Gullit, Frank Rijkaard and Marco van Basten – and that was just the Milan side. Between 1952 and 1992, football's world transfer record was broken 16 times. Fourteen of those times it was by an Italian club, with the only two outliers in that list coming from Barcelona – signing Johan Cruyff from Ajax in 1973 for £922,000, and Diego Maradona from Boca Juniors in 1982 for £3m. In 1992 there was another reason that the Italian football rights were so attractive to a UK broadcaster, and that reason was a Newcastle United legend.

In 1991 Paul Gascoigne had signed an £8.5m deal that would take him from Tottenham Hotspur to the Italian club Lazio. Then, in the FA Cup Final versus Nottingham Forest, set to be his last game in the white shirt of Spurs, he arguably made two of the worst tackles ever seen at Wembley. First was a horrific studs-up challenge on Garry Parker, and then a leg-breaker on the Forest full-back Gary Charles, in which he ruptured his own cruciate ligament in the process and was stretchered off after just 15 minutes. If that wasn't bad enough, Gazza would then re-injure that knee some months later after a nightclub incident in Newcastle, and in the most Gazza way possible (falling down the stairs after some bother). The Dunston lad had turned up to St James' Park that day, complete with 'Howay The Lads' bucket hat (or psycho hat as they were called around our way, for some reason) and found a spot in the Gallowgate Corner to watch a strangely dour 2-2 draw with Derby. He revelled in the attention that day, but then his presence was actually far more exciting than the game itself. Later I somewhat bizarrely saw him in town offering to race a man well into his 60s across Pilgrim Street to the old Odeon Cinema and back. I watched the race with a few others, slightly bemused, wished him well in Italy and got the bus home. Gazza, meanwhile, went clubbing and, well, we all know the rest.

By late 1992, however, Gazza was finally ready to make his Lazio debut (a 1-1 draw with Genoa), but he never settled in Italy. His fleeting moments of brilliance were all too often cancelled out by errors in judgement. Like the time he met the club's owner Sergio Cragnotti with the line 'Tua figlia, grande tette', roughly translating to 'your daughter, big tits'. Paradoxically, thanks to the calming, cosmopolitan vibe of host James Richardson, usually found outdoors at a nice cafe, sipping an espresso and going through a pile of newspapers, *Football Italia* on Channel 4 became a roaring success. All the more surprising when you consider that, despite the big names, famous stadiums and legendary strips with iconic sponsors (Pirelli, Mars, Parmalat, Nintendo, I could name them all back then) Italian football was always kind of boring to watch.

If *Football Italia* was all smart Milanese style and nonchalant shrugs, then *Fantasy Football League* – the BBC2 comedy show inspired by the new craze of the same name – was an Inspiral Carpets T-shirt in your front room with a can of cheap lager. Something that fitted quite nicely with the lifestyle I was working on at the time. Not only that, but the programme featured three Newcastle references in the opening credits alone – Keegan and Terry Mac in the dugout, Rob Lee powering past Arsenal's Paul Merson, and Andy Cole's sharp finish against Sheffield Wednesday when, for some reason, we wore our blue Asics away kit at home. It sounds silly, but just as I eagerly scan every new season's *Match of the Day* opening credits to make sure there's a reasonable amount of Newcastle featured, seeing my team so prominently in a programme that wasn't just about north-east football felt huge. We were now relevant to other football fans, and not simply ourselves.

Fantasy Football League felt like a show that had been written just for me. My parents hated it which meant, crucially, I wasn't yet turning into them – an important cultural signpost when you're young. The script, with its improvised delivery by Frank Skinner and David Baddiel, felt like a conversation I'd have with my mates down the pub. Looking back, some of the gags are a bit hairy. It's fair to say that the programme was firmly of its time, but in the mid-90s it very quickly became essential viewing, attracting a staggering calibre of guests. It's easy to forget that, in its first series alone, and to the backdrop of the newly launched Premier League, this late-night show had a guest manager roll-call including Bob Mortimer, Peter Cook, John Motson, Basil Brush (his team was called PSV Boom Boom), Sue Johnston, Roddy Doyle, Des Lynam, Andrew Ridgeley, Lennox Lewis, and Mandy Smith. Eventually Skinner and Baddiel also helped usher in the next rush of excitement over English football, and the collaboration with Ian Brodie of the Lightning Seeds on the anthemic 'Three Lions', a song that soundtracked the summer of Euro 96, when football nearly did, but then definitely didn't, come home. It's been very nearly, but not quite, coming home ever since.

If this new media attention taught us anything, it was that branding was now all-important, even if we didn't always see how it dripped into our psyche. Things like the Entertainers, 'Football's Coming Home' and 'Have You Ever Seen a Mackem in Milan?' stayed with you. OK, so that last one isn't technically branding, but I would like to think that the song and slogan, created to disparage Sunderland's very poor record in European competition, will remain in all of our consciences. But smart marketing will only take you so far. Past the slogans, and beyond the myths and legends, at some point the football has to do the talking.

If you utter the words 'the Entertainers' to football fans of a certain age, they immediately think of the team from the 1995/96 season that blew the title in spectacular fashion. That's not surprising. But there was devilment up front, too. An attacking line-up that consisted of Les Ferdinand, Peter Beardsley, Faustino Asprilla, David Ginola and Keith Gillespie was never going to be shy in coming forward. Still, their 66-goal haul was utterly eclipsed by the 82 plundered by the Newcastle side two seasons earlier, spearheaded by Beardsley and Andy Cole. Although that team had four more games to boost their goal tally – the league had been reduced from 22 teams to 20 in 1995/96 – that would still have required four 4-0 wins for the later group to even match it. There were some big wins in that earlier season, too. We put seven past Swindon, five past Aston Villa, and four past each of Wimbledon, Sheffield United, Sheffield Wednesday, Coventry and West Ham United. There was also an Andy Cole hat-trick against Liverpool – a team I had never even seen us draw with in the flesh – but it was probably a night at Oldham that truly birthed Kevin Keegan's Entertainers.

Newcastle were sitting ninth in the Premier League by the time they travelled to Boundary Park in November, a night under the lights so cold that you could see the players' breath push out into the air. The stadium was the type of football ground rapidly disappearing in the top flight: old, slightly ramshackle, but full of character and with four separate stands of differing heights covering the perimeter and plastered with sponsorship logos. Although Newcastle went a goal down against the run of play, in the second half they absolutely blitzed their opposition, with lightning-fast attacks and slick passing movements that left Oldham's beleaguered defence chasing shadows. In a record-breaking goalscoring season, Andy Cole got two – an audacious lob and then a trademark quick shot in the box after twisting and turning the defence – but it was Peter Beardsley's goal that night, a rocket of a shot into the top corner after a dipping, dodging run, that really shone. The night confirmed, at least to my mind, that Newcastle had become truly box office.

I suppose that if Oldham Athletic away in 1993/94 was the Entertainers' origin story, then Liverpool away in

1995/96 was us sharing that gift with the world. That's literally the best spin I can put on what was, in essence, a devastating evening of football. Originally I toyed with the idea of packing this part of the story full of rich detail, to convey the 100mph, breathless madness of it all. But then I thought, bugger that. I absolutely hate it when I catch sight of these goals on a football show now, it brings the heartbreak rushing back to me. It's bad enough that we have to endure Ronnie Radford's thunderbugger for Hereford on FA Cup third round day. So instead, I've summed it all up for you in one paragraph.

Keegan sent his side out to be resilient that night. To keep things tight. The only problem was that, after two minutes, Robbie Fowler headed the home team into the lead, sending that plan firmly out the window. Eight minutes later, Les Ferdinand's close-range shot somehow slipped through David James's fingers to equalise and, four minutes after that, David Ginola's surging run and shot put Newcastle 2-1 up. It felt like 'The War', when Marvin Hagler fought Thomas Hearns in 1985, where two legends simply slugged all hell out of each other. Fowler equalised on 55 minutes, only for Asprilla to push Newcastle back into the lead two minutes later – a sublime shot with the outside of his right boot that curved into the corner. Coming back so quickly in a match like this often means it's game over, with the stuffing knocked out of the opponent. But then came Stan Collymore, first with an equaliser on 68 minutes, before famously 'closing in' to score a 90th-minute winner at the Kop. It left Keegan hunched over an advertising board, famously collapsed by the defeat. I was in a Durham pub watching the game, the result made all the worse when a Sunderland fan burst in bang-on full time, doing celebratory forward rolls while shouting 'yee-ha'. He rolled in, did the entire perimeter of the bar, and then rolled out again. It was annoying but, in hindsight, athletically impressive.

It's moments like this which made me think that the 'Everybody's Second Team' tag which grew up around the Entertainers didn't really exist. Certainly not on Wearside, Teesside, and probably Merseyside and Greater Manchester, too. I have a problem with 'second teams' in general, actually. If you know the energy, pain and heartache involved with supporting one club, then how (and why) are you asking for second helpings? I imagine that the majority are looking to supplement a team that never wins with one that possibly does. Or is at least good to watch. Well I've got news for you, friend, if that's your game. Those second-club highs will never feel like they would with your *real* club. If they do, then you weren't doing it right in the first place. Full disclosure, I did once write in a school football fanzine interview that Spurs were my second team. In my defence this was in the immediate aftermath of Paul Gascoigne's move to north London and I was feeling a little bit woozy. When it comes to Newcastle United, I'm sure that thousands of people around the world enjoyed the occasional kamikaze football of Keegan's men during the three and a half seasons he guided them in the Premier League. But I'm equally positive that the vast majority also took great pleasure in our demise, too. Fair play to them. In all honesty I would have done the same. In my opinion the human psyche is conditioned to quietly revel in the downfall of others, and nowhere more so than in the world of football, where one team literally can't succeed without another failing.

The defeat at Liverpool may have sealed our tragically beautiful fate, but it also gave it a cinematic edge. A success-starved club finally looks set to win the big trophy its fanbase deserves, only to be undone at the very end, leaving their dream in tatters. Throw in a love interest and a last-minute dash through an airport and you've got a Working Title movie. The team is remembered for being fallible, for that big fuck-up. People can relate to a fuck-up. And it feels far more romantic to narrowly miss out on glory than to boorishly hoover up success continuously for decades. At least so I'm told.

I could have done without the romance of it all. I'd have been very happy for the Premier League's greatest-ever game to have been an absolute stinker, strewn with errors and thoroughly lacking in creativity and shots at goal. A drab 1-0 away win. As it was, Newcastle came through another gut-wrenching 90 minutes and had, once again, been found wanting. It all took its toll eventually, of course. But things weren't over yet. For the time being we were still fighting for this title. Something that Keegan himself was about to impress upon the waiting world.

22

Adios, Pet

12 May 2019
Fulham 0 Newcastle United 4
Shelvey, Pérez, Schär, Rondón

For a good three or four months after Rafa Benítez left Newcastle, I was traumatised by anybody fiddling with a snappy glasses case. It reminded me of what we had lost. I know that the Spaniard's trademark removal of specs after a game didn't involve a case, he just took them off and popped them in his top pocket. I think I must have added the snapping shut of a case to punctuate my grief. Perhaps if he had stayed, the casual swinging of a glasses chain, for example, would have suddenly brought me joy? But we shall never know. In many ways it also signposted the pain yet to come. Benítez has gone. Now you've got to have Steve Bruce … SNAP!

One of the most frustrating things about being a football fan is the utter helplessness of it all. While the supporters remain constant, key players and managerial appointments come and go with alarming regularity. And for the most part you just have to sit there and take it, hoping that there is some grand plan. So, it mattered not that Newcastle fans didn't really want Steve Bruce as gaffer.

The Corbridge-born former Manchester United centre-half was in charge at Sheffield Wednesday at the time, his tenth managerial job in 20 years. In a depressing indictment of Newcastle's status, it appeared that we were next.

The departure of Benítez didn't come as a major surprise. In fact every close-season since his arrival had brought with it increased speculation that he was on his way out. A man known for the canny ability to draw attention to his needs at a football club, Benítez often publicly decried his resources and maligned missed opportunities, in the hope that this application of pressure would help get what he wanted. In Mike Ashley, however, he had finally met his match. On 24 June 2019, six days before his three-year contract with Newcastle was set to expire, the news broke that Benítez had decided to leave the club.

It was a crying shame. Benítez had stuck with us through relegation, guided us straight back into the Premier League after winning the Championship, then gave us a tenth-placed finish in the top division. This season had ended in promising form, too, picking up ten points from a possible 15 in our last five matches. Although that was only enough to reach 13th spot, there felt a quiet confidence among the supporters that this was a team on the up. That misplaced optimism was thanks largely to an emerging connection between the attacking trio of Miguel Almirón, Ayoze Pérez, and Salomón Rondón. For a while, the Paraguayan, Spaniard and Venezuelan had something cooking, with an irresistible combination of lung-busting runs, cute touches, and brute force. It was quite the scene. But it could never last.

On a final day of the season trip to Fulham, Newcastle were resplendent in the burgundy and blue hoops so reminiscent of Kevin Keegan's Entertainers, and for once they put on a performance worthy of the name. From a first-corner-of-the-game, one-touch-then-bang volley from Jonjo Shelvey, to a sneaky tap-in by Pérez, Newcastle were two up inside ten minutes at Craven Cottage. Thanks largely to Matt Ritchie's fist-clenching energy, a comfortable win over Scott Parker's already relegated side was completed in the second half, first with a towering header from dreamboat centre-half Fabian Schär, and finally from a Rondón goal where time appeared to stand still. Newcastle's number nine took a shot that left him on the ground. It was saved, but bobbled up just a few feet away. Fulham's defenders appeared bewitched by some otherworldly forces. So Rondón slowly got to his feet and found the net at the second attempt. Job done and hopefully a precursor to a happy summer of smart recruitment and carefree cocktails. That's when it all went tits up.

I know what you're thinking. How did Figs take all this? Well, the man whose graffiti-pleading on Byker Bridge was, in my opinion, a crucial factor in Benítez staying in the first place, was pretty philosophical about it all. In what had become some sort of football-based *Sleepless in Seattle*, Figs opened his heart once more on the stained concrete walls of the bridge, 'Sorry Rafa, we understand and buena suerte [good luck] gafa'. He closed things out nicely with a throwaway 'Ashley = Curse'.

Things got ugly in the end between Benítez and the club, with managing director Lee Charnley even using the programme notes ahead of the following season's first home game against Arsenal to take a swipe at his former manager, claiming that the Spaniard had moved to the Chinese Super League outfit Dalian Professional 'purely for the money'. It was a typically classless move by Charnley and the regime. A public airing of dirty laundry that made headlines for all the wrong reasons, and once again left a bad taste in the mouth of the fans – but then I guess that was the point.

Not one to be cowed, Benítez was quick to respond, with a column on the sports website *The Athletic*.

'Newcastle's board had a year to sort out my contract but, when we met after the end of last season, they didn't make me a proper offer. They told me they didn't want to invest in the academy or the training ground – if they like, I can explain the reason why Mike Ashley refused to do that,' he wrote.

'After that meeting, I knew they would not come back with a serious offer and, when it arrived 19 days later, it was for the same salary as three years earlier and with less control over signings. After three years of unfulfilled promises, I didn't trust them.'

And who could blame him?

Money was occasionally available to spend at Newcastle, but it came with a host of caveats. And while we had a Champions League-winning manager sitting in the dugout, Ashley preferred to take his transfer advice off Charnley – a figure described by one club insider as originally an 'office boy that handed out the team sheets' – and the long-time scout and now head of recruitment, Steve Nickson. So, while the on-loan 29-year-old Rondón's 11 goals in 32 games had gone some way to helping retain the club's Premier League status, his release clause at West Bromwich Albion – set at £16.6m – was deemed too high for a player of this age. For Benítez the striker represented a real chance for Newcastle to progress. His hold-up play in a team built for the counterattack had proved effective, while his football intelligence brought team-mates around him into play. His goals, meanwhile, around one in three, were solid enough in a struggling team. But his permanent signing was an absolute non-starter, and strictly against the buy 'em young and sell on for a profit Ashley blueprint. Eventually the frustration simply became too much, and Benítez was off.

Three months later, in a left-field move even for Ashley, he sanctioned the £40m club record signing of a 22-year-old Brazilian centre-forward called Joelinton. He apparently even offered to pay for the striker himself. The man from Hoffenheim and £20m capture Allan Saint-Maximin from Nice were technically the first signings of the Steve Bruce era. Not that the incoming manager knew much about either of them. Their arrivals had long since been in the pipeline, and they were actually players Benítez had pushed against signing in the first place. Then his renewed contract offer from Ashley popped into his inbox, giving him even less control over who he could sign, and that was that. Although both players ultimately succeeded at the club, at least in their own way, it still feels staggering to me that the structure of modern football often dictates that a manager must work with any player they are given by a sporting director, whether they want them or not. Surely that's incongruous to success?

In Benítez we had a manager with the tactical ability to win games against the odds, along with the big-name pull to build an increasingly attractive squad. There had been glimpses of what was possible under his guidance: the 3-0 battering of Chelsea in 2018, and the never-say-die 2-1 home win over Manchester City the following year. Rare sunny days that broke through the clouds. But while you hoped for a prolonged stretch of good weather, deep down you knew the rain was always coming. And when it did it poured pure Steve Bruce. Another stellar decision based on, well, nobody is quite sure what.

Unfortunately Mike Ashley could never see the bigger picture when applying his business principles to the football world. While buying players with a resale value is undoubtedly a huge part of building a successful club, it cannot be the sole transfer strategy. A refusal to buy players over a certain age, or to disregard players with Premier League and big-game experience, comes at a cost. It leaves the club in a constant state of inertia, with new signings falling into one of two camps. If a signing doesn't work out you're left with a squad member likely on decent wages but who doesn't contribute on the pitch. If they excel then they're on borrowed time, and available to the highest bidder in the next transfer window. We will never see them reach their peak in black and white. Once the money is banked, it's back to the coal face, scrabbling away in the dirt and trying to unearth the next great undervalued talent ahead of the chasing pack, and for the whole thing to begin again. In many ways it's a strategy that plays Russian roulette with the club's top-flight future, but that was a risk Ashley was always willing to take. As for the fans, well it remained two steps forward and two steps back (a Paula Abdul-based football reference), stuck on a constant cycle of rinse and repeat. To be honest, we were all pretty fed up with being rinsed.

23

The Passion of the Keegan

29 April 1996
Leeds United 0 Newcastle United 1
Gillespie

I played football against Kevin Keegan once. Not in a professional capacity of course – although I couldn't have been taking it more seriously – but as a competitor at his Soccer Circus venture of the early 2000s. We bonded over *that* Dennis Bergkamp goal for Arsenal at Newcastle in 2002. Both of us were in agreement that the Dutch striker had not intended what is considered to be one of the finest Premier League goals of all time, but instead reacted quickly to a misplaced first touch. I feel confident that I speak for both Kevin and I when I say that it remains a hill we are both prepared to die on.

Soccer Circus was something of a side hustle for Keegan, an idea developed in retirement that he eventually part-funded into existence 20 years or so later. It was billed as the world's first interactive football attraction, and the deal was that you went from station to station, testing your passing, shooting and dribbling skills against various obstacles. The first venue opened in Glasgow in 2008. Then, 18 months after the god-awful mess Mike Ashley made of Keegan's second spell in charge at Newcastle, both he and his Soccer Circus pitched up to the ever-expanding landscape of Dubai. At the time I was the editor-in-chief of the Middle East edition of *Men's Fitness* magazine, and naturally felt it my duty to offer it my fully impartial review. I turned up wearing my 1995/96 season NUFC shorts, feeling as excited as I had done 18 years earlier, ahead of his Second Coming as manager of Newcastle in 1992.

That day in Dubai, Keegan was everything you would imagine him to be: charismatic, enthusiastic, energetic, bouncy. Taking my place as one of seven journalists trialling the venue, he promptly picked me as his opposing team captain, leaving me to fight back tears of pride as if he had just given me the armband for the Sunderland game. Things only got better from there, as he also chose me to take a fitness test on a theory about a certain part of the game (that carrying a ball between two points would be quicker than running with it at your feet). I genuinely don't think that I've tried harder at anything in my life. 'If I can just impress him by running between these two flashing lights,' I thought, 'then who knows what might happen? Maybe it's not too late for me to make it.' I was quickly brought down to earth by Keegan exclaiming that the team I was to captain would be Watford (seriously). His team of choice? Newcastle United.

The relationship between Keegan and the Magpies has always seemed on a metaphysical level to me, an understanding he has about the people and their football team that goes way beyond actual words. He was born in Armthorpe, Doncaster, signed his first professional contract with Scunthorpe United, and would not leave that part of the world until Bill Shankly's Liverpool paid £33,000 for him in 1971. But the north-east was always in Keegan's blood. His grandfather, Frank, had saved lives there during the West Stanley pit disaster of 1909, while his father, Joe, and his uncle – also called Frank – were huge Newcastle supporters, and would regale a young Keegan with stories of legendary St James' Park number nines, such as Hughie Gallagher and Jackie Milburn.

When Keegan made his final career stop at St James' Park in 1982, it affected him deeply. Of course he was no stranger to hero worship, but the love he received on Tyneside cut deeper. At Liverpool he was adored, and it's little wonder. In 1973 he helped deliver the club's first league title since 1966, and he won it twice more with them for good measure. He also won the FA Cup (scoring two goals against Newcastle in the 1974 final), the UEFA Cup (twice) and the European Cup, too. Next up was Hamburg, and Keegan may have taken some time to win over the players – a few of his team-mates eventually adopted his trademark curly perm as a sign that he had finally been accepted – but he was loved dearly by the supporters, who nicknamed him 'Mighty Mouse' on account of his size-to-power ratio. He won the Bundesliga with them in 1979, and was also named European Footballer of the Year in both 1978 and 1979, joining Alfredo Di Stéfano, Franz Beckenbauer and Johan Cruyff as the only players at that point to win the trophy more than once. Never one for the predictable, Keegan then pitched up at Southampton, helping take an unfashionable side to sixth position, their highest-ever First Division placing at the time, as well as winning both the PFA Players' Player of the Year award in 1980/81 and the Golden Boot for his career-high 30 goals the following season. But none of that compared with how the love of the Geordie faithful got under Keegan's skin.

Maybe this was all preordained, Keegan and Newcastle. Part of some grand plan. Certainly he always felt he would play for the club at some point in his career, it was just a shame that we were so abject for the majority of it. But when he did finally make it up to Tyneside, dropping down a division for the privilege, everything changed. You could see that from game one. When Keegan scored a goal – for anyone – he always ran away really fast. Possibly with high knees. When he scored on his Newcastle debut against QPR, however, he headed straight for the Gallowgate End. As far as I can tell this was one of the only times he did something like that in his entire career. Keegan later told the press that it was to show the fans that he was 'one of them.' And that he 'wanted to stay there for ever'. He also explained that he felt that he had been sent there to help the Newcastle fans start believing in themselves, like the curly permed messiah that he was. For me, this was how Keegan saved Newcastle United not once but twice. His understanding of what the people wanted. Yes, a football team that won would be nice, but perhaps even more than that they wanted to feel special ... to be wanted.

I often wonder what it must be like as a chairman or owner hiring a manager like Kevin Keegan. You need to think it through because, if you're aiming at the PR coup and nothing more – like Mike Ashley did with Keegan's later Third Coming, or Alan Shearer's ill-fated stint in the manager's office – then there's a good chance that you're going to be called out on it pretty soon. In 1992, at the time of Keegan's first return to Newcastle as manager, you could argue that he still had more clout than the club, even though he had been out of the game for eight years. Newcastle needed Keegan more than Keegan needed Newcastle and, as a man used to winning, he would not be shy in calling problems to order. As a result, hiring him effectively gave Sir John Hall no place to hide when it came to his ambitions for the club (as he would quickly find out following the Swindon game featured in chapter three).

Ten years earlier, when Keegan had left Southampton for Newcastle as a player, the then-Saints manager Lawrie McMenemy (shout-out for getting Sunderland relegated to the Third Division in 1987), said it was largely down to the fact that Keegan was unhappy the club would not match his own ambition. So, while Sir John Hall knew that he – and Newcastle Breweries who helped broker the deal – had a genuine coup on their hands, they also knew that they could not rest on their laurels. And if they weren't quite aware, they need only have checked out an interview with Keegan from 1989, after his appearance at St James' Park in Kenny Wharton's testimonial. 'Great players don't come along very often,' said a fairly brusque Keegan that day. 'They've been very privileged here [Newcastle] that they've had four or five in the last five years, but they sold them all. You've got a nice stand [the recently opened Milburn Stand] but this won't look very good in the Third Division, will it?'

From the moment Keegan returned to the city he made every Newcastle fan stand that little bit taller. The club had been largely forgotten as a footballing force, but Keegan was having none of that. In his first interview he said, 'We're sitting on potentially the biggest club in Britain here.' His first interview! There was no 'hoping to steady the ship', or going to 'do his best' rubbish. For Keegan it was all or nothing. Interview one, the club facing relegation to the Third Division and the words coming out of his mouth were that 'we could be the biggest side in Britain'. I dearly loved that. We all did. Even if it was far from accurate, it gave me goosebumps just watching it. And if Keegan *did* believe it, then shit, maybe it was even true. He wasn't finished.

Immediately after the success of his first game in charge, Keegan hyped things up further. When asked about the impact of the crowd, he said, 'I can't think of another word [to describe them]. I've used them all. You'll have to invent one.' This was not a prepared speech. Not like the depressingly templated 'thanks for your support' messages we now see plastered on social media. This was pure heart. He continued. 'We had a 15-minute spell which would have been as good as anything they've ever seen here, I think.' Now this was plainly not true. Keegan knew that. But, at that moment he believed it, so the players and fans bought into it too.

Players often say Keegan didn't come to the table with complex tactics, but instilled confidence in everybody who pulled on that black and white shirt. He looked them in the eye and told them that nobody was better in their position. If they weren't already an international, he assured them that it was only a matter of time before they would play for their country. He made the team feel like they were unbeatable. According to John Beresford, Keegan had a method where he would walk into the changing room ahead of a game with the opposition team sheet in his hand. He would study it for five seconds before crumpling it up and exclaiming, 'If we're not two up before half-time against this lot then there's something wrong.' Many times the game was won before they had even walked on to the pitch.

But there was more to Keegan than just how he got results. It was his desire to put a smile on people's faces, too. That was central to everything that he did at Newcastle. Whether it was chatting to fans who had made a pilgrimage to watch the team train at Maiden Castle, visiting children in hospital, sticking the Honey Monster on in his Sugar Puffs advert (why wouldn't you start the Honey Monster?) or, in 1994, picking the team best equipped not just to win the club's first European tie in 17 years but to win it 5-0 away from home. It was all done with a profound sense of joy, and everybody picked up on that. When Kevin Keegan shook hands with the opposing manager after a game, he almost always put his hand to their head in a moment of kindness. For a lot of people that might have looked patronising. But for Keegan it was genuine emotion.

After Newcastle lost at Anfield in 1996, they won three of their four games leading up to their clash with Leeds United at Elland Road. The only reverse had been yet another heartbreaker, this time being 1-0 up at Blackburn Rovers with only four minutes to go, only to lose 2-1 thanks to two Graham Fenton goals in the 87th and 89th minutes. Fenton, a Newcastle supporter from South Shields, received death threats after that. In fact in a local paper he was later named as the second most hated figure in the world after Saddam Hussein. Adolf Hitler came in at number three.

With Newcastle sitting in second place as they went to Leeds, Keegan knew that victory was paramount. No matter how they got it. They went out, once more, with the brief of being tighter at the back. But by the time the clock hit nine minutes, the home side had already hit the woodwork twice. Eight minutes later Newcastle were in front. A corner from Beardsley found Ferdinand, who directed a header on the edge of the box towards Gillespie. The winger, just back in the starting line-up after a nine-game absence, headed home unmarked from six yards out for his fifth goal of the season. After that it was all Newcastle, but Ferdinand, Lee, and Gillespie spurned great chances to put the game to bed. As the clock ticked down Newcastle became increasingly anxious, in the way that only a side who has conceded last-minute winners in its last two away games could do. As they saw out the final few moments, surviving a late David Wetherall header, nerves were utterly frayed. That clearly translated to the bench, and it quite possibly led to what is now considered one of the most iconic post-match interviews in Premier League history.

The image of Kevin Keegan, with his oversized headphones, black Adidas sweater and look of pure rage, is for ever burned into my brain. Close my eyes now and I can see it, feel it, even. It's been dissected numerous times over the years, and explained by Keegan as not realising how loudly he was talking, as he spoke to Richard Keys in the Sky Sports studio. But I dearly hope that he never looks back on the event with any embarrassment, as it was utterly brilliant.

'I think things have been said, I think you've got to send Alex Ferguson a tape of this game haven't you? Isn't that what he asked for? We're playing Notts Forest on Thursday and he objected to that – it was fixed up four months ago. We're bigger than that.'

Keegan quickly took the interview with Keys from zero to 100mph. Suddenly his anger rushed out. All the desire, all the passion, all the pain. Keegan moved through the gears towards full flow.

'When you do that with footballers like he said about Leeds, and when you do things like that about a man like Stuart Pearce, I've kept really quiet but I'll tell you something – he went down in my estimation when he said that. We have not resorted to that.'

Keegan was now pointing, jabbing his finger and revealing everything he was putting into Newcastle's title push. He continued.

'You can tell him now: We're still fighting for this title and he's got to go to Middlesbrough and get something.

'I'll tell you, honestly, I will love it if we beat them, love it.'

'YES KEVIN!!! LET'S GOOOOO.' I don't care if this was psychological warfare or not. In that very moment he said what all of us were thinking, and I defy anybody who watched it not to have silently wished for Kevin Keegan to be the custodian of their football club. If you are looking for the complete and utter antithesis of Steve Bruce's tenure at Newcastle then this moment is it.

It's often said that many Newcastle players at the time signed purely because of Keegan. That an idol from their youth, whose poster they had on their walls, wanted them. But it wasn't just that they loved him as a player, it was because he was utterly unabashed in what he wanted them to do. 'Come and join Newcastle,' he told them. 'Because we're aiming to win the whole thing, and we're going to do it beautifully.'

24

The Bacon of the Bruce

12 January 2021
Sheffield United 1 Newcastle United 0

I had an issue with Steve Bruce long before he became manager of Newcastle United. I feel quite bad as I've never even met the bloke, but there you have it. Football is a game of opinions. It had nothing to do with his time at Manchester United, even though they pinched the Premier League title from under our very noses in 1996. And it wasn't because he had previously been manager of Sunderland, either. I know the tabloids love to push this angle, anything to wind up the keyboard warriors, but it's so lazy. I can't speak for other supporters, but I couldn't care less if you've played for or, in this case, coached that lot down the road. All I'm interested in is what you do once you're in black and white. That said, my concern did come from something I saw during his time managing on Wearside, and specifically a game on 31 October 2010, you might remember it: Newcastle United 5 Sunderland 1.

I have many friends who support Sunderland. I'm what they call a 'Durham Mag', you see. Someone who lives in a county that, historically, included Sunderland as its biggest settlement. As a result I would be outnumbered roughly ten to one in the playground when I was a kid, as to the team I followed. If anything that made me want to support Newcastle even more. As far as I was concerned, there were two reasons that you supported someone: first, your family supported them, and, second, geographical location. While my dad only ever considered taking me to St James' Park, the stadium is also two miles closer to my home in Sacriston than the old Roker Park. If you required a clincher, well, Sir Bobby Robson was born there, before growing up down the road in Langley Park. So anyone who still views me with suspicion can bugger off. I still love my Sunderland-supporting friends dearly, of course. Except on derby day. Then I want to see their complete and utter head-in-hands devastation. Not crying, but kind of close to crying. A watery tear duct and a chin wobble is probably the sweet spot. I know this might sound cruel, but after the rather shameful six derby defeats in a row we suffered at their hands between 2013 and 2015, I know that the feeling is mutual – and that is exactly how it should be.

Although derbies are usually tight, grindingly cautious affairs, where both teams are far too scared of losing to try and win, the game in 2010 just clicked for Newcastle. Andy Carroll swatted away defenders with a big-kid-versus-small-kid energy, and Kevin Nolan popped up in places that only Kevin Nolan *could* pop up in. I'm not actually sure what I mean by that, but the upshot was that he scored a hat-trick. Meanwhile, Shola Ameobi carved his name into NUFC folklore with two goals and the sort of performance that helped forge his now iconic 'Mackem Slayer' nickname. As a football fan you dream of days like this. But rather than simply enjoy a historic win I became weirdly incensed by Steve Bruce's post-match interview.

In lieu of being able to go to the match – my last in-person derby was a 1-1 home draw in 2007, just before I left for Dubai – I had decided to watch it in a beach bar called Barasti, a somewhat legendary rite of passage venue found at the marina end of town. It's a bit of a weird place, Barasti. Or at least it was in 2010. It featured one main building with a straw-fringed roof, lots of day beds, beach access, and an intriguing green-ish pool/swamp area. It was the sort of place where lazy sun-drenched afternoons slipped into rowdy drunken nights, and where genuinely weird shit occasionally happened. My friend Neil once arm-wrestled the brother of Osama bin Laden in there.

When the full-time whistle blew, I basked in the warm glow of victory (assist: six pints of Magners). As my shoulders loosened, the derby day tension melting away like the sun behind me into the Arabian Sea, Steve Bruce appeared on screen for his obligatory post-match interview. After a result like that these chats usually go one of two ways: a furiously monosyllabic conversation where the manager bristles at every question, or a weirdly cheerful 'we'll get them next time'. But Bruce didn't seem angry or optimistic, he looked broken. With sunken eyes and a low, almost trembling voice, his head remained bowed as he talked about 'taking wor medicine'. Apart from the hilarious reality of using that level of colloquial Geordie in an international TV interview, I was staggered by his reaction. If you're a fan of a club that has just been taken to the cleaners by your local rivals, you want your manager to come out fighting, all fiery, furious, and threatening to 'get the fuckers in for training right now!' At least I do. But here was Bruce with the look of a man whose tortoise had died in a suspicious caravan incident. My anger receded when I remembered that he was Sunderland's manager and not our own. I breathed a huge sigh of relief that he had turned down the manager's role at St James' Park in 2004, when Freddie Shepherd came knocking after relieving Sir Bobby

Robson of his duties. But that had seemingly only delayed the inevitable. Fifteen years later, and with the departure of Rafa Benítez still raw in the hearts and minds of Geordies everywhere, Mike Ashley named Steve Bruce as manager of Newcastle United.

In truth it felt like Bruce was a dead man walking from day one at the club. Not that this was a gig for the fainthearted. Anybody who followed Benítez into St James' Park needed real credentials to be given some breathing space by the fans. But Bruce felt like an Ashley choice. A stooge, a patsy. Someone grateful for the gig who wouldn't rock the boat. That's not a stamp of approval you want where the Newcastle fans are concerned. But of course, just as Bruce brought a low energy to the job, so did his teams. Tactically confused, risk-averse, and playing without any real identity. Unless their identity *was* to be tactically confused and risk-averse? In which case they absolutely nailed it. It speaks volumes that, when I look back at the games under Bruce's tenure, I cannot remember any of the football. It's all one long sludge of lifeless grey. And few were sludgier than a night in South Yorkshire.

When Newcastle headed to Bramall Lane in early 2021 they were six games into what would become a nine-game winless run. It was January, a month in which Newcastle traditionally lose football matches. But even the most pessimistic of supporters fancied their chances at relegation-threatened Sheffield United, a side that hadn't won for 20 games. So, what did Steve Bruce do when presented with such an ideal game in which to kickstart our season? He played five at the back and stuck Callum Wilson up front on his own. A formation guaranteed to gift possession to the opposition, invite pressure, and lead to trouble. As a result the Blades, without a Premier League win all season, pinged the ball around like vintage Barcelona, while Newcastle took on the air of one of those football teams you see in a movie or on *Ted Lasso*, where they're essentially pretending to play football. Ryan Fraser was sent off for a second bookable offence, and the game was settled late on by a slightly dubious penalty – the ball brushing Federico Fernández's arm inside the box – for a shattering defeat. And without the heroics of Karl Darlow in the Newcastle goal, it would have been a heck of a lot worse.

'We were absolutely shite,' bellowed Bruce after the match. 'Frigging hopeless,' he added. 'The gloves are off now and we'll do it my way.' Which made you wonder just what the hell he'd been doing up until this point.

Sometimes I feel a bit sorry for Bruce. Despite his often ill-judged comments and defeatist manner, being offered the manager's job at Newcastle must have meant a hell of a lot to both him and his family. You grow up supporting Newcastle, work hard to become a footballer and then one day, against the odds, get the chance to manage your hometown club in the top flight. It's utterly Boys' Own stuff, but it pisses me off that he didn't approach it with more public passion, and showed everybody just what it meant to him.

What makes Bruce's public demeanour as manager all the more galling is that it seems in total opposition to his attitude as a player. At 19 he was on the verge of quitting football altogether, having no luck finding a club and with work at the Swan Hunter dockyard on the horizon. A last-ditch trial with Gillingham changed the course of his life – one he attended with a young Peter Beardsley. But while Beardsley was sent home, Bruce, playing in midfield, was signed up. From there to Norwich to Manchester United, his game was defined by a willingness to scrap for everything, putting his body on the line in pursuit of victory.

He appeared utterly overwhelmed by the Newcastle job. Where Keegan was all too ready to walk out if he didn't get the tools he needed to help the club survive, and then thrive, with Bruce the power felt at the other end of the scale, and that he wanted to keep the job above all else. As a result there seemed an apathy about his tenure … an acceptance that this was as good as things could be, and that we should all just get on with it.

This could be what led to my own loss of passion, but I doubt it. That was in the post long before Bruce showed up. He simply delivered it. Maybe the ambition under Benítez was an illusion. A dream of success that we projected on to the Spaniard simply because we were so desperate for something to cling on to. Considering the doom loop under Ashley, is it any wonder that my enthusiasm waned?

It tended to start in the summer with a link to any big-name player on the market. I knew it was rubbish, but still, with every social media post I would start to wonder, well, maybe this time. None of the *really* big names signed, of course, and we'd start the season in abject form. Chances are we would scramble a few results together, but it's always in chunks. A few wins, a few draws, then a run of five defeats in a row. Why is it always five? The winter transfer market is the same as the summer, only colder and darker. Unless we're looking in danger of the drop. Then Ashley spends for fear of losing the Premier League broadcasting riches. We go out of the FA Cup around the third or fourth round (chances are we're already out of the League Cup) and then we toil until the end of the season. Maybe there's a big scalp in there to keep us going. After that we'll hover around 17th, save for an unexpected late surge that pushes us up towards the glory of 13th.

Either that or we go down. Following relegation, Ashley will claim that he wants to sell, and that there's big interest from the Middle East, thus defusing our immediate anger in the hope that he might well soon be off. But he doesn't go, and the interested buyer turns out to be a fake sheikh. So, with no new owners on the horizon, Ashley sanctions a quite reasonable spend on decent Championship-level players who steer us towards promotion, but then remain in the squad for far too long on incessant one-year contract extensions. Other things probably happen, of course. Wild, cartoonish things. Maybe he bans yet more local journalists after they print a story about him in a Chinese restaurant seen laughing at that picture of Kevin Keegan slumped behind the hoardings at Anfield, or perhaps he insists on a contract clause where every new player has to change their name to Sports Direct by Deed Poll. You know, typical Ashley stuff.

Maybe you could call Bruce a victim of circumstance. He was a manager with a reputation for jumping rather quickly from club to club in the Championship and with no real record for major success. Now he was following a Champions League-winning manager who the fans had turned into a deity for their feverish idolatry. Even then it's hard to feel too much sympathy for the guy, as he often dealt with the whole thing so petulantly. Any press conference mention of Benítez was met with a mocking reverence, while he described Eddie Howe as 'that fella from Bournemouth that got a team relegated' when asked about him being his potential successor, at a time when the club was on the verge of a takeover from the Public Investment Fund of Saudi Arabia.

The fact is that Benítez's Newcastle and Bruce's Newcastle were remarkably similar in many ways. Stylistically, Benítez played a low-possession game which, admittedly, wasn't always great to watch. It was about being organised and difficult to score against, then having the players who could operate a swift counterattack and, hopefully, make the most of limited chances. Bruce's Newcastle seemed to operate in much the same way, only without the organisation and stoutness at the back. As a result they conceded goals like nobody's business – almost double that of his predecessor's sides. Despite that fact, they both accumulated similar final league positions and total points counts. But in the end, one man was viewed as tactically outperforming his circumstances, while the other was seen as blundering his way through the fixture list, taking long holidays, and a 'how's the bacon?' meme. If nothing else, this goes to show that what happens on the field and in the league table is only a part of being a success as Newcastle manager; how the boss conducts himself, connects with the city and people, carrying himself with pride, and most of all the emotion he instils in this most passionate of supporters is everything.

As for me, well this was quite possibly my lowest point as a supporter of Newcastle. Whereas once I lived for the fixtures between August and May, it had now become a grinding slog through each and every season. I expected defeat, and victory was met with genuine surprise. Even if we managed to get three points, I knew that nothing was genuinely geared to success. There would be no hunt for trophies, or star signings. No big nights under the lights or exciting cup runs. Dreams had been cancelled for the foreseeable future in favour of the bottom line of a balance sheet. Newcastle United were now there simply to make up the numbers.

25

Night of the Living Dead

20 March 2021
Brighton & Hove Albion 3 Newcastle United 0

When your football team loses, it briefly feels like the sky has collapsed. After the full-time whistle, nothing else matters. People talk but I don't hear them, and I secretly wonder just how they can ask normal questions at a time like this. Can't they see what I am going through? I replay the disaster over and over in my head, hoping that if I do it enough times there might be a different outcome. Instantaneously I scan social media, in a sadomasochistic desire to not only wallow in pain, but also have my anger stoked. As it all becomes too much, I search in vain for a positive spin. Something, anything, anyone who might sensibly explain why things went wrong, but also not to worry because, hey, it'll definitely be all right in the end. I'll need this take later on to soothe me to sleep. Because I know that when I wake up the next day there'll be a two-second grace period before my brain reboots the pain of the previous day's defeat. A feeling to deaden the stomach and weigh heavy on my limbs before I've even set foot out of bed. At this point, only the cold reality of the fixture list keeps my head above water, with its relentless march offering another game, and another chance to put things right. Win and everything is forgotten. Lose and I'm back where I started.

As Newcastle trudged lifelessly along in 2021 – all of us blissfully unaware that we were experiencing the last few months of the Mike Ashley era – it felt like this football club had been losing almost every week for years.

It has occurred to me, on more than one occasion, that this is all whining and I should really just shut the hell up. After all, successful clubs are few and far between in this world, and the vast majority of football fans see precious little silverware during their lives. Only seven different teams have won the title since the Premier League began 33 seasons ago, along with nine winners of the FA Cup. Only Blackburn, Leicester, Wigan and Portsmouth have interrupted the stranglehold of Manchester United, Manchester City, Arsenal, Liverpool and Chelsea on English football success. You can cast the net a little wider if you like, include the League Cup and add Middlesbrough, Swansea, Aston Villa, Tottenham Hotspur and Birmingham City to that list. It makes things a little more palatable, but essentially it remains a closed shop. So, why did I deserve more?

Last year, while attending a wedding set around a beautiful Norwegian fjord, simultaneously wondering about Newcastle United and Norwegian players (only an end-of-career Ronny Johnsen and the midfielder Travis Hernes, yet to make a first-team appearance), I was asked a question, 'Was your time following Newcastle under Mike Ashley really the worst that the club has ever experienced?' This came from a Sunderland fan, so I have to assume there was a certain amount of fishing going on here. But it is an interesting point. Two relegations aside, Newcastle under Ashley were a mid-table Premier League team. These are simply the facts. They were a god-awful, ruin-your-weekend team, but more often than not they ruined it from the relative comfort of English football's top flight. Now contrast that to when I began supporting the club in the mid-to-late 1980s, that saw us sell off our great homegrown talent, suffer relegation, endure play-off heartache (to Sunderland!), wallow in Second Division mid-table mediocrity, and go damn near relegation to the third tier. Attendances were low, with season averages hovering around the 17,000 mark. New signings were rare, and new signings that worked rarer still. It was hardly *Roy of the Rovers* stuff. Go back further. After the Fairs Cup success in 1969 the club was relegated in 1978, and didn't get back in the top flight until the first coming of Kevin Keegan, and a promotion at his second attempt six seasons after they had gone down. Go back further still, to 1962. Charlie Mitten's post-Jackie Milburn side concedes 117 goals and goes down. They were away from the top flight for four seasons. So what was it about life under Ashley that made following Newcastle so unbearable?

The thing about football is that it's not about the numbers. Not really. And while points may well mean prizes, the real beauty of the game lies in its intangible elements. For my friend Neil (you might know him on NUFC Twitter as @GeordieDentist), who has followed the Magpies through similarly disinterested chairmen in the 1970s and 80s, it's all about aspiration and association. Newcastle United and its city should be one, while everything else runs off pure hope. I tend to agree. It's about finding a community that accepts you without prejudice, and the friends you make (often forged in the furnace of a relegation scrap), that stay with you for the rest of your life. It's unbridled joy en masse and collective pain. It's about living through the natural peaks and troughs of a football fan, but still being able to dream that one day, it *will* be your day. That's what we lost between 2007 and 2021. Newcastle under Ashley were dead behind the eyes.

My disconnection from the team didn't happen instantly, or intentionally for that matter. It was a slow erosion. First a geographical separation, then a mental uncoupling. In between that, hope, belief, and passion were gradually choked out by a misguided owner. It's only natural that your relationship with football changes over the course of your life. It has to, right? It's all well and good being obsessed with something when you're a kid, in fact it's actively encouraged, unless that thing is sniffing glue or punching cats. But try and dedicate the majority of your life to a football team when you're an adult, with both professional and familial responsibilities to bear, and people will probably look at you a bit funny.

By my reckoning I've seen ten seasons of good football at Newcastle. Ten seasons out of 41. That's a 24.39 per cent goodness ratio if you're wondering. But then, eventually, the lights went out. It was like a relationship that isn't working – in fact it *is* a relationship that isn't working – but you tell yourself it'll get better, even though you know it won't. So you end up living in a constant state of heartache. Then, out of nowhere, a switch flicks and you're done. You realise that you're worth far more than this and so, now, the whole thing washes over you like you're immune to the pain. And you are. At least for a while.

Things came to a head against Brighton in 2021 on the south coast. Newcastle had already lost 3-0 to the Seagulls at St James' Park earlier on in the season – a spiritless debacle with zero shots on goal for Steve Bruce's listless mob. So, imagine my surprise when, in the reverse fixture and with relegation a distinct possibility, we lost 3-0 thanks to a spiritless debacle with zero shots on goal for Steve Bruce's listless mob.

Brighton, by contrast, looked sharp and focussed. It was quite amazing to think that Graham Potter's side were at the wrong end of the table, too, as they comprehensively outplayed, outfought and outthought Newcastle from first whistle to last. A pre-Arsenal Leandro Trossard pulled the strings, as the hosts dominated possession (Newcastle had just 25 per cent of it in the first half, and managed only two touches in the Brighton box). The second half started a little better, a Miguel Almirón cross finding Ryan Fraser whose shot brushed the post, but the comeback was short-lived. Goals for Danny Welbeck and Neal Maupay finished off a comfortable, confidence-boosting night's work for Brighton, leaving Newcastle well and truly in the clarts. The whole thing felt so typical of a Steve Bruce side, like they had gone into battle without any real plan. In his post-match press conference the beleaguered manager spoke of his surprise at how far ahead Brighton were in everything that they did. The Newcastle fans were considerably less shocked.

In 2019, shortly after the club hired Steve Bruce, scores of Newcastle supporters made a real sacrifice, voting with their feet and choosing not to renew their season tickets while Ashley remained at the club. I think the power of that often gets lost amid the noise of his subsequent 10,000 free season tickets giveaway that followed. These people made a decision to cut loose one of the most important things in their lives in protest at the running of their football club. In many cases these tickets will have been in the family for decades, with their stadium 'neighbours' almost like a second family. That decision makes me awestruck. If I had been a season ticket holder at the time, I'm not sure I could have done the same. Then again, maybe I could. It had got to the point where I would utterly dread the weekends, because defeat made me feel so miserable. Fatalism dogged even the good times. In the cups, if we somehow managed to make it to the later stages it wouldn't matter, because I knew that as soon as we drew someone decent we would limp out of the tournament anyway. Whereas I once lived for the fixture list, now I look forward to the off-season. Three months without any Newcastle United: bliss.

Despite such a comprehensive victory, Brighton ended the season four places below the Magpies, with the wild form of an on-loan Joe Willock (eight goals from 17 shots) a return from injury for Allan Saint-Maximin and Callum Wilson, and five wins in the last eight games improbably pushing the team to the dizzy heights of 12th place on the final day of the season. It was great, but it didn't *really* register with me. Maybe it was because this was football in the time of Covid. There were no fans in the stadium, no noise, and no real passion. Don't get me wrong, I was pleased that we had stayed up, even finishing half-respectably, but the whole thing was like background noise. I had entered my zombie era.

Without Newcastle to dominate my thoughts life would feel good, at least for a while. But I was discombobulated without the constant rhythm of my football club. It was unusual and unsettling and, in truth, I felt lost. I had removed an annoying, yet fundamental part of my personality. I didn't watch the games, I didn't buy the shirts, I didn't obsess over the minutiae of each Newcastle match in forensic detail. I didn't even play football any more. One year earlier I had moved to Amsterdam, where none of my new friends were football fans so, apart from WhatsApp, I didn't even talk about football. It got to the point when I had to ask myself the question: if I'm not into football any more, and don't have this team, people, and city to care about then who the hell am I? I didn't have an answer to that. The more I thought about it, the more I realised that my whole personality had been constructed around supporting Newcastle. Let me tell you, discovering that you're made up of 85 per cent underwhelming football club is a pretty sobering thought 48 years into your existence. I couldn't construct a new personality from scratch. Not now. The one I had was ropey enough, and I'd been working on that for ages.

I had always used football as a social crutch, a way to connect with new people and sidestep social anxiety in the blink of an eye. Even to this day upon meeting someone I try desperately to remember that person's name, and then wonder how quickly we can change the subject to football. If they're not interested in the game I break out into a cold sweat, terrified at the possibility of having to dredge up some form of real conversation in its place.

At this point my future looked uncertain. I had quickly realised that a life without the Magpies wasn't possible, not fully. The club was buried too deep under my skin for that. But did I really want to be one of those people who takes only a passing interest? The type who spends weekends with friends, or at B&Q, and perhaps checks the scores, but perhaps they don't, and it's all OK because they'll probably catch it all on *Match of the Day* later on? Nah. Not really.

I did know that things had to change. I couldn't keep going the way things stood, investing my heart and soul in a club that didn't seem overly interested in success. The way I looked at it was this: if I was to reignite my passion in Newcastle United, then the spark needed to be of epic proportions.

26

Dreams Warriors

5 May 1996
Newcastle United 1 Tottenham Hotspur 1
Ferdinand

By the time Newcastle kicked off against Spurs on 5 May 1996, we were looking for snookers if we were going to win the league; that's never easy when you're playing football. The route to victory was simple enough, at least on paper. Manchester United lose at Middlesbrough, we beat Gerry Francis's Spurs at home, and everybody gets drunk on the Quayside for a week and a half. But as Sir Bobby Robson once said, 'We don't play the game on paper.' The reality was that it would take almost divine intervention if our dreams were to be realised. And that almost never happened on Teesside.

You know what annoyed me that day, lack of possible miracle aside? The fact that somewhere inside of St James' Park lay a fake Premier League trophy. I mean, I get it, you never know right? If we did happen to win the league it would be nice to have something shiny to hoist up in the air, to kiss on a victory lap, and to definitely do that thing where the captain keeps the trophy low, but then suddenly lifts it high, taking the fans from 'ooooooh' to 'heeeeey!' But am I the only one who thinks there's something inherently sarcastic about it all? A *fake* trophy. I expect that Premier League head honcho Rick Parry handed it over with half a snigger. 'OK, boys, you can have one too, just in case,' saying the 'just in case' part using air quotes and then performing a dramatic eye roll in the direction of Alex Ferguson. Was it made out of tin foil like fans make for an FA Cup tie? Had they spelled Premier with just the one 'e'? Perhaps it was inflatable, for maximum comedy value? Maybe I'm overthinking it.

To be honest, mental gymnastics should have been the order of the day leading up to the Spurs match. I should have thrown myself into it, desperately working on permutations of how we could still win the title, getting by on two or three hours of sleep a night. But you know what? I didn't. I'm not sure any of us did. Perhaps that's because we had all seen it coming.

Newcastle saved their worst run of form for the title run-in, managing just five frazzled wins from their final 12 games (along with five defeats and two draws). Maybe it was exhaustion. Perhaps it was stress. Trophy-winning pressure can crush a player if they haven't already been there and done it. The fact is that, until the arrivals of Faustino Asprilla and David Batty, the only members of Newcastle's first-team squad with any experience of winning major domestic silverware were Peter Beardsley, David Ginola and Philippe Albert. Manchester United, meanwhile, were old hands. They'd won two out of the first three Premier League titles, had recently picked up an FA Cup, and even had a clutch of core players in Denis Irwin, Steve Bruce, Gary Pallister, Lee Sharpe, Brian McClair, and Ryan Giggs who remained from the European Cup Winners' Cup-winning side of 1991. So, while Keegan's team began to limp when it came to the business end of the season, Alex

Ferguson's grew tall, with ten wins, one defeat and one draw from their final 12 games.

The manner of how these results played out probably didn't help much. The body blow of Manchester United at home, the spirit-crushing late reverses at both Anfield and Ewood Park, followed by a desperate draw at Nottingham Forest. Newcastle dominated that game, missed a hatful of chances before Ian bloody Woan (why always you, Ian?) equalised Peter Beardsley's opener with just 15 minutes left to play. There had been wins against West Ham, Queens Park Rangers, Aston Villa, Southampton, and Leeds in that time, too, but aside from the game against the Hammers, they were narrow, plodding, and tired.

Even though we could have still technically won the title, the mood inside the stadium ahead of the match against Tottenham bore little comparison with the raw desperation that met Manchester United just two months earlier. In most people's hearts and minds the championship had gone. There was no anger, no frustration, it all felt a little numb. The unusually passive mood on the terraces was mirrored on the pitch, too. It didn't help that David May had put Manchester United 1-0 up after 14 minutes down the road at Middlesbrough, of course, but the apathy of the 12th man left the home team short from the start. As a result, the verve and urgency which had defined Newcastle's season was sorely lacking. David Batty pinged a snapshot over Ian Walker's bar – and then stared at the ball with disdain for not going in – but nothing much of note happened until Jason Dozzell sent Darren Peacock the wrong way and curled a shot past Shaka Hislop on the hour. The home crowd rallied. The general consensus after a goal being that if you didn't start singing immediately – thus showing your support for the temporarily beleaguered players – then you were an arsehole and could just about bloomin' well fuck off. So, for a moment the reflexes kicked in, and we all forgot the bigger picture in favour of trying to win a football match. It had an effect, too.

Ginola popped up on the right, taking a ball on his chest with the sort of leap that got Nureyev his gig at the Royal Ballet, before lashing a volley at goal. Moments later the Frenchman picked up the ball again, this time on his more familiar left flank. He bamboozled a couple of Spurs players before threading a lovely through ball to Faustino Asprilla. The Colombian, fresh on for Peter Beardsley, yet somehow looking like he had just got in from Julie's nightclub, promptly staggered towards a forlorn-looking Gary Mabbutt. He dropped a shoulder, did a sideways Cruyff turn and squared the ball across the box to Les Ferdinand – who duly thwacked it home from two yards out. At this point the title was gone. Manchester United were now 2-0 up at the Riverside (the second scored by Andy Cole), and they were 17 minutes away from a third. But we had all left that reality. The pressure mounted. Lee Clark dropped a lunging volley on to the top of the Gallowgate bar, while Ferdinand had a diving header saved at point-blank range by Walker. Finally, Asprilla hit a right-footed volley with the outside of his boot that was so staggering it probably still requires a full investigation. And then, suddenly, the whistle went. There was a lull, an intake of breath, and that was it. It was all over. Nobody knew what to do because, well, we'd never been *here* before. Then the applause came.

So, what went wrong? The reasons behind Newcastle's capitulation have become the stuff of urban legend. Asprilla blew it! They should never have dropped Keith Gillespie. No, it was losing Lee Clark that did it, and Batty coming in, don't forget Batty. The shape of the side was all wrong after that. The defence went to pieces, Fergie used mind games

… WE'RE CURSED! It was all bollocks of course. The fans who watched Newcastle play that year know Asprilla adapted almost instantly to the Premier League, and he was outstanding in games against Middlesbrough, West Ham, Manchester United, and Liverpool in particular. They would have seen Batty's quality shine through, too, adding a toughness and no little skill. The only problem was that these tweaks to the squad simply happened to coincide with a wide drop of form from almost everybody else.

People quickly forget that this season was also pivotal for Manchester United. Fergie had gambled by letting big-name players go – Paul Ince to Inter, Mark Hughes to Chelsea, and Andrei Kanchelskis to Everton – choosing not to replace them with new signings but rather promote from within. This was the season that David Beckham, Nicky Butt, Paul Scholes, and Gary and Phil Neville were thrust into first-team prominence. Fergie's Fledglings they called them, which is admittedly hard to say without getting a little bit of sick in your mouth, but hey, the lads could play. Alan Hansen wasn't convinced, of course. 'You can't win anything with kids,' he rather famously explained to *Match of the Day* host Des Lynam, after Manchester United had been trounced 3-1 at Villa Park on the opening day of the season. They went unbeaten for the next ten games. Which goes to show that the pundits didn't have a clue in the 90s either.

After stumbling through two wins in seven games between 27 November and 30 December (one of them against Newcastle at Old Trafford, naturally), Manchester United hit their stride in the final few months of the season, winning 13 of their last 16 games. While an energetic mix of old heads and youthful zest took them forward, it's hard to look beyond the efforts of two players in particular.

Peter Schmeichel kept a staggering 12 clean sheets in those final 16 games of the season. Colossally annoying for opposition fans, colossally annoying for opposition players. Let's be honest, probably colossally annoying for his own players, too, but as for his performances in goal that year, simply colossal. By October the talismanic Eric Cantona had returned from his nine-month suspension, too. Banned for, as he put it, 'kicking the hooligan', a moment he has since rated as his finest in a Manchester United shirt. Just to be clear, he claims launching into the crowd with a flying kick aimed at the leather-blousoned Matthew Simmons – who had shouted 'Fuck off back to France you French motherfucker' – as more satisfying than winning four Premier League titles and two FA Cups. You can't help but like the guy for that; despite the fact that he played with his collar up and scored a goal that utterly crushed my dreams. But it wasn't just Cantona's bouncing winner at St James' Park that killed our season. He hit ten of his season's 14 goals in those last 16 games, including four times as the match-winner in 1-0 victories. If you contrast that with how Newcastle ended the season – with seven wins in 16, five clean sheets and Les Ferdinand hitting only six of his 25 – you start to see things a little more clearly. Ultimately when the title pressure came, Fergie's team thrived. That's no slight on the Newcastle squad, every single one of them were utterly heroic that season. They simply ran out of steam.

I remember reading an interview with Ray Parlour in the summer of 1996 (it was in *90 Minutes* or some such football magazine) and he offered what I took to be the most ridiculous statement ever. 'Look at Newcastle,' Parlour said. 'They should have won the league this year. They didn't, and they might not get close to it again.' That absolutely blew my mind. This was in the days before the multimillion-pound spending sprees that clubs now go on between seasons, so it felt utterly ludicrous to me that we would not be up there challenging for the title once again the following year. 'What do you know Ray, ya prick?' I thought, in an imaginary conversation that got out of hand pretty quickly. While we would go on to finish second again in 1996/97, the truth is that Ray was right (the prick). Newcastle were never in with a shout of winning the title that year. And have never been close in the 27 years that followed. You'll be pleased to know that I have since had a follow-up conversation in my head with Ray Parlour, in which we eventually settled our differences, fair play to him.

By the end of the 1995/96 season we were all exhausted – Keegan included. He talks in his autobiography about how he struggled for weeks at the end of that campaign, analysing every missed chance, misplaced pass, and fumbled save in a bid to find out where it had all gone wrong. In typical Keegan fashion he talked of leaving. If he can't give everything, he shouldn't give anything. Ultimately he was only brought out of his funk by the world record signing of Alan Shearer. And even that would only give us six more months of Keegan at St James' Park.

I think that this team in particular is so fondly remembered because of what it came to represent: one built to score goals, to win matches, to entertain. This was the message from the top down. Keegan wanted his players to go out and give the fans something to shout about, to know that the hard-earned cash they spent each year on a season ticket was worth it. There's a kind of purity in that – perhaps mirrored in how it all turned out, too, with the full-blooded passion of Keegan tripped up by a managerial naivety that had long since left Ferguson. For some fans there was an element of tragic comedy to our downfall, and that's OK, too. I know that this team will live longer in the memory of football fans everywhere than umpteen Premier League title winners that followed it.

I advise those people looking for a fully immersive 90s experience to play 'Born Slippy' by Underworld while reading this next part (seriously, you'll get more out of it in the end).

There were no tears as the reality of our failure to win the Premier League sank in. No bouts of rage, or screaming into the void. Just gratification. In a little over three years, Newcastle had gone from the very brink of existence to a whisker away from winning the whole damn thing. I mean, how was that even possible? So, while the disappointment of that missed opportunity will stay with me for ever, at the time I was strangely OK with it. Keegan had given us something that would live long in our memories. He had made us feel relevant again, and that affected how we looked at not just our football club, but our city, ourselves, and our very place in the world. That season might well have ended in failure. But sometimes (and I do mean sometimes) even failure can be glorious. More than anything else I look back at it all with a smile. Not thinking about what might have been, just happy that I was there to enjoy the ride.

27

Seventeen Years Later

4 October 2023
Newcastle United 4 Paris Saint-Germain 1
Almirón, Burn, Longstaff, Schär

On 7 October 2021, Newcastle United became the richest football club in the world. It was something of a shock, I don't mind telling you. In all honesty, I had long since disengaged with the idea of a takeover. Mike Ashley had cried wolf too many times for it to feel plausible any more. I did still occasionally dream about the club being owned by some deep-pocketed investor with a desire for greatness. He would have an unnerving year-round tan, own a gigantic multinational shrouded in mystery, and would come in all guns blazing – sanctioning the signing of a tricky Brazilian before he'd even set foot inside St James' Park. As it turned out, the reality was even more bizarre.

Newcastle were sold 18 months after a consortium of Amanda Staveley's PCP Capital Partners, Reuben Brothers, and the Public Investment Fund of Saudi Arabia (PIF) first requested the Premier League's Owners' and Directors' test in April 2020. Although the departure of Ashley was celebrated by fans outside St James' Park with a mini-rave, the process from bid to sale was protracted and ugly. It was on, and then it was off. There was talk of piracy and dodgy streaming channels. Discussions in parliament were had, and challenges in court were made. There were reservations about degrees of separation between PIF and the Saudi government, while Hanan Elatr, widow of the murdered journalist Jamal Khashoggi, spoke out about the implications of the club being associated with the Saudi regime. For many supporters it was a time of conflicting emotions, where morally complex ideas about the suitable ownership of a club at the heart of the community butted heads with football dreams we had held dear for a lifetime. Questions about geopolitical tension suddenly became commonplace in pre-match press conferences, and a new man was required in the hot seat after the club parted company with Steve Bruce. But even that was a decision fraught with danger. We were owned by a sovereign wealth fund with net assets, at time of writing, of $940.26 billion. We required a manager who could eventually take us on to glory but who, right now, was also willing to get stuck into a relegation scrap. Thankfully, my mate Spugsy and I had some thoughts (and no, the money wasn't going to change us).

> Me, 'So, who would you have in as gaffer, then?'
> Spugsy, without hesitation, 'Antonio Conte.'
> Me, 'Aye, same, Conte.'
> Spugsy, 'Of course I would take Zidane, too. If he could prove capable of keeping us up. But he's my reserve, shall we say.'

For context, the previous week there had been a detailed defence of why we should give the job to our current joint first team coach Graeme Jones. Now, here we both were, evaluating a former Real Madrid boss and football legend with all the aloofness of Sir Alan Sugar in the latter stages of *The Apprentice*. It was a crazy time. But then crazy is often what Newcastle does best. Some days later there was footage on Twitter of a guy in the Bigg Market on an evening out, asking the boxer Chris Eubank Jr. to sign his microwave oven. Why did he have a microwave with him at the time? I fear we shall never know. I probably have more questions about that than I do the takeover. I expect you're the same. We can discuss it later.

On 7 November 2021, Eddie Howe was named as the Magpies' new manager. It was an appointment that, at first, underwhelmed parts of the fanbase. We were too busy fawning over Champions League-winning gaffers at the time. But Howe was a sensible choice, a man who knew the league, knew the players, and knew his way around a relegation dogfight. His effect on the club would be nothing short of staggering. After zero wins in the opening 14 games, Newcastle won 13 of their remaining 23, with the team transformed from relegation certainties into 'proper shithouses' as the phrase goes, ultimately finishing 11th. The new owners came to the table with cash, too, providing £90m for the transformative January signings of Kieran Trippier, Bruno Guimarães, Dan Burn and Chris Wood and, the following season, a further £153m for Nick Pope, Sven Botman, Alexander Isak, and (in January) Anthony Gordon, as the club started to move with menace. In 2022/23 Newcastle finished fourth and qualified for the Champions League, losing just five league games all season. They also reached the League Cup Final (a first final of any sort since 1999), losing 2-0 to Manchester United. But while the action on the pitch was way ahead of schedule, it was also a year that saw football change irrevocably for me.

In December 2022 my dad passed away. Although he was my very first connection with football, he was never really a Newcastle United fanatic. They were his team, but he would always impress on me the importance of each and every north-east side doing well, and how that was good for the region. I scoffed at that sentiment with as much scoff as I could muster at the time. But, as usual, he was right. He had some very specific opinions about football, my dad. Including, but not limited to, how beards on players were awful. Tattoos were even worse. Anybody who knee-slides after a goal is going to get injured (see also somersaults), and players who celebrated goals by removing their shirts were idiots, as they know they're going to get booked. He was a joyful old bugger. Even for us football was the great connector, and when I was a moody teenager we could still talk about Newcastle. I have those chats in my head sometimes, even now, where his opinion remains as irrepressible as always. I wish we had gone to the match together more often, and that I had watched *Match of the Day* with him regularly when I was a kid, rather than pretending to be asleep so I could lazily watch it in my room instead, when all he wanted was to spend some time with me. It's been three years since his death, but I still occasionally reach for my phone to text him after a big win, only to realise my mistake milliseconds later. Should Newcastle go on to achieve success, it breaks my heart that just a little bit of that moment won't be shared with him.

In the future, I hope that Newcastle's glory will include a trophy, rather than just the occasional triumph over a big club. But still, it would have been difficult to find a game that better encapsulated the exultant release of pure joy felt by supporters post-Mike Ashley than the game at St James' Park on 4 October 2023. Newcastle United 4 Paris Saint-Germain 1. A night under the lights, with the supporters close to frenzy at a first Champions League occasion on Tyneside in two decades. The opposition boasted a generational talent at number nine in Kylian Mbappé, but the youngest Frenchman ever to win the World Cup didn't quite live up to the hype that night, frozen out by Dan Burn, Fabian Schär, and some pure Geordie aggro. Tackles were cheered like goals, as the home side tore into the French champions from the off. Miguel Almirón scored Newcastle's first Champions League goal in 20 years, curling a sublime shot past the giant frame of Gianluigi Donnarumma on 17 minutes, and there was no looking back. Twenty minutes later, after a chaotic scramble in the box, Guimarães dinked a ball invitingly across the six-yard line for Dan Burn, who launched himself at it like a massive salmon (from Blyth) to make it 2-0. Five minutes into the second half and it was three, as Sean Longstaff's low shot squirmed under the dive of Donnarumma for a local-lad double. And although PSG pulled one back it didn't matter. Schär would later rattle a shot into the top corner of the Gallowgate End goal from 25 yards, sealing a stunning victory and a party years in the making on Tyneside.

As for my own love of the Magpies, well, rather predictably, the upturn in performances did pique my interest. How could it not? After years of utter mediocrity it felt borderline sadomasochistic to avoid watching the team now it boasted genuinely exciting talent. I had more than done my time as a long-suffering fan, and deserved a modicum of joy when it came to watching my team on the pitch. Any decisions on ownership were never mine to take. When it comes to the crunch, the fans have no control over who runs their football club. We have no way of influencing interested parties, or indeed the outcome of a takeover. Not really. We can protest, of course, or choose to vote with our feet. But expecting people to turn their back on a club that means everything to them is unrealistic and unfair. Newcastle United is intrinsically woven into the fabric of life on Tyneside. It's our past, present and future. But while we are fated to eternally care about the fortunes of this football club, we don't have to revel in its ownership. We can make it our business to understand the social, historical, and political context behind the current controversy, and be mindful of that. I think that's fair.

When it comes to Mike Ashley, I actually think that there is some contrition there. That's often what made his tenure so confusing. Occasionally he would accept liability, like when he spoke of his regret at buying the club in 2009 by stating, 'I never said I was an expert in football clubs. I tried my best. But I accept my best was woefully short.' The problem was that his next move would generally be something even worse. After eventually selling up to PIF for £305m, he made a surprising £50m bid for Derby County, then withdrew the offer amid rising costs and the administrators allegedly rejecting his original proposal. Kevin Keegan, meanwhile, has been something of a football recluse since leaving Newcastle, making just a handful of pundit appearances over the course of nine years. You are now more likely to see Keegan on the corporate speaking circuit than offering his thoughts on Eddie Howe's current side.

In the cold light of day the whole thing occasionally feels like some sort of tragic comedy. You are now the richest club in the world, but those riches come from one of the most controversial nations on Earth. I suppose it's not like football hasn't always had dark affiliations. Rumour has it that Adolf Hitler was a big FC Schalke 04 fan for example, while Benito Mussolini was the original Lazio ultra. If you're looking for something a little closer to home, well, Prince William supports Aston Villa so, y'know, there are skeletons in a number of cupboards. But even if you make your peace with it all, PSR has strangled big-spending options for quick progress on the pitch anyway, at least for those clubs outside the traditional Big Six in the Premier League. So, we now have to mentally compartmentalise that controversial ownership with, perhaps, just a sixth-, seventh-, or eighth-placed finish. Would a trophy make the deal we have struck more palatable? I don't know. But then winning silverware is uncharted territory.

I have only recently started to consider success and what it's worth as a football fan. Being a supporter and winning trophies every year feels like something of a paradox to me. On one hand the game is entirely about winning. But on the other your worth as a supporter is judged on pure loyalty. It's about being there on the worst days and still coming back for more. This journey we're all on is a love story. And love is pain. But that pain is also what makes the bright days even more brilliant. How can I truly appreciate the joy of Liam O'Brien's free-kick winner against Sunderland at Roker Park in 1992 without knowing the devastation of Sunderland's play-off victory at St James' Park two years earlier? Supporting a team that wins trophy after trophy isn't fandom, it's entertainment. When fans are disinterested after winning the League Cup for the tenth time, only reserving their doe-eyed excitement for the Champions League, then their success has well and truly jumped the shark. Of course if you follow a winning club then this is simply your life, and I wish you well. But I would be willing to bet that Manchester City's first Premier League title in 2012, for example, felt sweeter than all of the others combined, simply for those fans for whom life in the third tier was still a recent memory.

So, here I am writing a book about the heartache of Newcastle United's lack of success, paralleled by the joy of its glorious failure. A fan of a team without a major trophy since 1969, who's worried that winning too much silverware might potentially ruin his experience. I realise that I've got some complicated issues to work through. One thing I know for certain is that Newcastle will always be an essential part of my life. There is no alternative, but then having something to care about is what makes life worth living. When you think about it, it's not just the winning that makes football so compelling. It's not the amount of finals you reach, or a list of major honours, but the journey you take to get there in the first place. And while every year we pray that our name is on the cup, it's the passion *and* the pain which makes the whole experience truly worthwhile.

Epilogue

Welcome To Your New Life

16 March 2025
Liverpool 1-2 Newcastle United
Burn, Isak

When the full-time whistle blew at Wembley on 16 March 2025 I didn't quite know how to react. Newcastle United were trophy winners, we were in uncharted territory. So, in lieu of any better ideas, I just stood there with hands on head, borderline catatonic.

Everything you have read so far was written prior to that glorious Sunday. Prior to Eddie Howe's side bullying Liverpool into submission in the Carabao Cup Final, and prior to generations of men being reduced to blubbering wrecks as a result. I'm not ashamed to say that I was one of them. After the enormity of it all sank in, the tears came.

As you may have gathered from the previous 266 pages, success is rather at odds with my identity as a Newcastle United fan. I think, in some ways, I got a perverse kick out of that. Passionately supporting a club that could never quite reciprocate with a major trophy. The north-east is built on struggle and sacrifice. But pride, too, burning and fierce. It all felt rather on-brand.

Now, perhaps, a new reality.

People have since commented that the final hit differently this time. Something had clicked, the players were better, wiser, more experienced. There was adversity, but even that got a glow-up. Playing the best side in the country, with Anthony Gordon suspended, and Lewis Hall and Sven Botman injured. It felt like our bad luck was going so far that it might just come full circle as good. Victory against all the odds, and one of those great football stories. If Dan Burn's colossal header made me dream, then Alexander Isak's typically cold finish dared me to think that victory could actually be real.

But it was the events off the pitch, afterwards, that really hit home. All those things I had seen a million times after a cup final, now happening to my club. Our name being engraved on the trophy, black and white ribbons carefully attached. Newcastle United players walking up the Wembley steps – second, not first – thunderously holding a trophy aloft. I was desperately happy that I had lived to see it and terribly sad for those who hadn't. I raised a glass to my dad, and wondered how young supporters might experience this great club in the future.

Those just embarking on a journey to follow Newcastle United will likely have a very different story to tell. They already do. Success and glory are now realistic aims, a million miles away from the austerity of Gordon McKeag and Sack The Board, or Mike Ashley and his Cockney Mafia.

Yet I would never trade this brave new world for my own. Loyalty, passion, resilience – core requirements of a football fan – I learned those things on the Gallowgate End. And you never know; on a beautiful day some time in the future, you might just be rewarded. Like Newcastle United in March 2025. Eyes wild, laser-focused, utterly unwilling to let the moment slip through their fingers. No glorious failure today, lads, just glory.

Acknowledgments

(Don't just skip this bit, there's some good stuff)

Now I'm no expert, but I've always believed the first debt of gratitude for any book is owed directly to you, the person holding it in their hands. So, with that in mind, dear reader, I say thanks! It sounds a bit underwhelming when I write it like that, kind of flat, but you should know that I truly appreciate you spending your hard-earned cash on it, and taking a leap of faith on me. Unless you're reading this bit in a shop, or over somebody's shoulder. In which case I urge you to spend your hard-earned cash on it, and take a leap of faith on me. Literally everybody else is doing it.

When I was younger and thought about a situation where I might have to thank people publicly, I would always imagine some sort of glamorous awards ceremony. I would walk to the stage, looking wise, yet approachable, and proceed to show my appreciation for a completely random selection of people who had nothing to do with me at all. Mr T, Zammo from *Grange Hill*, and the romance novelist Dame Barbara Cartland, for example. I don't know why that idea always tickled me when I was younger, or indeed why it still does now. But you can't fight who you truly are. That's something I learned in the process of working on *The Battle for Newcastle United*, actually.

I have always wanted to write a book. To get my thoughts down on paper, stick them in a grandiose-looking hardback and get it in a shop alongside the greats. But I never thought I would actually do it. It was just one of those things I said in order to sound like a real person with healthy ambition (see also scaling a mountain and getting a six pack). I never previously acted upon it because, well, it's hard isn't it. So, with all that in mind, it's good that I have some pretty amazing people in my life who have helped make this a reality, whether by gentle coaxing or less-gentle kicks up the arse. The best part about it all is that I get to tell you about them, here, now, in this bit below.

To begin with, my thanks must go to Jane Camillin and the good people at Pitch Publishing, for believing that this story was worth committing to paper in the first place. Without you my unusual thoughts on Newcastle United would have remained hidden to the world, and that surely would have been a tragedy.

Of course unusual thoughts are all well and good, but without any semblance of order they can occasionally turn into chaos, like when the Happy Mondays toured their *Yes Please!* album in '93. So, it's only right that I thank Philip Connor for his wise edits and honest opinions; and Mark Evans for his wise edits, honest opinions, and constant derision in his role as 'Mag-hating Mackem' for more years than I care to remember. Along with improving my grammar, you both gave me the confidence that this book could resonate beyond St James' Park into the wider football world, and that's a pretty great thought.

The biggest problem when it comes to writing a book such as this is that the memory can play tricks. The fog of time swirls everything together, like the scent of cigar smoke and Brown Ale that formed the olfactory backdrop to my early experiences at St James' Park. The key is to have the assistance of your football community to confirm or deny; people who lived through the same things as you, even if you didn't know them at the time. So, I'm very grateful to Peter Redding and Neil Mitchell for helping to clarify moments that I couldn't quite recall, and to Newcastle United historian Paul Joannou for when I needed the club's often complicated past cleared up in no-nonsense style. To Dave Spours (aka Spugsy), I thank you for the social media designs, and for the great stories. But we can never go to the match together again. Three games, three defeats, it's just not working out, pal.

Football is all about family, so it goes without saying (even though I'm saying it) that I should thank my mam, Cathy. There's a good chance she will never fully read this book (her taste is more Catherine Cookson than Kevin Keegan), but she has always supported me wholeheartedly. Case in point, the time she sent me a congratulations card even after I failed some exams at school. I have to presume that this wasn't sarcasm on her part so, Mam, I thank you for that, and for every other bit of help you have ever sent my way.

A few years ago I found a postcard that my sister wrote to me when I was about 19 (no idea why she was sending me postcards, but there you go). In it she urged me to study journalism, and even suggested some useful reading. It would be a long time before I acted upon that advice but, Andrea, I thank you for the encouragement that was always there. I thank you less for *still* laughing at the season I stood up through every Newcastle away game in my bedroom, wearing my full matchday outfit, boiling hot, and terribly hungover.

To my amazing wife Alexandria, I once took you to arguably the worst Newcastle match I have ever witnessed (a 1-0 home defeat to Sheffield United in 2006), yet still you agreed to marry me. I thank you for being the finest person I know. For believing in me and encouraging me, for getting up early to read the drafts of this book, and for offering what always appears genuine interest when I drone on about the latest crisis at St James' Park. Quite simply nothing in my life works without you.

When it comes to football fandom, however, there is always one person who sparks everything off. For me that was my dad, József. The man who made the wise decision that Newcastle United would become my team. I truly wish that I could have told him about this book, and that he could have had an opportunity to read just a little bit of it. At least any bit after the word 'wank' appears in the first sentence (which wouldn't have gone down too well). Writing *The Battle for Newcastle United* has made me realise just how many of his football opinions I have taken as my own, and how entwined my journey as a supporter really is with him. In truth that wasn't something I expected to find, but it has been a genuinely heartwarming discovery nonetheless. It's one that I will take with me for ever.

Finally, I would like to thank Mr T, Zammo from *Grange Hill*, and the romance novelist Dame Barbara Cartland.